Struck by Apollo

SUNY series, Insinuations: Philosophy, Psychoanalysis, Literature

Charles Shepherdson, editor

Struck by Apollo

Hölderlin's Journeys to Bordeaux and Back and Beyond

DAVID FARRELL KRELL

Cover: Winter sunset on the *Massif Central*, Auvergne. This and all the photographs in the book were taken by the author.

© 2023 State University of New York

All rights reserved

Printed in the United States of America

No part of this book may be used or reproduced in any manner whatsoever without written permission. No part of this book may be stored in a retrieval system or transmitted in any form or by any means including electronic, electrostatic, magnetic tape, mechanical, photocopying, recording, or otherwise without the prior permission in writing of the publisher.

For information, contact State University of New York Press, Albany, NY
www.sunypress.edu

Library of Congress Cataloging-in-Publication Data

Name: Krell, David Farrell, author.
Title: Struck by Apollo : Hölderlin's journeys to Bordeaux and back and
    beyond / David Farrell Krell.
Description: Albany, NY : State University of New York Press, [2023] |
    Series: SUNY series, insinuations: philosophy, psychoanalysis,
    literature | Includes bibliographical references and index.
Identifiers: LCCN 2022062174 | ISBN 9781438495026 (hardcover : alk. paper) |
    ISBN 9781438495040 (ebook)
Subjects: LCSH: Hölderlin, Friedrich, 1770–1843—Travel. | Poets, German—
    19th century—Biography. | LCGFT: Biographies.
Classification: LCC PT2359.H2 Z74 2023 | DDC 831/.6 [B]—dc23/eng/20230404
LC record available at https://lccn.loc.gov/2022062174

10 9 8 7 6 5 4 3 2 1

Photo 1. January sunset at Soulac-sur-Mer, where Hölderlin may have first seen the Atlantic Ocean. *Source*: Photography throughout is by the author.

For

Françoise and Sarosh Dastur

and Joe Kemming

Contents

Preface	ix
Prologue: Who Is This Hölderlin?	1
1. The Achievement	35
2. The Journey to Bordeaux	49
3. "Its Floor Is the Sea"	109
4. The Journey Back	145
5. Heroic Tenderness in the Louvre	171
6. Beyond Bordeaux and Back	197
Epilogue: *Viva la joia!*	217
List of Illustrations	223
Index	229

Preface

For many years I dreamed of repeating the journeys of Friedrich Hölderlin—one of the great poets not only of German literature but of world literature—from Nürtingen (near Stuttgart) to Bordeaux and then back home. The dream became something of a plan in the early 1990s when I visited the father of colleague and friend Pascale-Anne Brault. Her father Pierre Brault was an administrative engineer for the SNCF, the French railway system, and he had an avid interest in the old post-coach system that the railroad replaced in the course of the nineteenth century. He and his daughter helped me think more concretely about the post-coach route from Strasbourg to Bordeaux that Hölderlin must have followed in December and January of 1801–1802. It was especially the stretch between Lyon and Limoges, which took the poet over the mountainous Massif Central and the forbidding Auvergne, that was difficult to ascertain. And the return journey, from Bordeaux to Stuttgart by way of Paris, was shrouded in even greater mystery. At all events, my dream and the plan did not become a reality until decades later.

My neighbor and friend Jürgen Heinrich Kemming, known as "Joe" (the hero of his childhood was Michael Landon's "Little Joe" Cartwright, inasmuch as *Bonanza* was as big a hit in postwar Germany as it was in the United States), invited me to make the trip with him in the winter of 2017–2018. He had recently purchased an RV, a Fiat Hymercar, and this was to be, if not its maiden voyage, its longest trip to date. We started from Nürtingen, the town of Hölderlin's childhood, in mid-December—Hölderlin having started out sometime between December 6 and 10—and made our way to Strasbourg, Lyon, Limoges, Périgueux, and Bordeaux during the next three weeks; we returned to our homes in St. Ulrich (in the German Black Forest near Freiburg-im-Breisgau) during the first week of January. In late May and early June 2018, at about the same time of year when Hölderlin made his return journey, we traveled to Bordeaux to duplicate the homeward journey, this time, to repeat, by way of Paris. During both trips I took hundreds of photographs, some of which accompany this text.

x / Preface

Hölderlin traveled to Bordeaux, arriving there on January 9, 1802, part of the way on foot but mostly by post-coach, to become a tutor to the children in the household of the Hamburg consul to Bordeaux, Daniel Christoph Meyer (1751–1816). Although the conditions of his employment were by all accounts excellent, Hölderlin decided to return to Germany—for reasons we do not know—around May 10, 1802, after only four months in Bordeaux. His twenty-eight-day journey homeward, much of it presumably on foot, took him north to Paris and its Louvre, then east to Strasbourg and the German border at Kehl.

Obviously, there was quite a difference between Hölderlin's post-coach trips or long hikes and our voyages in the Hymercar. In the two centuries that separated Hölderlin from us, an enormous amount had changed, especially in the cities along the route. Yet enough remained to enable us to feel justified in making the trip. Above all, it took us to the sea, to the Atlantic Ocean west of Bordeaux, where Hölderlin beheld the sea for the first and only time in his life. He never forgot this goal of his journey, no doubt because, as one of his poems says, the sea both takes and gives memory. The journey also took him into foreign lands—into Alsace, Burgundy, Limousin, and Gascogne, where a foreign tongue and its many different dialects were spoken. He sensed that this journey to the southwest of France was as close as he would ever get to Greece, that is, to the Greece of classical antiquity, which he had loved all his life. French and Gascognais phrases began to find their way into his notebooks. The journey made him realize that whatever might have been German about him had to be discovered abroad, or at least far from home. Bordeaux, the great port city, opened up more than one new world to him.

In an earlier book on Friedrich Nietzsche's "work sites in word and image," I spoke of Nietzsche as "the good European," which is what Nietzsche very much wanted to be. Something similar happened to Hölderlin as a result of his travels, it seems to me, especially the journey to Bordeaux. Almost a century separated his and Nietzsche's experiences, to be sure, but travel and foreign residences were crucial for both of them. This is why the use of either of the two as a "national poet" or a "national thinker" is a misuse. Or so it seems to me.

My text has the following structure: the Prologue, asking the question, "Who is this Hölderlin?" examines the poet's correspondence to get some sense of his life prior to the Bordeaux trip—he was thirty-one when he began the trip and arguably at the peak of his powers as a poet and thinker. Chapter 1 tries to offer a sense of the achievement that this journey represented: to set out on foot for Strasbourg in winter, with only a rucksack and a walking stick (his luggage had been sent ahead to Bordeaux), to travel then by post-coach from relay station to relay station in the France of the

Preface / xi

post-Revolutionary and early Napoleonic period all the way to the Atlantic coast, all of this was surely a daunting enterprise. The post-coach route over rough roads, with perhaps the occasional boat trip along the rivers when they were not dangerously swollen, and then, during the final days of the trip, walking into the city of Bordeaux, well over a thousand kilometers from home—Joe and I learned, no matter how comfortable our own trip was, just how hazardous and strenuous the trip must have been for Hölderlin. Chapter 2 follows the main way stations of his journey, from Nürtingen to Strasbourg; from Strasbourg to Besançon, Beaune, Mâcon, and Lyon; from Lyon to Clermont-Ferrand, across the Auvergne to Limoges; and then finally from Limoges southward through Périgueux to Bordeaux. Chapter 3 reports what we know and what we may speculate about Hölderlin's four months in and around Bordeaux and on the Atlantic coast. Chapter 4 retraces Hölderlin's homeward journey, taking him and us from Bordeaux to Paris—where he spends some two or three days visiting the collection of Greek antiquities in the Louvre—to Strasbourg and eventually home. Chapter 5, the final chapter, says just a few things about Hölderlin's final years of illness and isolation, thirty-five of them spent in confinement in the Tübingen Tower. A brief epilogue, perhaps a reprise of the "Ode to Joy," concludes the book.

Nothing in my text speaks to Hölderlin as a distinguished thinker, which he surely is; in my view, he is the most creative thinker of that famous generation after Kant, very much equal in stature to Schiller, Fichte, Schelling, and Hegel—not shabby company. His ideas about Greek tragedy and the poetic arts in general are among the most original and radical ideas we have. Neither do I, nor can I, say much about the qualities of his poetry, simply because of my own lack of special training in poetics and in literature generally. Yet it is universally accepted among the Germanists of our time, and not only among them, that Hölderlin is one of the "greats"; if during his lifetime he wished to be in the company of Schiller and Goethe, he certainly has joined such company by now.

It is impossible to say what exactly Hölderlin may have been working on during his voyage to Bordeaux and his stay there, except that we know he labored on his translations of Sophocles during the time he was a tutor at the Meyer residence in Bordeaux. Among the many poems he may have been working on, only two have prominence in my own text: the poem in which he remembers some significant details about his time in Bordeaux, *Andenken*, "Remembrance," and—for reasons I am unable to explain even to myself—the poem "The Wine God," *Der Weingott*, which he composed before the journey and which, revised after the journey, became the hymn "Bread and Wine," *Brot und Wein*. It has always seemed to me that these poems are among his finest and that the alterations to "The Wine God," while intriguing, do not alter the

xii / Preface

impact of the original poem. And so, it was the original, *Der Weingott*, that accompanied Joe and me during our journey. It may well have been because the wines of France too accompanied us every evening of our trip.[1]

It is also impossible to say with certainty what these journeys to Bordeaux and back ultimately meant to Hölderlin. My own surmise, confirmed by many other researchers, is that they offered him an insight into what he called "southerly humanity," which he associated with the Greeks of antiquity. And my further surmise is that such humanity offered him insight into what he called the "heroic body," the kind of body that he saw represented in the Greek antiquities section of the Louvre. Remarkably, such bodies, while undoubtedly "athletic," mirrored to him what he called "tenderness," *Zärtlichkeit*. If the present book has a philosophical kernal, it is this riddle of "heroic tenderness," the riddle that Hölderlin brought back home with him from the south.

Perhaps it is obvious with a project of this sort, but I should say explicitly that for me the photographs are essential. To be sure, I am not a professional photographer. Many of these photos are simply snapshots, although this is not the fault of my Canon T1i/EOS 500D and two very fine lenses, the Sigma LH780-07 (18–300 mm) and the Canon EF-S (60 mm) Macro lens. Even so, whether snapshot, Kodak moment, or more studied landscape or cityscape, it is the photographs that provide a sense of Hölderlin's adventure, and the words I have added remain approximations. My friend Helmbrecht Breinig pointed out to me that my presenting here my own photographs rather than reproducing archival prints from Hölderlin's time shows that my own effort is a romantic rather than a scientific

---

1. Throughout my text I translate the passages from Hölderlin's works. Only rarely do I cite the German, using principally the Carl Hanser edition cited below. Let me also mention at the outset that my text owes a special debt of gratitude to the research of Jochen Bertheau. Joe and I based our route on many different sources, which I will cite as we go along. Yet the source from which I learned most, not only about the route but also about the significance of Hölderlin's journeys and about his relation to France in general, is Bertheau, *Hölderlins französische Bildung* (Frankfurt am Main: Peter Lang, "Heidelberger Beiträge zur deutschen Literatur," 2003), which I cite in the body of my text as JB with page number. The editors of the five current historical-critical editions of Hölderlin's works and letters— Friedrich Beißner, Adolf Beck, Jochen Schmidt, D. E. Sattler, and Michael Knaupp—have made essential contributions to what we know about Hölderlin's journeys. The edition of his works and letters that I cite most often is that by Knaupp, *Friedrich Hölderlin Werke und Briefe*, 3 vols. (Munich: Carl Hanser, 1993), cited in my text as CHV with volume and page numbers. For readers who wish to pursue further study, I recommend Bertheau's exhaustive (at least up to 2003) bibliography. See also the detailed bibliography in Thomas Knubben, *Hölderlin: Eine Winterreise* (Tübingen: Klöpfer & Meyer, 2012).

or historical one; I have tried, through the use of my own imagination and perception, to venture a guess as to what Hölderlin may have seen on his journeys, what may have gripped him. My attempt is, to say the least, highly speculative. Yet is that not what philosophers do? What, for scientists, is irresponsible is the philosopher's virtue and métier.

I have tried to be as precise as possible about the routes Hölderlin followed, but even there a great deal of guesswork is involved. Precisely what his travel schedule and his many stopovers may have enabled him to experience involves even greater guesswork. All we really know about the journey to Bordeaux is what he tells his mother, namely, that he had "many experiences," some of them granting "pure joy," others exhausting or even terrifying him. Joe and I set out to see if we could learn what some of his experiences—with luck, the more joyous ones—might have been.

I want to express my gratitude to the personnel at the Bibliothèque historique des postes et de télécommunications in Paris, in particular to the directrice, Anne Dauga-Pernin, and Catherine Chauvière, who were prompt and generous with their counsel and assistance. The map they placed at my disposal, which has their catalogue number 10123, reprinted here with the generous permission of the Bibliothèque, is from 1812, a decade after Hölderlin made his trip but showing the routes that were already well established by the time of his Bordeaux journey. All the remaining maps in the book are enlargements of certain portions of the 1812 map.

Over the years, my brother Jonathan F. Krell and my colleagues Pascale-Anne Brault and Michael Naas, along with Françoise Dastur, have aided me in all things French, and I thank them warmly for their counsel. My friend Helmbrecht Breinig read the entire manuscript and made countless improvements. Juliana Cárdenas Toro produced an electronic version of the project, integrating the photographs, maps, and text into a whole, and she has my deep gratitude. The entire staff at SUNY Press made the publication process a joy: I thank especially Rebecca Colesworthy, Senior Acquisitions Editor; Jenn Bennett-Genthner, the Manuscript Editorial Manager; Susan Morreale, book designer; Julia Cosacchi, Sue Kauffman, Kate Seburyamo, Aimee Harrison, and Sharla Clute. Charles Shepherdson, the editor of "Insinuations," has lent generous support over so many years now, and he has my gratitude. Finally, my thanks go to the Dasturs for their hospitality and friendship and, of course, to the very big-hearted Little Joe.

D. F. K.
Strobelhütte, St. Ulrich,
and Akrotiri, Santorini

Photo 2. Tübingen cemetery. "Friedrich Hölderlin, born March 29, 1770; died June 7, 1843."

Prologue

Who Is This Hölderlin?

Who is this Hölderlin, the man who travels to Bordeaux in the winter of 1801–1802 at least part of the way on foot? If we are to spend weeks attempting to accompany him on his journey, setting off from Nürtingen, his hometown, we ought to learn something about our travel companion. Let me therefore provide a biographical sketch based on some passages from his letters. True, many of his letters may be presumed lost. Yet what we do have, and it fills hundreds of book pages, sheds the brightest light on Hölderlin's life. In what follows I will cite mere fragments of the letters; when we arrive at the period of the Bordeaux trip, I will cite at least a few letters in their entirety.

Photo 3. Nürtingen on the Neckar River.

2 / Struck by Apollo

The first letter that we have, written by the fifteen-year-old Hölderlin, tells of his love of nature and of solitude. Indeed, he cannot abide having anyone around him during his walks through the woods and fields that border the Neckar River near his childhood town of Nürtingen (see photo 3). Thus he "seemed, as it were, to despise humanity" but also to suffer from his extreme sensibility, so extreme that "the least little thing struck me to heart" (CHV 2:393). Two years later, he confirms that he prefers to be anywhere else than in "human society" (CHV 2:399). He attributes his moodiness and unsociability to the early deaths of his "two fathers," that is, both his biological and his adoptive fathers, the first of whom died when he was two, the second when he was eight. "Have I not borne enough? Did I not experience as a boy what would make a man sigh? And now that I am a youth, are things any better? And they say this is the best time of our lives! My God! Am I the only one who feels this way? Is everyone else happier than I am? So what have I done to deserve this?" (ibid.).

Furthermore, a certain prudery, the inheritance of his Pietist upbring-ing and schooling, is always present in the letters. He abhors Christoph Martin Wieland's literary eroticism (CHV 2:400), and his own tendency with the young loves of his life is to pass them on to a friend. Later he will fall desperately in love, yet one senses that his ability to express love never equals the intensity of his feelings—something that he would share with a significant portion of humanity, to be sure, even if the Pietist upbringing adds appreciably to his burden.

Another trait that is visible early in his life is his ambition to become a poet—and thus to resist his mother's wish for him, a wish she never surrenders, that he become a Pietist pastor. True, he writes to his mother from the seminary school in which she has placed him that he would never dream of rejecting the call to be a clergyman, inasmuch as a "village pas-tor" is so "useful" to humanity that surely no one could be "happier" than a man of the cloth (CHV 2:404–5). Yet Hölderlin has been so miserable at the seminary schools of Denkendorf and Maulbronn, where his mother has sent him on a scholarship—a scholarship that requires that he become a pastor, otherwise the mother has to pay back his tuition stipend—so mis-erable that one has the sense that Hölderlin is trying to convince himself of what he knows is not the case. He will in fact spend the rest of his life trying to escape from his mother's frugality, not to say parsimony, and her relentless dominance. Here is the seventeen-year-old writing from Maulbronn to a friend: "I will never be able to hold out here! Truly, never! I have to leave—I've firmly decided either to write my Mother tomorrow to take me out of the cloister, or to ask the prelates for a sick-leave of several months,

Prologue / 3

because I have often been coughing up blood.—You see, my friend, that I am gradually heading toward repose" (CHV 2:407–8). By *repose*, of course, he means the requiescat of the grave.

This is the first and last reference to what looks like tuberculosis—or, just as likely, a bleeding ulcer. Or perhaps he is merely imagining grounds to request sick leave from his superiors, which would be preferable to his having to write his mother. He apologizes to his half-brother Carl for his "eternal, eternal griping" (CHV 2:408), a word he uses again two years later in Tübingen, where the Evangelical *Stift* or seminary is no more congenial to him than the earlier "cloister" schools.

He confesses his "melancholy mood," *trübsinnige Laune* (CHV 2:439), to his first girlfriend Louise Nast. The only two things that seem to relieve the young man's persistent melancholy are his long hikes into the Swabian countryside and his occasional outings with friends. When he is eighteen, still at the Maulbronn cloister, he takes an unaccompanied trip (by rent-a-horse, apparently) to Speyer. There he marvels at the Romanesque cathedral, contrasting it with the miserable chapel back at Maulbronn. At Speyer he crosses the Rhine for the first time: "You have to imagine—a river that, where it is widest, is three times the breadth of the Neckar, shaded on both banks from top to bottom by forest—the prospect as one looks downriver extends so long that your head spins. That was a view! I will never forget it; it touched me deeply" (CHV 2:424–25). He tours Heidelberg—its famous *Tun* or wine cask and its "new" bridge—and Mannheim, with its perfectly squared-off streets and its luxurious *Nationaltheater*, and he admires the ships that line the wharves along the Rhine.

The more one reads Hölderlin's letters, which are often epistolary travel journals, the more one regrets that we do not have such a journal from the Bordeaux trip. Either that journal is lost or, if it was never written, such an omission would speak volumes about Hölderlin's altered mood by the end of 1801. Only extreme weariness, I believe, would have prevented him from writing about the places and people he was seeing for the first time in France. At all events, here is one last passage from the Speyer diary, again about crossing the Rhine, which seems to him a kind of ocean:

> Think of the majestic Rhine, so wide that you scarcely notice the ships out there on it, so wide that it seems to be a kind of azure wall, and on the opposite shore thick, wild forests—and above the forests the shimmering mountains of Heidelberg. Downriver an immeasurable plain, everywhere so full of the Lord's blessings—and all around me so much activity, the ships

4 / Struck by Apollo

discharging their cargo; over there some of them are plunging into the sea, and the evening wind wafts and swells their sails– –. (CHV 2:429)

In the spring of 1789, he breaks off his puppy-love relationship with Louise, returning to her the ring she has given him and the letters she has sent. He promises that he will congratulate her heartily when a worthy young man proposes marriage to her; she will then see that she never could have been happy with her erstwhile friend, who is so "peevish, glum, and sickly" (CHV 2:446). Notably, he now attributes this prevailing melancholy to "unsatisfied ambition" (ibid.). He will often say this about himself, and his friends will confirm that ambition—to be a poet, and a great poet at that. The initial and enduring frustration of his ambition, however, derives from his mother, who doubtless takes poetry, if she takes it at all, to be frivolous. Later frustrations will be the aloofness or reserve toward him of most of the "greats" of his time, partly due to the overweening earnestness of Hölderlin's demeanor and his poetic themes and partly because of the daring twists and turns, never before seen or heard of, in his German syntax and vocabulary. When toward the end of his letter to Louise he writes, "my love is not for this world!" the allusion is to a Jesus who will never find his Magdalene and who lives solely for the sake of his poetic mission.

Louise will be easier to leave behind than his mother, however. Hölderlin's university years in Tübingen are marked by his continued efforts to convince Frau Gock (she keeps the name of her second husband, Hölderlin's adoptive father) that he is a poet and that she must abandon her plans to make a country parson out of him. One early letter, written from Tübingen when he is nineteen, is quite revealing in two respects. First, he reports a conversation with Christian Friedrich Daniel Schubart (1739–1791), the remarkable poet, musician, and social critic and political activist. Schubart had been released from prison only two years prior to their meeting, having spent a decade in the Hohenasperg dungeon because of his criticism of the local duke and of the Jesuit Order. The political prisoner still bore the scars of that imprisonment at the time of Hölderlin's visit. He received Hölderlin "with fatherly tenderness," and there can be no doubt that the older man increased the younger man's disaffection from the politics of the German lands, especially his own Württemberg. Hölderlin tells his mother that Schubart asked him whether he had sufficient support from his parents to enable him to be a poet and that of course he answered "yes." More remarkable than this gentle hint to his mother are his words to her about her chronic "mournfulness," which has given him many "gloomy hours"

(CHV 2:450). Even though he begins the letter with apologies for his own "bad behavior," in what context we do not know, he now has the temerity to scold his mother, begging her to put off her gloominess: "I conjure you to fulfill your duties as a mother and a Christian, which up to now you have fulfilled so conscientiously but with excessive mournfulness—be of good cheer, enjoy the lovely spring, take joy from the greening that gives us hope, the greening that God has bestowed on our fields and trees" (ibid.). One can imagine his mother's face as she reads these lines; she may well have passed from gloom to dudgeon. Hölderlin did not often show such boldness. In his next letter to her, he confesses his own propensity to sadness, remarking "of course, it is innate in me that I take everything too much to heart, but I thank God for the fact that it prevents me from being frivolous" (CHV 2:452).

Shortly before his twenty-first birthday, when he should be celebrating his maturity, he writes to his mother, "Your goodness to me has shamed me. I am so far behind you in goodness, and you give me so many opportunities to imitate you. Forgive me, dear Mother!" (CHV 2:467). Indeed, the word *shame* appears over and over again as the response to his mother's "goodness" to him, that goodness consisting principally in her never releasing his paternal inheritance to him, her controlling the purse strings until her death. As a result, Hölderlin dies a nominally wealthy man but lives his entire life as a pauper, whereas she is and remains a wealthy widow to the end of her days. He never seems to have discovered this fact, never seems to have learned of his mother's having withheld from him the monies that his stepfather had intended him to have: all his life he struggles to keep his expenses low, begs her for pittances, and feels ashamed to have to ask her for money at all. He never escapes the feeling that he is "indebted" to her, that he must "pay recompense for her labors" (CHV 2:490). When he is twenty-five years old, working now as a tutor in Waltershausen, he adds a bizarre postscript to a letter written to his friend Neuffer: "P.S.: One more favor! Could you maybe visit my Mother, and if you find that she is not entirely satisfied with the change in my situation, calm her down? I want to do everything not to be a burden to her, and so I am living very frugally; I eat only one meal a day, and that one quite plain, and whenever I have a pitcher of beer I dream of our Neckar Valley wine and the lovely hours that were blessed by it. Farewell, dear friend!" (CHV 2:567). During that same year he writes to his half-brother Carl, "Our dear Mother's goodness makes me infinitely ashamed" (CHV 2:576). A psychologist would have to ask whether the mother's goodness is a *Gift* that keeps on *gifting*—the German word *Gift* means "poison."

In the summer of 1791 Hölderlin confesses to his mother that he will never marry. It is an essential part of her plan that he marry, since a country pastor has to have a chaste and pious helpmate like herself. Hölderlin tells her: "My peculiar character, my moods, my obsession with my projects, and (to tell the whole truth) my ambition—traits that cannot be eradicated without endangering my life—all these things do not allow me to hope that I can be happy in a tranquil married state living in some peaceful parish" (CHV 2:473). Lest his mother take the news too badly, he immediately adds, "but maybe the future will change that." To his friend Neuffer he is more candid: "The reason for the fact that I am in a cloister is my Mother's pleading; for her sake one can allow a couple of years to go sour" (CHV 2:476). The years turned into decades.

In his early novel *Hyperion*, Hölderlin suggests that every life is shaped as an ellipse—that is, it follows not a circular but an oval-shaped orbit, one that has two centers or foci. One center is "the school of nature" into which an individual is born and where he or she is most likely to find happiness; the other is the "school of destiny," which tweaks and twists the natural

Photo 4. The Sankt-Remigius-Kapelle near Wurmlingen dates from 1050, in its present form from 1685. After the ascent to its 475 meter summit, one enjoys fine views of the Schwäbische Alb to the southeast and the surrounding vineyards—even in winter.

inclinations and talents of the individual in what is otherwise called "rearing" or "education." A "rounded" or "centered" existence is rarely if ever achieved; normally, only the elliptical or "eccentric" orbit, which pertains to Kepler's imperfect planets, literally, the "wanderers," is ours. Hölderlin's outings into nature, his walks along the Neckar River or into the hills of Tübingen, often taking him to the chapel overlooking the neighboring town of Wurmlingen (photo 4), are desperate efforts to enable the school of nature to prevail.

To his sister "Rike" (Ulrike), he writes more candidly than to his mother about his need to dedicate his life to poetry, which for him is the curriculum of the school of nature. He must find another "situation" than the one he finds himself in, even if he has to earn his living by the sweat of his brow. "God knows how much I love my family," he adds, "and how much I want my life to conform to its wishes, but it is impossible for me to impose on myself nonsensical and useless laws and to remain in a place where my best powers will wither" (CHV 2:479).

He also notes more explicitly than ever before that he can never "become a man" in the present political situation. Here he shows how strongly he and every gifted student of the Tübinger Stift have embraced the ideals of the Enlightenment, the "Rights of Man," or rather of "Humankind," and the goals of the French Revolution. The local duke of Württemberg, alerted to the unrest among the university students, has recently taken repressive measures; the university administrators and most of the faculty knuckle under. The only members of the faculty that the students respect, however, are those few who are reading Kant's critical philosophy. Hölderlin and his friends Schelling and Hegel follow events in Paris as closely as they can, hungry for information. In the summer of 1793, after the September Massacre and the establishment of the Directorate and the Committee of Public Safety (the machinery of the Terror), Hölderlin writes to his brother, "It hangs from a thread whether France will perish or become a magnificent state" (CHV 2:496). It is not until 1802 and his Bordeaux sojourn that Hölderlin becomes entirely skeptical about the chances of revolution in the German lands, especially if it is being exported forcefully by First Consul Napoleon Bonaparte.

Jochen Bertheau argues quite convincingly that Hölderlin's politics were always Girondist rather than Jacobin and that his heroes were Montesquieu and Helvétius even more than Jean-Jacques Rousseau. Bertheau emphasizes that Hölderlin had no sympathy for the more radical Jacobin party led by Marat, Danton, and Robespierre; unlike his friend Sinclair, an avid Jacobin, Hölderlin did not try to justify the Terror (JB 20). In June

8 / Struck by Apollo

1792 he urges his sister, "Pray for the French, who are fighting for human rights" (CHV 2:489). His enthusiasm for the Revolution clearly arose from his devotion to its ideals of liberty, equality, fraternity—and most of all to its Declaration of the Rights of Humanity and its celebration of peace.[1] Hölderlin's hope, shared by most of his friends, was that peace would soon be restored to a France riven by civil strife. He and his friends felt that by 1791 the Revolution had been accomplished, its victories for the French people secured. The reign of peace would now begin—the three versions of Hölderlin's "Celebration of Peace," *Friedensfeier*, reflect that hope (JB 28). The Jacobin plan for something like "permanent revolution" was thus far from Hölderlin's mind (JB 23–24). His early enthusiasm for Napoleon was based on his hope that Bonaparte would secure the Revolution in France and then bring it to Germany and Austria; to repeat, that enthusiasm did not die until 1802, with his stay in Bordeaux and the May 1802 referendum that made Napoleon consul for life. By that time, it had become clear that the Corsican was a despot. The despair of Hölderlin's friend Johann Gottfried Ebel in Paris and, even prior to that, the political cynicism of Bonaparte's *Consulta* in Lyon were ultimately enough to disabuse Hölderlin of his enthusiasm (JB 36).

For the three friends of the Tübinger Stift (photo 5), Hölderlin, Schelling, and Hegel, the peace that Revolution would imminently introduce was nothing less than the veritable "Kingdom of God," an odd mix of Revolutionary, Anarchist, and Pietist ideals that we today can hardly understand. At the very least, the religious language would serve as camouflage for the political intent, and such camouflage was necessary in the despotic duchy of Württemberg. Yet it was more than camouflage. The underlying attitude of Hölderlin and his friends toward matters political is best expressed in "The Oldest Fragment Toward a System in German Idealism": the machinery of the state, operated by the aristocrats and their priests, says the Fragment,

---

1. In his third chapter, Bertheau argues convincingly that Hemsterhuis, Montesquieu, and Helvétius, rather than Jean-Jacques Rousseau, are the most significant contributors to Hölderlin's political ideals—this in spite of the heroic stature that Rousseau has in Hölderlin's poetry (JB 49). Rousseau's *Julie ou La nouvelle Héloïse* is less important in this respect than Helvétius's *De l'esprit* (JB 51). As for the epistolary style of Hölderlin's early novel *Hyperion*, Goethe's *Werther*, claims Bertheau, is more influential than any text of Rousseau. As for Rousseau's *Émile*, Hölderlin's appreciation of that work is tempered by a number of criticisms (JB 78–79) that stem from his own experience as an educator. And yet Hölderlin's mentions of Rousseau in his poems, as the spokesperson for and the figurehead of *les droits de l'homme*, are surely heroic celebrations.

Photo 5. Main courtyard of the Tübinger Stift, the Evangelical seminary where Hölderlin and his roommates Schelling and Hegel studied in the early 1790s.

needs to be dismantled (JB 28).[2] Ironically, the absolutist princes of Württemberg and the other German lands looked back to Louis XIV as their model, and they tried to speak his French in their own courts (JB 40). For the young Hölderlin, politics was a matter of Revolutionary France versus the ancien régime that still prevailed in the backward German princedoms. There can be no doubt that as he set out on his journey to Bordeaux he still looked to France as the harbinger of whatever political hopes his generation entertained. Even if he feared the effects of war on his family and friends, France remained the only hope for his fatherland.

Heidegger was fond of saying that Hölderlin, *his* Hölderlin, represented a "test" for the German nation, and perhaps he was right. Yet the test was not what Heidegger thought it was. The test was that Hölderlin's German fatherland look to France for inspiration in the task of achieving radical political and social reform—to be sure, always in the Girondist "republican"

---

2. For the text of this fascinating "Fragment," the authorship of which is claimed by the editors of the works of Hegel, Schelling, and Hölderlin alike, see the opening chapter of my *The Tragic Absolute: German Idealism and the Languishing of God* (Bloomington: Indiana University Press, 2005), esp. 25–26 and the accompanying commentary.

10 / Struck by Apollo

direction, signposted by the Declaration of Rights of Humanity. The test for Germany, in other words, was that it become more French.

In September 1792 Hölderlin expresses his unhappiness with the Tübinger Stift to his friend Neuffer: "Here I have absolutely no joy" (CHV 2:492). He tells Neuffer that he is planning to write a hymn to "boldness"; imagine, "boldness," he says, "in this my life as a vegetable" (ibid). In May 1793 he writes to his half-brother Carl about his "wretched finances," which condemn him to stay in his room at the Stift. Going out, except for walks, means spending money. He gives us a peek into the daily routine of his university years: "It's four in the morning and I'm up preparing my coffee myself; then I sit down to work. Usually I stay in my cell until the evening, often in the company of the sacred Muses, often with my Greeks. At the moment I'm attending the school of Herr Kant" (CHV 2:496). These are the months when he is working on the first drafts of his novel *Hyperion*. In addition to his attendance at the school of Kant, he is often in the company of Plato's Socrates, wandering through the shady grove of Plato's *Phaedrus* or attending the *Symposium* on love in the company of "that wag Aristophanes" (CHV 2:499).

His efforts to declare his unhappiness to his mother intensify now. In November he writes her, "My youthful ardor took the path of melancholy" (CHV 2:493). That is of course the path that in his view she had mapped out for him: an early poem of his, "My Family," describes her "lying senseless in the dust" at the time of her second husband's death (CHV 1:22–23):

> That she in many melancholy hours
> Weeps silently in her widow's pain!
> When all my wounds gape again
> And memories of mourning are ours.

In late summer 1793 he tells his mother of his plan to continue his philosophical studies in Jena (CHV 2:506). "Is it my fortune or misfortune that nature gave me this unconquerable drive to develop further and further the forces that are in me?" (CHV 2:509). He promises her that he will cover at least half of his expenses by taking on a tutorship. Such tutorships were common for recent graduates of the Stift who did not immediately receive a parish or vicarage; his friend Hegel, for example, was about to leave for Berne to take up such a tutorship. Normally, a tutorship was an interim job, not a professional goal for someone who had the training that a Stiftler received. Yet tutorships turned out to be the only source of Hölderlin's independent income until his active years came to an end. He would later defend tutoring as an "innocent" occupation, knowing however that for his mother it was simply the sign of a wasted life. When he tells Carl about his decision to search for tutorships, he defends that modest profession by saying that he believes in "the generations of the centuries to come" (CHV 2:507) and that he will endeavor to become their educator: "We live during a period in which everything is tending toward better days. The seed of Enlightenment, these silent desires and strivings of individuals to shape the human race, will expand and grow stronger, and they will bear splendid fruit" (CHV 2:508). Carl understands better than anyone else Hölderlin's pedagogical drive, since he has been on the receiving end of his older brother's pedagogy for a decade now.

Why is Jena the goal? Principally because the school of Herr Kant is expanding its horizons there under the guidance of Johann Gottlieb Fichte and also because Schiller and Goethe are active either there or in nearby Weimar. These are the "greats" whom Hölderlin dreams he might some day accompany. With the help of a Professor Stäudlin, Hölderlin soon receives an offer from Schiller's friend Charlotte von Kalb to tutor her son in Waltershausen, not far from Jena, in the Gotha district of Thuringia, and by January 1794 Hölderlin finds himself in Waltershausen. When he is not tutoring young Fritz von Kalb, Hölderlin studies Kant's third *Critique*, focusing on Kant's aesthetic theories and the reply to Kant that Schiller had made in his *Aesthetic Education of Humanity*. Charlotte von Kalb shares with Hölderlin her notes from Fichte's lectures. By November he himself is in Jena. He attends Fichte's lectures, held spellbound by this man "of such depth and intellectual energy" (CHV 2:553), and on occasion he speaks with the philosopher. He visits Schiller several times, and one may assume that the two grow closer, even if Schiller is troubled by Hölderlin's unrelieved intensity and gravity, not to say melancholy.

During one such visit a minor catastrophe occurs—not so minor for the ambitious yet diffident poet (CHV 2:553–54). A stranger is in the room with Schiller when Hölderlin arrives. Schiller neglects to introduce him, so that the situation becomes awkward. At one point Schiller leaves the room, and the stranger fills the empty time by picking up an issue of Schiller's journal, *Thalia*, the very issue that contains Hölderlin's recently published "Fragment of *Hyperion*." The stranger thumbs through the journal, scanning those pages that are so important to Hölderlin—his first attempt to go public with his novel. The stranger says not a word until, as though only small talk will rescue the situation, he asks Hölderlin about the health of Charlotte von Kalb and the Major, her husband. Hölderlin answers the query in two or three words, and the small talk dies. Schiller returns, and

12 / Struck by Apollo

the three are then joined by another friend of Schiller's; there is talk about the theater in Weimar and about the arts in general and then the meeting dissolves. Later that afternoon Hölderlin learns that the stranger was Goethe, the greatest of the "greats," the man whose works Hölderlin had been reading for years now, but whom he had never met and therefore could not have recognized. Schiller no doubt assumed that everyone would recognize Goethe, the superstar of his time—or the *other* superstar of *their* time. Hölderlin confesses his gaffe later that night to Schiller, who finds it hilarious. He tries to console his young friend, but it is a wonder that the humiliated Hölderlin does not flee Jena the next morning.

Later letters inform us that the gaffe was soon forgotten. Hölderlin emphasizes that his subsequent conversations with Goethe were fruitful and rewarding. He writes to Hegel in January 1795: "O my brother! I have spoken with Goethe. It is the greatest joy of our lives to find so much humanity alongside such greatness. He conversed with me in such a gentle and friendly way that he made my heart smile, and when I think back on it I am smiling still" (CHV 2:568). Hölderlin compares Goethe to Herder, with whom he has also spoken, saying that Herder is more urbane, more "a man of the world," and much more inclined to use high-blown metaphors in conversation than Goethe is (CHV 2:568, 564).

During those weeks in Jena, Hölderlin is living in a small garden house, a kind of cabin or modest chalet, high on a hilltop overlooking Jena, but he often meets with Schiller and Goethe in the city. On January 19, 1795, he writes to his friend Neuffer:

> I went to visit Herder, and the warm-hearted way the noble man received me made an unforgettable impression on me. . . . I will no doubt visit him often. I also met with Goethe. My heart was pounding when I crossed the threshold—that you can well believe. I did not meet him at his home, however, but, after our first meeting [at Schiller's], here at the von Kalbs' house. Tranquillity and great majesty are in his gaze, but also love; he is utterly uncomplicated in discussion, but with the occasional bitter jab at some of the foolishness that surrounds him and an equally bitter expression on his face—but then illuminated by flashes of the genius that is far from extinguished in him: that's the way I found him. Some people say he is proud. But if by that they mean that he is domineering, or that he keeps people at a distance, then as far as I am concerned they are lying. Just yesterday I spoke with him here at the club. (CHV 2:564)

Prologue / 13

In a later letter to Neuffer he writes, "I often make my way to Schiller's, where I usually also find Goethe, who is spending a lot of time in Jena these days" (CHV 2:583). The tone of these letters suggests that Hölderlin is finally beginning to be accepted by the "greats" and that he feels more at ease with them, if not by any means equal to them.

His situation changes abruptly in June 1795. Suddenly, without advance warning or explanation, he leaves Jena without telling anyone, heading back to his mother's house in Nürtingen. Why? No one really knows. Yet the psychiatrists, Jean Laplanche among them, are inclined to take this as a sign of Hölderlin's emerging illness—they do not shy from calling it an early symptom of schizophrenia.[3] But why does Hölderlin abandon Schiller, Goethe, Herder, and Fichte, the giants of his time, and return to the seclusion of his mother's house—which in the meantime has been sold but where she still occupies several of its rooms? Could it have had to do with the student revolt of May 27 in Jena? It is not too far-fetched to imagine that Hölderlin would have joined the radical students in their political protests and that the police would then have become "interested" in him. (This "interest" of the police in Hölderlin was indeed awakened ten years later.) Or could it have had to do with Wilhelmine Marianne Kirms, the companion of Charlotte von Kalb?

Kirms and Hölderlin had become close at some point during the year 1792, and later rumors suggested that she may have had a child by him. To his sister on January 16, 1794, Hölderlin wrote that Kirms, whom he calls "a widow," is a woman "of intelligence and heart," one who speaks several languages and who is at the moment reading Kant's most recent publication. He adds, "In addition, she has a very interesting figure" (CHV 2:518). The remark is notable as the only such remark we have from Hölderlin. It is perhaps a sign of his affection for his sister, whom he then teases by saying that she should not worry, Frau Kirms is "promised" to someone else, and in any case, she is far more intelligent than he is, even if he himself has become "wiser" since becoming a tutor. Nevertheless, Kirms did give birth to a child (Louise Agnese) sometime in 1795; a year later the child

---

3. I will discuss Jean Laplanche's views in the final chapter of my text. I am happier with Françoise Dastur's insight that Hölderlin's flight from Jena, after weeks of contact with the "greats," results in a period of withdrawal and intense solitude, perhaps Hölderlin's first real experience of radical solitude. Yet even radical solitude, especially for a writer and a poet, need not be (to put it mildly) an expression of schizophrenia. See Dastur, "Hölderlin's Solitude," in *The Philosophy of Creative Solitudes*, ed. David Jones (London: Bloomsbury Academic, 2019), 163.

14 / Struck by Apollo

died. Hölderlin seems to have had no further contact with Kirms once he left Waltershausen for Jena, however, and it seems highly probable that he knew nothing about the pregnancy. It is quite possible that the rumors were merely that, baseless rumors. And yet on January 19, 1795, from Jena, he confides to his friend Neuffer: "The girls and women here leave me ice-cold. At the house in Waltershausen I had a friend that I was unhappy to lose, a young widow from Dresden who has now become a governess in Meinungen [i.e., Meiningen]. She is a wonderfully bright and serious person, and a good-hearted woman, made unhappy by a bad mother. It will be interesting for you if some other time I tell you about her and about her fate" (CHV 2:566–67). One suspects that he knows something about her "fate" but also that he almost certainly does not connect himself with her pregnancy, otherwise he would never refer to her fate as merely "interesting." His affection for Kirms appears to have been genuine, and in any case, his superb training in guilt would never have allowed him to be so frivolous and flippant about a possible paternity.

Finally, to add another name to the gossips' list, there are various reports, all of them unconfirmed, that in Jena, Hölderlin fell in love with Schiller's beautiful personal assistant, Sophie Mereau, later the wife of Clemens Brentano. Such an infatuation would likely have made the relationship with Schiller even more difficult than it already was. In any case, Hölderlin later tells his friend Neuffer that he cannot write to Mereau (regarding some literary matter) because of these rumors—the truth of which he of course denies (CHV 2:689).

Yet the most likely reason by far for the "flight" from Jena has to do with Hölderlin's relationship with Schiller, with whose "genius" he finds himself engaged in "secret struggle" (CHV 2:690). Hölderlin writes about this struggle and the emotional confusion resulting from it in a remarkably candid and insightful way. On July 23, 1795, he tries to explain to Schiller himself the reason for his abrupt departure that past June:

> It is quite remarkable that one can be very happy under the influence of an intelligence even when that intelligence works its effects not by speaking but merely by proximity, so that one suffers a loss that increases with every mile of distance that opens up between them. And with all the motivations that I had, I could scarcely have brought myself to leave were it not for the fact that, on the other hand, this very proximity so often disquieted me. I was constantly tempted to visit you, but then when I did, I always felt that I could mean nothing to you. I had to

pay for the intense demands I was making with the pain that I often had to bear; because I wanted to be so much for you, I had to tell myself that I was nothing to you. (CHV 2:589–90)

In a later letter to Schiller, Hölderlin repeats this self-analysis, and his quandary expresses itself in a remarkable metaphor:

Can you believe that I still have to tell myself that being near you is something I must forbid myself? Truly, you enliven me too much when I am around you. I remember all too well how your presence ignited me so much that for the rest of the day I couldn't entertain a single thought. As long as I was in your presence, my heart was almost too small, and when I was away I could not hold things together. In your presence I am like a plant that has just been transplanted into fresh soil: it has to be covered during the noonday heat. You may laugh at me; but I am telling the truth. (CHV 2:665)

In that first letter to Schiller after his flight from Jena, Hölderlin goes on to say that it was not mere vanity on his part, not a matter of craving a friendly glance from the great man, whether deserved or not. "I would despise myself very deeply," he writes, were that the case (CHV 2:590). Rather, he speaks of his hope to achieve a true "affinity" with Schiller, as though he might even attain a kind of kinship, *eine Verwandtschaft*, in their common service to "the good, the beautiful, and the true" (ibid.). He asks whether he may visit Schiller from time to time in the future, but for the moment he stresses his need for solitude. "I live a very lonely life, and I believe it does me good" (ibid.). In his next letter to Schiller, on September 4, 1795, he describes himself as a *res nullius*, "a thing belonging to no one," and he describes his solitude in terms borrowed from Goethe's *Wilhelm Meister's Apprenticeship*, terms that Nietzsche will later use to describe himself: "I believe it is the property of rare human beings that they can give without receiving—that they are able to 'warm themselves with ice.' All too often I feel that I am not one of these rare human beings. I freeze and stiffen in the winter that surrounds me. As my sky is of iron, so I am of stone" (CHV 2:596).

Something happens to Hölderlin's world of ice, iron, and stone, however, when he takes up a tutorship at the Frankfurt house of Jacob Gontard and his wife Susette Borkenstein Gontard in January 1796. Already by February he tells Carl that he is suddenly growing younger. He senses some sort of

16 / Struck by Apollo

"rejuvenation" in his life, although he is not well prepared for the love that is about to shape and shake the remainder of that life. (And who is ever prepared for it?) "It was also time for me to feel a bit younger," he tells his half-brother, adding, almost prophetically, "in only half the days that might be allotted to me I would already have become an old man" (CHV 2:612). A later letter, one that is reminiscent of the difficult relationship with Schiller, once again puts the matter in terms of horticulture: "At all events I am like an old flower stalk that has been dropped in the street amid the shards of its pot, stripped of its new growth, roots damaged, to be rescued only if someone very carefully repots it in fresh soil—but even so, to a certain extent the stalk is still stunted and crippled, and it will remain so" (CHV 2:622).

Meanwhile, Hölderlin asks his brother to send him his flute—he clearly wants to participate in the musical evenings at the Gontard residence, no doubt encouraged to do so by the mother of the children he is tutoring. It is a period in which he is thinking a lot about education, including the "education of the populace" referred to at the end of "The Oldest Fragment Toward a System in German Idealism." He is also thinking specifically about the education of Susette's son Henry, to whom he grows close—as he becomes increasingly close to the boy's mother. The boy's father, the banker Jacob Gontard, is soon out of the picture, except as a rival. The three points of the triangle are the boy, the boy's mother, and the boy's tutor. To make a long and scandalous and very tender story short, Hölderlin and Susette soon confess their love for one another.[4]

Hölderlin writes to his friend Neuffer, "I am in a new world" (CHV 2:624). Later he enhances the image: "Since I last wrote I have circumnavigated a world of joy" (CHV 2:649). Soon enough, however, the rumors begin to fly. The world cannot bear the sight of other people finding love; its ressentiment wants the destruction of such love and works to achieve it. Soon enough the husband hears the rumors. A fractious scene ensues between the husband and the lover in September 1797, in Susette's presence, and Hölderlin is banished from the house. He and his Diotima exchange letters, magnificent love letters, and they meet secretly from time to time until May 1800. Yet the defeat is too much for the two of them. Part of the reason Hölderlin elects to go to Bordeaux eighteen months later is surely

---

4. For Susette Gontard's remarkable love letters to Hölderlin, and the drafts of his letters to her, see Douglas F. Kenney and Sabine Menner-Bettscheid, *The Recalcitrant Art: Diotima's Letters to Hölderlin and Related Missives* (Albany: State University of New York Press, 2000), throughout.

Prologue / 17

this sense of defeat—the loss of the human being he loves and the loss of his own sense of direction. Not long after the scene, in November 1797, he asks Carl how one can build a wall around one's heart "when the world pummels" that heart "with its fists?" (CHV 2:668). In early 1798 he calls his life a "shipwreck" (CHV 2:680). For it is also at this time that severe doubts about his ability to be a poet and to be recognized as such plague him: he complains that his work lacks vitality or "liveliness," *das Lebendige* (CHV 2:710). He is crushed by the fact that the greats will neither support the literary journal that he hopes to found nor help him procure a lecture-ship in Greek literature at the University of Jena (CHV 2:794, 903–4). Only the stopgap profession remains for him, it seems: tutorships, the next one in Hauptwil, Switzerland.

That tutorship lasts only four months, from mid-January to mid-April 1801. Around this time, he writes to his friend Christian Landauer, "Tell me, is it a blessing or a curse, this being lonely? I am destined to it by nature, and whenever I choose the situation that I believe will help me best to learn about myself in this respect, I find that I am relentlessly compelled back to it!" (CHV 2:896). He has already complained to his sister Rike, in one of his most heart-rending letters, that he feels trapped in "a paralyzing restlessness," a paradoxical state that leaves him once again "as cold as ice," so that all he can hope for is the calm that continually eludes him (CHV 2:880). To Carl he confesses that his heart has been "torn to shreds" from attacks that have come from "more than one side" (CHV 2:897), meaning presumably both the personal and professional sides. It is in this frame of mind that he accepts the offer of a tutorship in Bordeaux. He will walk from Nürtingen to Strasbourg in December and then make his way to the Atlantic coast of southern France, hoping to find there a new life.

Hölderlin's long hike to Strasbourg in mid-winter was not the first such walk for him. Not one year earlier he had made the walk to Hauptwil in Switzerland. At that time, he left Stuttgart on January 11, 1801, in the company of some friends, walking the familiar path to Tübingen. On the next day, or the day following, he walked via Ebingen and Siegmaringen to Lake Constance. He crossed the lake by ferry and then walked the two-hour distance to the city of Constance; on the next day, he hiked to Hauptwil in Canton Thurgau, in the northeastern quadrant of Switzerland. His letters mention "sunny skies" (CHV 2:887) and his own "fine fettle" (CHV 2:889), so that one has the impression that the walk went without complications. Whether the walk at the end of that same year, in December 1801, from Stuttgart to Strasbourg went so smoothly and under such a blithe sky, we do not know. Certainly that was not the case for Joe and me.

Hölderlin's mood at the end of that year does not seem as ebullient as it was at the beginning, to say the least. The publisher Cotta had proposed that a volume of his poems be published, but after Hölderlin prepared a good copy of a number of them the proposal disintegrated. His desire to offer lectures on Greek literature at Jena had prompted him to write Schiller and Immanuel Niethammer at length, requesting their help. Those letters remained unanswered. The Hauptwil tutorship lasted only four months, perhaps because of the restlessness Hölderlin himself mentions, even though the work seems to have gone smoothly. In the letters leading up to Hölderlin's departure for Bordeaux, however, we sense a new level of unquiet, weariness, and desperate loneliness. Hölderlin has by now entered his thirties, and he is still trying to establish an independent existence. And still trying not to disappoint his mother more than he already has.

On October 22, 1801, Hölderlin's friend Christian Landauer writes him about the possibility of the new tutorship in France. Their common friend, Professor Stäudlin, who himself had held the post sometime earlier, is offering Hölderlin a tutorship in the home of the wine merchant and Hamburg consul to Bordeaux, Daniel Christoph Meyer. The number of children to be tutored is uncertain, but it most likely involved Meyer's

Photo 6. The Hôtel Meyer, Bordeaux, in the January sun. Consul Meyer had his home and offices here, and here Hölderlin tutored the Meyer children.

daughter, Anne Mathilde, and two or three more children from Madame Meyer's first marriage. In the aftermath of the Revolution and the civil unrest of the 1790s, the school system of Bordeaux is in shambles; it is therefore not surprising that Consul Meyer insists on having a German tutor for his and his wife's children. Hölderlin's travel allowance and the salary would be quite generous. Landauer begs Hölderlin to come and talk with Stäudlin about the position (CHV 2:910).

Hölderlin accepts the offer from Consul Meyer. Born in Hamburg in 1751, Meyer had become consul to Bordeaux in 1793, and at some point before his death in 1816 he became a naturalized French citizen. He was a leading member of the large German community there (Hamburg or Bremen was home to most of its members), which consisted of wine merchants and exporters—Bordeaux was the departure point to England and the rest of northern Europe for the fine clarets of the region. Consul Meyer's residences mirror his considerable wealth (see photo 6). Hölderlin writes to his mother and his siblings from Stuttgart sometime in October or November about his plan to go to Bordeaux. He begs them—but this means his mother—to take the most favorable view of the matter. "I would have a trouble-free existence in an occupation to which I am accustomed, and hopefully I will find fine human beings there. I have to start to lead an independent life, no matter what kind, and teaching children is now a particularly auspicious activity for me, because it is so innocent" (CHV 2:910–11). To Carl he is somewhat more candid, although the piety of the following letter is a sign that it is still a letter to family. On December 4, 1801, perhaps only several days before his departure, he writes from Nürtingen (CHV 2:911):

My dear Carl!

I am coming to take my departure [*Ich komme Abschied zu nehmen*]. But let us not complain! In such cases I prefer to maintain a contented spirit, one that, to honor God, remains silent about matters that are unfortunate and instead looks at the good side of things.

I have to concede this much, that in my life I was never very firmly rooted in my fatherland; in that life I have never esteemed very much my dealings with my fellows, never wished that much to preserve those dealings!

But I feel it—it will be better for me to be abroad [*draußen zu seyn*], and you, my dear brother, will feel it as well—whether

20 / Struck by Apollo

I stay or go, the one or the other, God's protection alone avails if we are to survive. Keeping busy is what particularly sustains you, that is your way. Otherwise things would be too oppressive. What I really need to do is make the right choice about what it is mine to do. Otherwise I would be driven to distraction.

May the old brotherly love between us not perish! It is a holy blessing when, whatever differences in their style of life may obtain, human beings are held together by a bond such as ours. That is the greater meaning, the one that energizes and rescues us. And especially for manly souls, it isn't necessary that they be like one another for love to prevail between them. Yet they will not be happy without this openness of heart. Oh, my Carl! forgive me, so that things between us are unsullied!

And so farewell! You will do well with our family, because you are doing well in your own matters. Think too of me from time to time!

Your

Hölderlin

One of the tragedies of Hölderlin's existence was his desperate attempt to be a good brother to his younger half-brother. Because their mother did not want to waste money on Carl's education, however, he was forced to pursue a life in business without his really having had the chance to try his hand at anything else. Hölderlin tried to convince his mother to give Carl too the opportunity to study toward a profession, but in this as in all such instances he did not succeed. He no doubt felt that he had not tried hard enough. At all events, Hölderlin hopes that it will be enough for Carl if he "keeps busy"; *Geschäftigkeit*, the "busyness" of business will have to suffice for him. This in spite of the fact that Hölderlin's letters to his brother had always been full of philosophy, replete with references to Kant and Fichte and whatever else belonged to the world of letters and thought. Yet Carl, as the letter says, will get on well with the "family," meaning again the mother, because he is doing what she wants. For Hölderlin himself, the black sheep, or the white sheep, since black is the noncolor of the cleric his mother wants him to be, it is better to be begone. The "fatherland" has no use for him. Nor the "motherland," if the truth be told.

The next letter that we have, from that same day, December 4, 1801, proves to be one of the most important in Hölderlin's correspondence (CHV

2:912–14). It is the first of two letters to Casimir Ulrich Böhlendorff, a fellow poet and the editor of a journal of poetry. It is a letter so rich in content that I will interrupt it from time to time, underscoring this or that aspect of it.

My dear Böhlendorff!

Your kind words, and the presence of you in these words, gave me much joy.

Your *Fernando* was a great solace to me. The progress my friends make is such a good sign for me. We have a destiny. If things move forward for one of us, the other will not be left behind.

Dear friend! You have gained so much in precision, skill, and agility, and you've lost nothing of your warmth; on the contrary, like a sharp blade, the elasticity of your spirit has only gained in strength from its submission to the school of hard discipline. It is for this that I congratulate you heartily. Nothing is more difficult for us to learn than the free use of what is native to us.

"What is native to us" tries to translate *das Nationelle*, which is not the same as *das Nationale*, "the national." The morphology of the word reminds us of Hegel's *das Naturell*, which is a kind of "second nature," or what comes *naturally* to someone, as though they were "born to it." *Das Nationelle* has been the subject of reams of commentary, but Hölderlin's own description of it is perhaps the clearest definition we have. For his letter continues: "And I believe that clarity of presentation [*die Klarheit der Darstellung*] is precisely what is originally as natural to us as fire from heaven was to the Greeks." "Fire from heaven" is related to the heat of the sun, which provides warmth and stimulates growth, but which can also scorch. Solar fire illuminates all things but also provokes ardor and even blinding passion; it is the heat of the heart and the flame of genius alike, as it were. In the notes and essays on the ancient Sicilian philosopher Empedocles that he had written some four years earlier, Hölderlin associated such fire with what he called *das Aorgischere*, whatever is "more intimate" and "more intense" in us, *inniger*, and therefore less amenable to our conscious organization and control. Such passion was native to the Greeks, even if their Homer seems to paint his pictures so lucidly and luminously, as though he were a German by prolepsis.—Yet now comes a reversal for which neither Böhlendorff nor we are prepared:

22 / Struck by Apollo

Precisely for that reason, the Greeks are to be *surpassed* more in splendid passion, the sort of passion you yourself have achieved, than in that Homeric presence of mind and gift of presentation.

It sounds paradoxical. But I assert it once again and I submit it to your examination and for your own use: what is properly native has less and less prominence as a culture progresses. That is why the Greeks are not so much masters of holy pathos, because pathos was innate in them; by contrast, they are exceptionally skilled in presentation from Homer onward, because this extraordinary human being was rich enough in soul to seize for his Apollonian kingdom that occidental *Junonian sobriety* and thus to appropriate what was foreign to him.

Apollo and Hera, or Juno, are in Hölderlin's view figures of light, of luminously clear presentation. The case for Phoebus Apollo is convincing, even if Apollo is also the avenging god of pestilence; the case for Hera, whose furious jealousy is fairly constant in the old stories, is far more difficult to make. In any case, it is important that, after Homer, such clarity of depiction or presentation becomes important for the Hesperian West in general and Hölderlin's own Germany in particular. Yet the Germans have their own problems:

With us, the reverse is the case. That is why it is so dangerous to draw up our rules of art solely and exclusively on the basis of Greek excellence. I have labored over these things for a long time, and now I know that, granted what has to be supreme in the Greeks and in ourselves, namely, the vital relation and skill [respectively?], we dare not try to be *like* them in these respects.

Rather, one's own has to be learned every bit as much as what is foreign. That is why the Greeks are indispensable to us. It is simply that we will not reach their level when it comes to what is our own, what is native to us, because, as I said, the *free* use of what is *one's own* is most difficult.

Clarity of depiction, with lines clearly drawn and figures precise down to each detail and by the book, may be as German as German can be, and yet it has to be learned in the school of hard knocks, and part of that discipline is what the Germans can learn from the Greeks, as though one were oneself a perfect stranger to these "native" skills. Furthermore, the "vital relation," fire from heaven, may well be foreign to the German, even the German of the Sturm und Drang period, so that it too will have to be learned. Yet what is native to the German, skill in presentation, will not be any more congenial for the learner to learn.

Hölderlin now praises Böhlendorff for the revisions he has made to his today forgotten play, *Fernando*, and he adds a remark on tragedy that is oddly compelling:

> Your good genius has inspired you, it seems to me, so that you have handled your drama more in terms of an epic. It is, viewed as a whole, a *genuinely* modern tragedy. For what is tragic in our case is that we depart from the kingdom of the living quietly packaged in some sort of container; we do not repent by way of all-consuming flames the fire we were never able to leash [*nicht daß wir in Flammen verzehrt die Flamme büßen, die wir nicht zu bändigen vermochten*].

Hölderin admired the Greeks' funeral pyres and funeral games for their closeness to the more "aorgic" element, to wit, the fire of heaven; yet he also respected the fact that for as long as they lived, the great Greek heroes were not scorched by that fire. Of course, some were—one thinks of Ajax—and all came close. In many of his poems around this time, Hölderlin speaks of the Greek capacity to protect its genius from fire and flame. Yet the lines we have only now read seem to reflect Hölderlin's inmost feeling about the Christian tradition in which he was raised. As fond as he was of the Jesus of his youth, he abhorred the pusillanimous and lugubrious four last things—death, judgment, heaven, and hell—on which so much Christian doctrine was and is founded. The games around Patroclus's funeral pyre, performed after his body has been destroyed by the flames, is the image that repeatedly occurs to him as affirmative of life on this Earth. In the lines that follow, at least as I read them, the funereal flames that go to meet death are somehow in balance with the fire from heaven that inspires life, not only in ancient Greek tragedy but even during Hölderlin's own Hesperian age:

> And, truly, the former [i.e., death in the Christian era] moves the inmost soul as much as the latter [death in the age of the Greeks]. It is not so imposing, but it is a more profound destiny, and a noble soul accompanies such a dying one in fear and compassion [*Furcht und Mitleiden*] and elevates one's spirit in anguish [*Grimm*]. Whenever the poet depicts such dying in the way he should, and in the way you clearly wanted to depict

24 / Struck by Apollo

it, splendid Jupiter is indeed the final thought concerning the downgoing of a mortal, whether he dies under the auspices of our own destiny or that of antiquity. In general, and especially in masterful traits, this is what you have achieved.

"A narrow path leads into a darkling valley,
Thither has treachery compelled him."

Here and elsewhere.— You are on a good path; stay on it. But I will now take your *Fernando* to heart and study it carefully; maybe then I'll be able to tell you something more interesting about it. In no case will it be enough!

Concerning myself, and how things have gone for me up to now, to what extent I have become and will remain worthy of your friendship and the friendship of others, and also what I am doing and the work I intend to bring forth, no matter how slight it is, I will write you soon from the neighborhood of your Spain, that is, from Bordeaux, whither, next week, I am traveling. I will be a tutor and a private preacher in a German Evangelical household. I will have to keep my head clear in France, in Paris; I am also looking forward to beholding the sea, and to feeling the sun of Provence.

"Provence" may simply be an indication of the state of Hölderlin's French geography, even if commentators try to justify it by remarking on the Languedoc and Gascogne languages and dialects and on the widespread tendency in many languages to refer to every rural area as "the provinces." It is notable that Hölderlin here seems to believe that he will have to prepare Evangelical sermons for Consul Meyer's family, even though the letter from Landauer has told him that he is dispensed from this hated activity. As it turns out, Consul Meyer and his family have joined the Reform (Huguenot) church in Bordeaux and hence have no need of an Evangelical-Lutheran preacher. It therefore does not seem that this threat could have been the reason for Hölderlin's abrupt departure from Bordeaux (JB 111). Also clear from these lines is Hölderlin's intention to travel by way of Paris, where, perhaps quite literally, he hopes he can keep his head. Only after his arrival in Strasbourg is the necessity of the alternate route, via Lyon, made clear to him. Yet his desire to experience "fire from heaven," if not in Greece or Sicily then at least in the neighborhood of "Spain," is expressed here, along with his desire to see—for the first time in his life—the vast reservoir where all the rivers run, the sea. And so Hölderlin comes to the final page of his letter:

Oh, my friend! The world lies more brightly before me than before, and more earnestly. Yes! I am pleased about how things are headed; it pleases me in the way that in summer "the ancient holy Father with effortless hand scatters blessed lightning bolts from red clouds."[5] Because, among all the things pertaining to God that I can see, this is the special sign for me. Furthermore, I could well sing a song of praise for a new truth, a better vision of what is over us and all around us; now I fear lest in the end it will go with me as it did with Tantalus of old, who received more from the gods than he could digest.

The "new truth," the "better vision," the greater brightness and higher seriousness, along with the "fear" expressed here are all difficult to understand, difficult and tantalizing. The story of Tantalus, the "lurching" or "most wretched" one, as Robert Graves understands his name, has several layers. Most commonly remembered is Tantalus's punishment, yet the crime for which he is punished is all about the fate of one who was once close to his gods—and that seems to be the point of Hölderlin's allusion. Graves reports:

Tantalus was the intimate friend of Zeus, who admitted him to Olympian banquets of nectar and ambrosia until, good fortune turning his head, he betrayed Zeus's secrets and stole the divine food to share among his mortal friends. Before this crime could be discovered, he committed a worse. Having called the Olympians to a banquet . . . Tantalus found that the food in his larder was insufficient for the company and, either to test Zeus's omniscience, or merely to demonstrate his good will, cut up his son Pelops, and added the pieces to the stew prepared for them. . . . None of the gods failed to notice what was on their trenchers, or to recoil in horror, except Demeter who, being dazed by her loss of Persephone, ate the flesh from the left shoulder.

For these two crimes Tantalus was punished with the ruin of his kingdom and, after his death by Zeus's own hand, with eternal torment. . . . Now he hangs, perennially consumed by thirst and hunger, from the bough of a fruit-tree which leans over a marshy lake. Its waves lap against his waist, and sometimes reach his chin, yet whenever he bends down to drink, they slip

---

5. The allusion (not a direct quotation) is to Goethe's poem "Limits of Humanity" (*Grenzen der Menschheit*), composed in 1781, published in 1789, and later revised. Thanks to my friend and colleague Alexander Bilda for locating the reference.

26 / Struck by Apollo

away, and nothing remains but the black mud at his feet; or, if he ever succeeds in scooping up a handful of water, it slips through his fingers before he can do more than wet his cracked lips, leaving him thirstier than ever. The tree is laden with pears, shining apples, sweet figs, ripe olives and pomegranates, which dangle against his shoulders; but whenever he reaches for the luscious fruit, a gust of wind whirls them out of his reach.[6]

Hölderlin too had been invited to the divine banquet by the gods of his youth. Did he fear now that such divine hospitality had turned his head and that he had proved unworthy? At all events, the letter to Böhlendorff closes with tears of parting:

> But I shall do what I can as well as I can. And whenever I see that I must make my way ahead just like everyone else, I think that it is godlessness and madness to seek a path that would be immured against *every* eventuality, and I know that death is a stone that gathers no moss.
>
> And so farewell, dear friend! Till next time. I am now full of parting. It has been a long time since I have cried. But my decision to leave my fatherland behind, perhaps forever, has cost me bitter tears. For what in all the world is more beloved to me? But they have no use for me. Otherwise, I will and I must remain German, even if the needs of my heart and my stomach should drive me all the way to Tahiti.
>
> Greet our friend Morbek. How is he doing? He will surely survive. He will be true to us. Excuse my ingratitude. I recognized you both, I saw you, but in a jaundiced perspective. I would have had so much to say to you both, my good friends. And you to me also. Where will you be living now, dear Böhlendorff? I worry about that. When you write me, address your letters to the merchant Landauer in Stuttgart. He will surely send them on to me. Write me your address as well.
>
> Yours,
>
> H.

---

6. Robert Graves, *The Greek Myths*, 2 vols. (Harmondsworth: Penguin Books, 1955), 2:25–26.

Strange that Hölderlin should be envious of or "jaundiced" toward Böhlendorff, whose work has been forgotten by later times. The jaundice seems to be caused by nothing more than the fact that his friends are evidently of some use to their countrymen, whereas Hölderlin feels that he himself is not. Even if he is buoyed by the prospect of a new and brighter world and inspired by what seem to be new insights, he has to fear that he is being tantalized. Once again, as in his letter to Carl, he is "full of parting," *Ich bin jezt voll Abschieds.* If Hölderlin is bound to remain German, devoted to his "fatherland," which in his case means the landscape of the Neckar Valley and the dialect that is spoken there, it seems that the larger fatherland has no use for him.

The next letter that survives, a letter to his mother, is written five weeks later from Lyon (CHV 2:915–16). It contains all we know—which is practically nothing—about his walking trip from Nürtingen to Strasbourg and his post-coach trip from Strasbourg via Besançon to Lyon. As usual, the letter—with its odd, staccato paragraphing—is guarded, written out of a sense of obligation and filial piety but also with hopes of satisfying someone he will never satisfy:

Lyon, January 9, 1802

My dear Mother!

You will be astonished to receive a letter from me at this time and from Lyon. I was forced to stay in Strasbourg for my travel visa longer than I thought would be necessary, and the long journey hither from Strasbourg was made even longer by floods and other unavoidable circumstances that delayed me.

It was an arduous path, my way here, and rich in experiences, but I found many things that gave me pure joy. Nor can I remain silent about the fact that I sometimes thought of you, my beloved family, and also of the One who grants me my courage, the One who has preserved me to this hour and who will lead me farther on.

I know that anyone engaged in a solitary life will have a difficult time out there in the wide world, but I believe that God and an honest heart will help me get through it all—that and humility in the face of other human beings.

I am still weary from the long, cold journey, dear Mother, and there is so much hubbub around me here and now that one

28 / Struck by Apollo

can return to oneself only by meditating on those who know us and are surely good to us.

Tomorrow I depart for Bordeaux, and I will be there soon, since the roads are better now, the floodwaters of the rivers having subsided.

I should also mention that the Strasbourg authorities advised me, as a foreigner, to make my journey via Lyon. So I will not see Paris. I have made my peace with that.

I'm looking forward to taking up my duties soon.

I'll write you and my other loved ones much more from Bordeaux whenever things settle down.

Greet everyone for me, everyone, and most heartily!

Our Carl will by now be in Nürtingen. Think of me now and then when you are enjoying your evenings together. I ask my dear sister to remember our best hours together, and to mention their uncle now and again to her little ones.

A thousand thanks for all your goodness and support and concern!

Farewell!

Your faithful son,

Hölderlin

The next letter we have is indeed from Bordeaux, dated January 28, 1802. This means that the third leg of Hölderlin's journey took some eighteen days. The bulk of the trip must have been by post-coach, even though it seems that Hölderlin walked during the final two or three days of his journey, as he approached Bordeaux. The letter (CHV 2:916–17), again addressed to his mother, contains only a few details about the trip, some of them hair-raising:

Finally, dear Mother, I am here, safely arrived. I am healthy, and I will not forget that I am indebted to the Lord of Life and Death.—For the moment, I can write only a little. I arrived just this morning, and my attention is too much claimed by my new situation for me to tell you about the interesting things that happened during the journey that is now behind me. Furthermore, I had so many experiences that I scarcely know how to talk about them.

"The Lord of Life and Death"? The debt that Hölderlin owes is to a very ambiguous deity, it seems. The brittle Pietist God, not some more gentle variety, is his own Lord and Master—inherited perhaps from the mother to whom he writes. And even though Hölderlin also worships other less frigid gods, the appearance of deity in the form of death itself remains a powerful and persistent thought for him. In the months to come, as he is translating Sophocles, who "wanders amid unthinkable things," he will note that the "boundless unification" of god and mortal, while intense, is invariably followed by "boundless separation," so that what mortals best remember is "divine infidelity" (CHV 2:370, 315–16). Ultimately, in Hölderlin's view, the god becomes present to mortals precisely "in the figure of death" (CHV 2:371). There were doubtless moments during his trip when Hölderlin felt close to a wintry death, even if he now mentions the promise of springtime. His letter from Bordeaux ends this way:

> These past few days I have been walking into a glorious springtime, although just before, on the fearsome snowy heights of the Auvergne, in storm and wilderness, in ice-cold nights and with a loaded pistol lying next to me on my rough bed—it was then that I prayed a prayer that is the best one I have prayed till now and one I will never forget.
>
> I am preserved—be thankful along with me!
>
> Beloved family! I greeted you as a newborn after I emerged from these dangers—and I immediately scolded myself for having forgotten in my last letter, from Lyon, to send a special greeting to our dear Grandmother. I spoke to you, dear Mother, I saw my sister's image, and in my joyous thoughts I wrote a letter in elevated tones to my brother Carl.
>
> I am now tempered and confirmed [*gehärtet und geweiht*], as you all wished. I believe I will remain so in the principal matter. Fearing nothing and putting up with many things. A deep, refreshing sleep now would do me a lot of good! I'm living almost too well. I would be happy with a certain secure simplicity. My duties here will, I think, go well. I will devote myself entirely to them, especially at the outset. May you all fare well! With all my heart, and most faithfully,
>
> Your
>
> H.

30 / Struck by Apollo

P.S.: The letter has been delayed for several days. A good start, I have gotten to know the people here and I am learning my obligations. Things could not be better. "You will be happy here," said my Consul when he greeted me. I think he is right.

Happy he may have been from time to time over the next four months, although the precipitation with which he left Bordeaux makes us wonder. True, Hölderlin's departures were always precipitous: one thinks of his leaving Jena so suddenly in 1795 or Hauptwil in 1801. Because he failed to keep his promise to write his family often while in Bordeaux, we have very little insight into his state of mind, and we know even less about his adventures there. The theories as to why he left Bordeaux so abruptly are many, the two principal ones being (1) that he was asked after all to prepare sermons for the family, an activity he found repulsive, and (2) that he received news, whether directly or indirectly, about Susette's terminal illness. Neither of these explanations is satisfactory. The truth is that we simply do not know why he left his post in May. His third and last letter to his mother, from Bordeaux, dated "Good Friday," which would be April 16, 1802, does not really give us any insight into his reasons for leaving so unexpectedly three weeks later. His purpose for writing her is that he has learned of his grandmother's recent death, the grandmother who he had recently remembered not to forget. His letter is filled with the sort of consolatory prose that a pastor manqué has been trained to write and that a pious mother so wants to read. Let us pick up the letter only at the point where it reports a word or two about his own situation in mid-April (CHV 2:917–18):

Things are going as well for me as I could wish! I also hope that I am gradually able to merit all the things that my situation is giving me and that, some day, after I return to my homeland, I will not have proved unworthy in the eyes of the truly excellent people here to whom I am so devoted.

Think of me, my dear family, only as much as will not disturb your own activities. I wish for my brother that he be content as he carries on with the affairs he has undertaken, and that he continues to be happy in his circles.

The good children will give you much joy, and you will be happy to have such lively images of hope around you, as I do with my pupils. Greet my friends, forgive my not writing:

the long distance and my duties convince me that for now I have to be sparing with letters. We remain together nonetheless.

Yours faithfully,

H.

This is all we have from Hölderlin's hand while he is in Bordeaux. Noteworthy in this last missive is his expressed intention to return to his homeland—a return that seemed doubtful at the time of his departure from Nürtingen. Is he intending after all to return to Frankfurt and Susette?

The next letter in his correspondence is not from him but to him. It is the letter from his friend Sinclair that reaches him in Stuttgart—we do not know exactly when—telling him of Susette's death on June 22, 1802. Here is that terrible letter (CHV 2:918–19):

Homburg vor der Höhe, June 30, 1802

Dear Hölderlin!

As terrible as the news is that I have to communicate to you, I cannot leave it to chance to inform you of something for which even the aid of friendship is too meager. I am all the more prepared to tell you the news, since a similar fate has befallen me, a destiny I did not expect, and one that has made me profoundly sick at heart. The noble object of your love is no more. Yet she *was* yours, and if it is more terrible to lose her, it is more galling when one is found to be unworthy of love. The first is your destiny, the second mine. I do not know how to console you, except to state the consolation that is already yours. You believed in immortality while she was alive; surely you will believe in it now more than before—now that the life of your love has departed from this world of transiency. And what is more grand and more noble than a heart that has survived its world, a heart that early on was attuned by destiny to that earnest feeling in which alone life, peace, and eternity are bestowed on us. I want to give you courage, and I do so with an intrepid heart. Because I am not afraid, I dare to speak the truth about love.

32 / Struck by Apollo

On the 22nd of this month, G. died of rubella, after ten days of illness. She had her children with her; happily, they survived her. During the past winter she suffered from a severe cough that weakened her lungs. She remained equal to herself up to the very end. Her death was like her life.

It has moved me deeply, and I weep as I write this. I had not seen her again after the time of your separation, and I felt that it would be unworthy of me to try to find out about someone who was living the immutable life of the Godhead. The news was therefore entirely unexpected, but I also received it with a heart that was made all the purer by its unsuspecting state, and I am telling it to you in a way that will not be unworthy of her.

Since you last saw me I have suffered some reversals of fortune. I have grown quieter, colder, and I promise you that you can seek repose in the bosom of your friend. You know all my faults. I hope that none of them will cause another disturbance between us. I therefore invite you to come to reside with me for the length of my stay here. If circumstances should call for a change in my situation, we can think things through together and make a collective decision; if destiny decrees it, we will be as two going together, faithful to one another. I can manage to set aside 200 florins a year for you, and I can set you up in an apartment with whatever you need. Do not take this merely as my plea to you, but also as my advice—even though I do not know what sort of state you are in, and it is difficult for me to advise you. It could be that you will find down there the peace you need. Let me know your decision. I'll also travel down to Bordeaux, if you like, so that I can bring you back.

Our friend Ebel sends greetings. Since January he has been in Frankfurt. He was with G. during her illness and consoled her during her final hours.

Yours,

Sinclair

An intense discussion among scholars involves whether or not Hölderlin knew of Susette's illness during the winter of 1801–1802 and her turn for the worse in the spring. Bertheau suggests that the Bethmann family

Prologue / 33

of Bordeaux, friends of the Frankfurt Gontards and Consul Meyer in Bordeaux, may have said something about it in Hölderlin's presence (JB 106–7). Bertheau even believes that Susette herself may have written Hölderlin in Bordeaux, begging him to return for a final adieu. The abruptness of Hölderlin's departure speaks for this—even though many of his partings were sudden. Furthermore, there is a period of several weeks after his arrival in Strasbourg that is unaccounted for; his exit visa from Strasbourg is dated June 7, yet only in late June or early July does he arrive in Stuttgart, walk to Nürtingen, and after a few days return to Stuttgart. What, then, about those days after June 7? Some commentators believe that he may have gone from Strasbourg directly to Frankfurt and that the two lovers could have met several times before Susette became bedridden in mid-June. She died on June 22, about a week into her final illness, the German measles that one of her children had communicated to her. Some commentators even speculate that Jacob, Susette's husband, may have had a change of heart or succumbed to a fit of either generosity or indifference and allowed his wife's lover to see her prior to those final days.

What speaks against all this is that Hölderlin spent at least two days in Paris visiting the Louvre. We have no evidence that he was in a desperate hurry to get to Frankfurt. Bertheau wonders (JB 111) whether the ostensible letter from her to Hölderlin (today lost, if it ever existed) did not mention her illness, but only a quarrel with her husband, thus giving him hope but no reason to be rushed. What is moving about all these theories is that those of us who comment on Hölderlin's life are so desperate to get Susette and Hölderlin back together again: Hölderlin would have been pleased by all this support and encouragement—if only it had come sooner, during his and her lifetimes. The truth is that his hasty departure from Bordeaux and the unhurried yet not unharried trip home are swathed in mystery.[7]

---

7. If readers would like to see the ways in which Hölderlin's editors and commentators are wont to project their own desires and fears onto the Hölderlin–Susette relationship, I invite them once again to read Kenney's and Menner-Bettscheid's comments and fictions in *The Recalcitrant Art.*

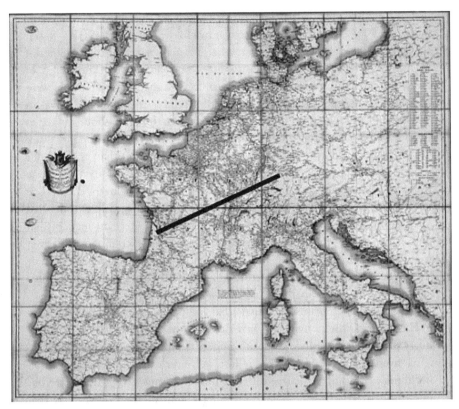

Map 1. Post-Coach Map of Europe in 1812, reprinted with the kind permission of the Bibliothèque historique des postes et des télécommunications, Paris. The dark line shows Hölderlin's route, without all its twists and turns, from Nürtingen to Bordeaux. All the remaining maps in the book are details, that is, enlarged portions, of this 1812 map.

1

The Achievement

Even if the travel times—two months from Nürtingen to Bordeaux and one month for the return—seem to us incredibly long, Hölderlin's achievement during these months of travel is extraordinary. It is difficult (really impossible) to calculate all the variables—the precise route, the exact number of days traveling, weather and terrain conditions, unforeseen delays, coach breakdowns, inundating rivers, and so on—but here is an approximation. Taking the greatest possible number of days for travel and the most economical route, the result for the journey to Bordeaux is as follows.

First, Hölderlin walks from Nürtingen to Stuttgart, heads south to Tübingen and Freudenstadt, then west to Strasbourg—this over a period of five to nine days, depending on the departure date of December 6 or December 10. To manage this, he would have had to walk about twenty-two to thirty-nine kilometers (some thirteen to twenty-four miles) per day, the latter extremely strenuous but doable. Second, after a two-week delay waiting for a travel visa, he journeys from Strasbourg to Lyon, some 650 kilometers, over a maximum period of eighteen days, some fifty-nine kilometers (about 39 miles) per day. Everyone agrees that he would have had to do the bulk of this travel, and probably all of it, by post-coach or perhaps also by riverboat; even then the distance covered is quite considerable, especially given the reported condition of the roads that winter.[1]

---

1. My calculation here may be off because of Joe's and my decision to follow the Doubs River all the way to its confluence with the Saône at Verdun-sur-le-Doubs, near Chalon, traveling through Dôle to Beaune and then directly south to Mâcon, rather than following the faster post-coach route from Besançon to Lons-le-Saunier and Bourg-en-Bresse. Some kilometers would have been saved by following the hypotenuse instead of the two sides of this more or less right triangle, although the road to Lons-le-Saunier is much hillier.

36 / Struck by Apollo

Finally, third, the stretch from Lyon, via Clermont-Ferrand, Limoges, and Périgueux to Bordeaux, some 590 kilometers, traveled over a maximum period of eighteen days and covering some thirty-three kilometers (about twenty-and-a-half miles) per day. If one speculates that he walked during the final days of his trip, from either Périgueux or Libourne to Bordeaux, the number of kilometers covered per day is much greater. In short, if one hopes to follow in Hölderlin's footsteps, it will not be at a leisurely pace. In the letters to his mother from Lyon, about halfway there, and then upon his arrival in Bordeaux, he tells of the joys, surprises, inconveniences, and hazards of the journey, but he does not offer any details, and he does not sound as utterly exhausted as I believe you and I would have been.

Certainly, like most people of his time, and like most country folk up to the mid-twentieth century in rural Germany, Hölderlin was accustomed to long walks. He generally measured distances by the hours it took to walk them. When his mother asked him how far it was from Waltershausen, where he had taken up a tutorship in the von Kalb household, to Jena and Weimar, he replied, "Jena must be about sixty hours from Nuremberg; from Waltershausen it is only thirty; from Waltershausen to Weimar is about four hours" (CHV 2:572–73).[2]

He means of course "by foot." He tells her that the winter weather has been harsh and that he has not yet made that proposed walk to Jena but that he plans to make it the following week. During the spring of 1795, when he is living in Jena, he takes a walking trip to Halle, Dessau, and Leipzig, following the Saale River Valley at least part of the way, the whole trip covering some two hundred kilometers as the crow flies. He calls it "a small hike" and remarks to his sister that if one follows the numerous river valleys and has a pair of healthy feet, one can walk much farther than anyone imagines (CHV 2:580). "I made this trip in seven days," he adds, "and I feel now how healthy and invigorating it was for me" (CHV 2:581). Thirty kilometers per day seems like nothing to him, apparently.

As for the much longer journey to Bordeaux six years later, if one simply takes the computer's word for it, having selected routes that avoid highways and toll roads, the total distance traveled in Germany would be

---

In any case, the number of kilometers from Besançon to Lyon, some 220 (rather than 270) kilometers by the shorter route, still would have meant a minimum of thirty-three or thirty-four kilometers per day—likely too much to achieve by foot.

2. Alexander Bilda, of Freiburg University, informs me that Google maps measures these distances differently, sometimes more, sometimes less, than Hölderlin's estimates. Clearly, Hölderlin neglected to google.

194.8 kilometers, in France 964.4 kilometers, a total of 1,159.2 kilometers—that is, over seven hundred miles. Yet that is a bare minimum, perhaps as little as one-half of the real distance traversed, as incredible as that may seem. Sinuous are the ways of mortals.

I was struck recently by the statistics for one of the Roman aqueducts that fed Lugdunum, the ancient city of Lyon: the aqueduct of Gier, the longest of the four, had its source some forty-two kilometers south of the Roman city as the crow flies; yet the distance actually traveled by the water, since the aqueduct's incline had to be adapted to all the obstacles on the route, crossing every hill and dale at the proper rate of declination, was more than double that length—some eighty-six kilometers of construction were necessary for the water to travel the forty-two kilometer distance. One might think that roads are more efficient than aqueducts, yet probably this is an illusion. The twists and turns of Hölderlin's route, which, as we learned, most often followed the meandering courses of rivers, would readily have increased, and perhaps even doubled, the distances I have cited. On our own trip, Joe and I tried to keep an account of the odometer's numbers, but we soon gave up: the distances covered were always far more than they should have been, indeed something close to double. And automobiles on paved roads are more efficient than people on foot or coaches on mud roads.

How many kilometers could Hölderlin's post-coaches cover in a single day without major stops? The only estimate I have seen in the literature, and that for the English post-coaches, which are said to have been far superior to those on the continent, is some twenty-five miles, or forty kilometers. This seems reasonable, except for the poor horses. And whether this was a blustery winter's day or a breezy summer's day would make all the difference. The average speed? The only guestimate I have seen is about four miles or six-and-a-half kilometers per hour. During an eight-hour winter day that would mean a bit over fifty kilometers a day without stops, but this seems wildly optimistic and cruel to both passengers and horses. What makes all these estimates even more fraught is Bertheau's remark that the route followed by Hölderlin was by no means an "express" route of the French post, but only an "ordinary" route (JB 94). This would mean that the roads taken were not thoroughfares and probably not in the best condition under winter rain and snow.

One last thought. If the average human walking speed is some five kilometers per hour, or a little over three miles per hour, one can imagine that Hölderlin might often have wondered whether he would do just as well to walk as to take the coach. He tells us that he was able to walk eight full hours a day (CHV 2:589). Forty kilometers per day, which would be

38 / Struck by Apollo

only ten kilometers less than the most efficient coach, seems too strenuous to me, but that may be one of the differences between Hölderlin and me. There can be no doubt that he was a robust walker. Would he have been afraid to walk alone? Probably not. The danger of meeting a highwayman would have been far greater for post-coach passengers, inasmuch as brigands always preferred groups of well-heeled passengers over solitary down-at-heel hikers. (Hölderlin himself was the victim of a post-coach robbery at some point during his homeward journey, but that remains a mysterious event to be discussed much later.) In any case, even though we are probably right to think that the first five days and several of the final days were done on foot, we actually have no idea which stretches of the route he may have hiked. My own surmise is that there were more such pedestrian stretches than recent commentators assume. Floods, storms, inconvenient coach schedules, and unpredictable coach breakdowns—all of these happenstances may have compelled or invited him to walk more than we imagine he did.

The "Precise" Route

Precision is impossible here too, because if Hölderlin kept any sort of travel diary—which to me seems certain—it has vanished. True, painstaking archival research could estimate the weather for each day of Hölderlin's journey, but even then, so many details and contingencies would escape us. We do not even know the precise dates of most of Hölderlin's rest stops and overnights. All we know for certain is that on December 15 he is in Strasbourg, on January 9 he is in Lyon, and on January 28 he arrives at Bordeaux.

That said, the main roads he would have taken, whether hiking or riding, would have been the ordinary post-coach roads, so the old post-coach maps are a great help to us. The Historical Library of the Postal Museum in Paris kindly sent me a map from 1812, the map to which I will be referring in the following chapters, suggesting that this would be the best approximation to Hölderlin's travel route. I worried that the dozen years between the map and Hölderlin's trip might have seen a lot of road construction in France, but a study shows that only in southeastern France were any real improvements in the road system made, this because of Napoleon's interest in integrating the newly conquered northern Italian states into what was becoming the Empire. I was also able to check the 1812 map against a less detailed post-coach map from 1720, and this older map confirmed that most of the roads Hölderlin would have followed had been long-established post-coach routes. Indeed, as I discovered at Lugdunum, the Roman Lyon, many of those roads, especially those between Lyon and Bordeaux, were ancient Roman roads—even if it is also true that the Romans most often followed the routes already established by indigenous peoples.

I had my first experience with these ancient Roman roads on the Via Augusta at Portofino, south of Genoa. I was following in Nietzsche's footsteps, and I was astonished to learn that the stones of the pavement on this narrow road—one of Nietzsche's favorite walks—were the original ones. Once again at Lugdunum I noticed the paving stones of the Roman roads: they were in fact small boulders flattened on top, each one about a foot thick—no wonder the Roman roads lasted so long! It would be instructive to learn how many of the national roads all over Europe today are Roman in origin. A great many of them, I suspect.

It is important that I mention here one significant decision on Joe's and my part: because of Hölderlin's fascination with the rivers of Europe, we found ourselves deciding to favor the river routes as often as seemed feasible. Usually, the post-coach roads followed the rivers in any case, so that our decision—not so much a conscious choice on our part but our following a kind of fluvial invitation—seems reasonable. If my count is right, Hölderlin traveled along or crossed over more than a dozen major rivers during his trip to Bordeaux, following the course of the Neckar ("Necker" on the 1812 map) for many hours of the initial days, the *walking* days, of his trip, then crossing the Rhine at Kehl, meeting the Ill River at Strasbourg and following it to Colmar; he then meets the Doubs at l'Île-sur-le-Doubs and follows its meander all the way to Verdun-sur-le-Doubs near Chalon (the 1812 map reads "Chalons"); there the Doubs joins the great Saône, which makes its way south to Lyon, where it meets the mighty Rhône; on his way west from Lyon, Hölderlin crosses the Loire at Feurs, then the Allier at Pont-sur-Allier, followed by the Creuse at Aubusson and the Vienne at Limoges; he then follows the Isle River from Périgueux to Libourne, where the Isle meets the Dordogne; and near Bordeaux he confronts the confluence of the Dordogne and the Garonne in what then becomes the Gironde, which flows wide into the Atlantic Ocean. Only in one case, I believe, is this river route controversial: as I mentioned earlier, Joe and I traveled along the Doubs River all the way to its confluence with the Saône at Verdun-sur-Doubs, only then, at Chalon, turning south and following the Saône to Lyon; true, there was a post-coach route connecting Lons-le-Saunier to Bourg-en-Bresse and that route would have been shorter, although over rougher terrain. Adolf Beck speculates that Hölderlin

40 / Struck by Apollo

took the river route,[3] and Joe and I preferred it as well, simply because the Doubs River Valley, although it is not well known outside of France, is so beautifully serene. It may be that the Burgundies of Beaune tempted us to travel farther westward as well.

Even if Hölderlin's precise route is perforce a matter of speculation, we may gain an idea of the achievement merely by listing the minimal distances from station to station on the way. To be sure, we do not know precisely which stations he stopped at or where he spent the nights. As a general term of measure in the French post-coach system, a *poste* is roughly six miles, a *demi-poste* three. But how many *postes* could be covered on any given winter's day is, to repeat, contingent on weather, roads, the stamina of the horses, and a dozen other incalculables. One may be certain that the towns and villages listed on the 1812 map had relay stations and inns where passengers could overnight, and I will list the major towns here, using the spelling that appears on the map and only occasionally offering the modern spelling. Several of the names seem to designate country inns rather than entire towns or villages, with the result that they cannot be found on modern maps; many of them also designate homonymous towns and cities that are quite remote from the route, so that the names can be misleading. I will indicate this only occasionally in footnotes. As for the places designated in the following lists, Hölderlin could have spent the night at any one of them, though certainly not all of them.

It seems clear that Hölderlin overnighted with friends after he began the trip, walking from his hometown to Stuttgart (see map 2). He probably stayed for more than a night in Tübingen. After that, it becomes impossible to speculate. It seems likely that Freudenstadt would have been a likely town to spend the night; but then comes the formidable climb up the Kniebis Mountain, then back down to the Rhine Plain and on to Strasbourg. As the following chapter relates, this may have been one of the most challenging segments of the journey, but we know nothing about where Hölderlin may have paused. The relevance of the post-coach map picks up only with his arrival at Strasbourg.

Between the cities of Strasbourg and Colmar we find on the 1812 map (see map 3) the towns of Benfeld, Schelestat (Schlettstadt/Sélestat), and Ostheim; between Colmar and Belfort (see map 4), Hölderlin may have stopped at Hastat (Hattstatt), Meyenheim, Isenheim, or Aspach-la-Chapelle; on his way to Besançon, he could have stayed in the towns of Tavey, l'Ile

---

3. Adolf Beck, *Hölderlin: Chronik seines Lebens* (Frankfurt am Main: Insel Verlag, 1975), 87.

The Achievement / 41

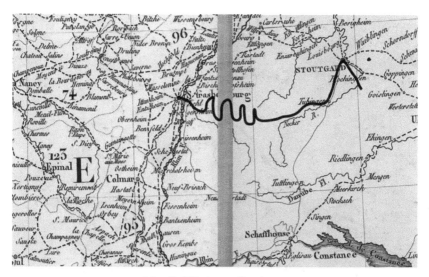

Map 2. Nürtingen-Strasbourg

sur Doubs (Isle-sur-le-Doubs), Clerval, Baume-les-Dames, or Roulans. From Besançon to Beaune in Burgundy (see map 5), he could have stopped at S. Vit, Orchamps, and Dôle; after Dôle, at Grand-Noir, Seurre, and Moissey; between Beaune and Mâcon, close to the vineyards of Burgundy and Beau-

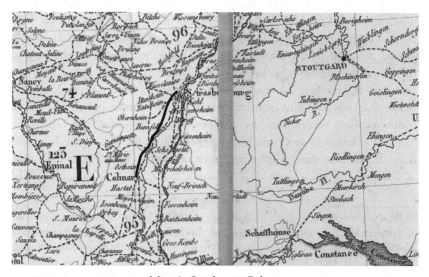

Map 3. Strasbourg-Colmar

42 / Struck by Apollo

Map 4. Colmar-Besançon

jolais (see map 6), the post-coach could have stopped and overnighted at Chagny, Chalons, Senecy, Tournus, or S. Albin; between Mâcon and Lyon, we find the villages or inns called la Maison blanche and les Tournelles de Flandre, along with the towns of Anse, Limonest, and Salvagny.[4]

According to the Bibliothèque historique des postes et des télécommunications in Paris, Hölderlin would most likely have followed two main postal routes from Lyon to Bordeaux, first, postal route number 91, which carried the mail (and passengers) coming from Strasbourg on the way to Bordeaux, passing through Lyon, Feurs, Thiers, Clermont, Aubusson, and Limoges; at Limoges, the mail and the passengers were transferred to the coach that was traveling southward on postal route number 44, which connected Paris to Bordeaux by way of Chalus, Périgueux, and Libourne.

As one travels west from Lyon, climbing into the hills of the Auvergne (map 7), the post-coach routes become more scarce. Indeed, the 1812 map at this point shows a great deal of empty space, which in nature is filled

---

4. There is a town on the Mediterranean coast east of Toulon by the name Les Tournelles de Flandre, which I suppose designates "the windmills of the Lowlands," but it is not the village or relais on Hölderlin's route. There is a Salvagny in the Canton de Fribourg, Switzerland, no doubt lovely, but not the right one for us. Françoise Dastur informs me that *Salvagny* (meaning "the domain of Salvinius") was the name given during the Revolution to a village called La Tour de Salvagny, seven kilometers beyond Limonest, a village that is now a part of greater Lyon.

The Achievement / 43

Map 5. Besançon-Chalon

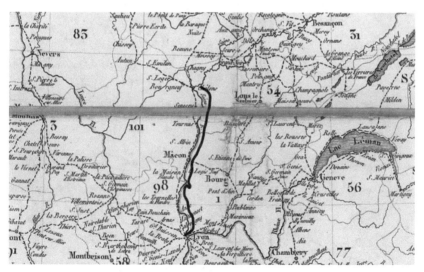

Map 6. Chalon-Lyon

by the wild volcanic countryside of the Massif Central. On the long way to Clermont the coach could have stopped at Gd. Buisson (not the one in the Jura mountains, however!), la Braly, Fenouilh (not the Fenouilh in the Maritime Alps west of Sisteron), Feurs, Roen, S. Thuriens (not the Saint-Thurien close to Le Havre, obviously), Noirétable, la Bergere, Thiers, Lexoux, and Pont sur Allier (not the Pont sur Allier that is eighty kilometers north

44 / Struck by Apollo

of Hölderlin's route, however). On the even more remote and forbidding road from Clermont-Ferrand west to Limoges (map 8) the coach may have stopped at "les Baragues" (not the town in the central Pyrenees), Pont Gibaut, Pont au Mur (not the Pont au Mur near Toulouse—but I will stop adding these parenthetical notes: readers will have seen how often place names are repeated in France as everywhere else!), S. Avit, la Villeneuve, le Poux,

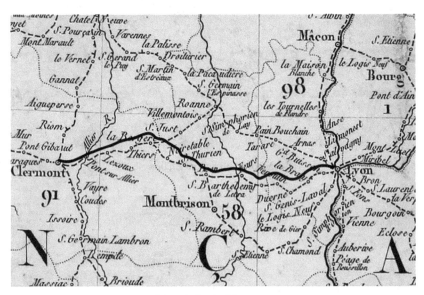

Map 7. Lyon-Clermont

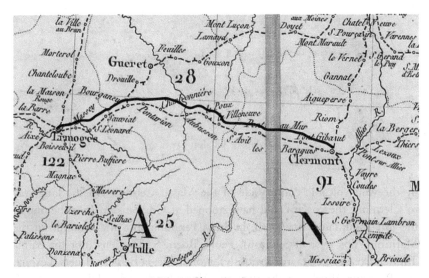

Map 8. Clermont-Limoges

The Achievement / 45

Map 9. Limoges-Périgueux.

Aubusson, Charbonnière, Pontarion, Bourganeuf, Sauviat, S. Leonard, and Massey. Heading southwest at Limoges (map 9), crossing the Vienne River at Aixé on its way to Périgueux, the coach may have stopped at Gatinaud, Chalus, la Loquille, Thiviers, "les Palissons," and "les Tavernes." Following the Isle River to Libourne (map 10), it could have stopped at "la Massouli," Mucidan, Monpon, and S. Médard.

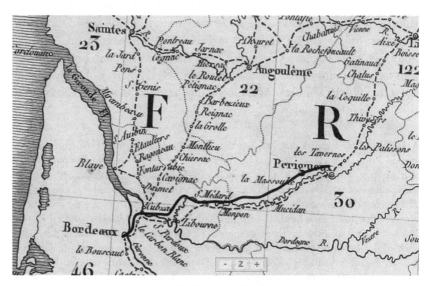

Map 10. Périgueux-Bordeaux.

46 / Struck by Apollo

By this time Hölderlin is probably walking again—perhaps he has left the post-coach behind at Libourne, if not earlier at Périgueux—and is passing through the towns and country inns of S. Pardoux and "le Carbon Blanc" on his way to Bordeaux. As Joe and I followed the national or departmental routes (all of them marked by the letters *N* or *D* on modern maps and road signs), roads that usually adhere quite closely to the traditional post-coach routes, we could identify most of these towns, villages, and inns listed on the 1812 map, even if the spelling of their names had changed in intriguing ways.

Perhaps it would be helpful to list here the national roads that best approximate the post-coach routes, the roads that Joe and I actually traveled. I will begin with Strasbourg, since Hölderlin's walking tour from Nürtingen to Strasbourg, via Stuttgart, Tübingen, Horb, Freudenstadt, Kniebis, and Kehl, did not necessarily follow any given post-coach route. From Strasbourg to Colmar, Belfort, and Besançon, there are two possibilities: one can stay closer to the Rhine if one follows departmental road D 468, passing through Rheinau and Marckolsheim to Neuf-Brisach, then heading west on D 415 to Colmar. Joe and I took the more direct route to Colmar, via Sélestat and Benfeld, on D 1083, mainly so we could visit the well-preserved relais at Benfeld. After Colmar the road becomes D 83 to Belfort, then D 663/683 to Besançon. There, one picks up the D 673, which follows the Doubs River, leading the traveler past Dampière, Rochefort-sur-Nenon, and Dôle to Seurre, at which point one takes the D 973 to Beaune. (If one chooses to travel directly to Chalon-sur-Saône, one follows the N 73.) At Beaune, one heads south on D 974 and D 933 to Mâcon, then on to Lyon on that same D 933.

From Lyon westward to Clermont-Ferrand, the route becomes more complicated: one can follow the D 24 due west to D 389, then head south, then west once again on D 81/89 to Feurs; D 1089 leads on to Thiers; D 2089 then takes one into Clermont.[5] From Clermont-Ferrand, one heads west into the mountains of the Massif Central on D 941, by way of Aubusson, all the scenic way to Limoges. At Limoges, one heads southwest on the N 21 to

---

5. Full disclosure requires that I confess that Joe and I departed from Hölderlin's route to spend Christmas Eve and Christmas Day with Françoise Dastur, one of finest philosophers and scholars of Hölderlin's work in France, joining her and her husband Sarosh in the lovely village of St. Pons in the Ardèche. This took us several hours south of Lyon. Readers of Françoise Dastur's books and articles on Hölderlin will call this a wise decision on our part. Joe and I then headed north to Clermont by way of Aubenas and Le Puy-en-Velay—which explains why there are photos of Issoire, a town that would have taken Hölderlin a bit farther south than his probable route. This was our only major sin, I believe. But we were happy to commit it, and we thank the Dasturs for their hospitality and friendship. One can only imagine what a lonely Christmas Hölderlin himself would have had in Strasbourg, as he waited impatiently for his travel visa for Lyon.

Aixé-sur-Vienne, Châlus, Thiviers, and Périgueux. From Périgueux, one takes the D 6089, following the Isle River past Saint-Astier, Neuvic, Mussidan, and Monpon to Libourne. From Libourne, the D 936 takes one to the suburb of Lormont, which Hölderlin visited on occasion during his stay in Bordeaux. At Lormont, one crosses the Garonne River into Bordeaux proper.

The following table presents the minimum distances between some of the major stopping points, "minimum" because—especially when one avoids major highways and toll roads—the genuine distance by foot or by post-coach, to repeat, would have been much greater than Table 1 suggests.

This comes to a total of some 1,159.2 kilometers, more or less as the crow flies, at least if the crow is using a computer map. But let us back up a bit. We are relatively certain that Hölderlin walked the entire way from Nürtingen to Strasbourg, so that the German post-coach routes are irrelevant for the first part of Hölderlin's journey. Thomas Knubben, who, younger and braver than Joe and I, actually walked much of Hölderlin's path from Nürtingen all the way to Bordeaux, is particularly helpful for the early stages of Hölderlin's journey. We may now take up our own detailed story of Hölderlin's journey to Bordeaux, with Knubben's, Beck's, and especially Bertheau's help.

Table 1. Minimum distances between major stops from Nürtingen to Bordeaux

Nürtingen to Stuttgart	37.3 kilometers
Stuttgart to Tübingen	34.3 kilometers
Tübingen to Horb-am-Neckar	34.2 kilometers
Horb to Freudenstadt	24 kilometers
Freudenstadt-Kniebis to Kehl	56.4 kilometers
Kehl to Strasbourg	8.6 kilometers
Total kilometers in Germany	194.8 kilometers
Strasbourg to Colmar	71.4 kilometers
Colmar to Belfort	71.3 kilometers
Belfort to Besançon	95.8 kilometers
Besançon to Beaune	110.7 kilometers
Beaune to Mâcon	91.8 kilometers
Mâcon to Lyon	74.1 kilometers
Lyon to Clermont-Ferrand	186.9 kilometers
Clermont (Auvergne) to Limoges	171.8 kilometers
Limoges to Périgueux	100 kilometers
Périgueux to Bordeaux	130.6 kilometers
Total kilometers in France	964.4 kilometers

Photo 7. The swollen Saône River flooding its banks in December.

2

The Journey to Bordeaux

Let us for convenience's sake divide the journey into three stages: first, the leg from Nürtingen, Hölderlin's hometown, to Strasbourg; second, the journey, principally by post-coach, from Strasbourg to Lyon; and third, the long final leg from Lyon west to Clermont-Ferrand and Limoges, then south, through Périgueux, to Bordeaux—with those initial and final days, at least, traveled on foot.

The First Leg: From Nürtingen to Strasbourg

Around December 10, 1801, according to Beck—or perhaps a few days earlier, December 6 or 7, according to Sattler—Hölderlin sets out from his mother's house in Nürtingen.[1] He heads down the cobblestone street toward the village church, its steeple soaring "into lovely blueness." The street gets steeper now, wending its way down through the town all the way to the river's edge. He crosses the Neckar to the farther side, close to the garden on the left bank where he played as a child (see photo 8). Today the land belongs to a society of local artists, who clearly remember him: the garden has a number of sculptures and fountains marked with his name—or names, inasmuch as the dweller in the Tübingen Tower often signed his name as Scardanelli or Buonarroti. The editors of his works and commentators on his poems have debated the meaning of these names for decades now. One editor says that Hölderlin was robbed on the hill of Scardanal, at the confluence of the anterior and posterior Rhine streams in Switzerland. The

---

1. Adolf Beck, *Chronik*, 86; D. E. Sattler, *Friedrich Hölderlin Sämtliche Werke, Briefe und Dokumente in zeitlicher Folge*, Bremer Ausgabe (Munich: Luchterhand, 2004), 9:185.

Photo 8. The garden across the Neckar where Hölderlin played as a child.

name remains nonetheless mysterious. As for Buonarroti, most commentators agree that Michelangelo's *Slaves*, which Hölderlin likely saw at the Louvre, haunted him. In any case, as he walks past that garden trellis of his childhood, Hölderlin may be thinking that his youth is finally over; he is entering the second "Half of Life," which is the final and more earnest half.

This poem, "Half of Life," becomes one of the "Nocturnes" of 1803, but Hölderlin had been thinking of this inevitability—his entering into the second half of life—since the mid-1790s, and it may have been on his mind as he was walking out of his home city and leaving his native land, Swabian Württemberg, behind. In its final form, "Hälfte des Lebens" (CHV 1:445) strikes us as one of Hölderlin's most expressionistic poems, itself divided into two starkly contrasting halves:

> Yellow pears hang suspended
> And full of wild roses
> The land stretches into the lake;
> You swans are so elegant,
> And, drunk with kisses,
> You dip your heads
> Into the sacred sobering water.

The Journey to Bordeaux / 51

Woe, where will I find, now
That it is winter, my flowers, where
The sunshine,
And the shadows of the earth?
The walls stand
Speechless and cold, in the wind
Weathervanes clatter.

It is impossible not to think of Franz Schubert's *Winterreise*, composed two decades after Hölderlin made his journey, the song cycle in which the weathervanes continue to clatter. Hölderlin's mood may not have been entirely dire; yet, as he himself said, "I am full of parting." He would be visiting friends in Stuttgart, among them Friedrich Matthison (1761–1831), whom he would see on his return to Stuttgart the next June or July, and Georg Christian Landauer (1769–1845), with whom he would be celebrating Landauer's birthday on the eleventh of December; and a few days after that he would be in France, the land that had publicly declared its commitment to human rights. There were adventures to look forward to, and yet the string of recent failures he was trying to leave behind, failures of love and of career, must have filled him with foreboding. The walking did him good, however, as it always had and always would, up to the end.

We picture him walking slowly at first along the left bank of the Neckar, reluctant to leave the garden of his childhood behind. Some kilometers down the road he picks up the pace; he turns left at the village of Köngen on what is today the Swabian Poets' street. He then passes through Denkendorf, trying to shake off the bad memories of the cloister school, crossing the river again at Esslingen and then following the road along its right bank into Stuttgart. It would have been a good day's walk, some twenty-five or thirty kilometers, but not overly strenuous for him.

Knaupp is probably right when he says that Hölderlin would surely have stayed in Stuttgart through the eleventh to help Landauer celebrate his thirty-second birthday. We may assume that on the twelfth of December he set out for the university town of Tübingen, where he also had friends. This is a walk about equal to that from Nürtingen to Stuttgart, perhaps a bit longer, and certainly a good day's worth of hiking. A more or less straight line would have taken him over the Frauenkopf, passing through or by Degerloch, Echterdingen, Steinenbronn, and Dettenhausen. There he would have begun a hike through the Seven Mills Valley in today's nature park of Schönbuch, arriving at Bebenhausen, which was dear to his friend Schelling, who had spent his childhood there. Hölderlin then would have

52 / Struck by Apollo

threaded his way uphill through the thick woods into the familiar town of Tübingen.

How long he stays in Tübingen we do not know. I imagine only one or two nights, even if the city is important to him because of his university years there. Although he complains bitterly about the Tübinger Stift, which is too much a continuation of his life in the cloisters of Denkendorf and Maulbronn, Tübingen is the site of his first love—and of his lasting love of both poetry and philosophy. During his student years (October 1788 to December 1793), Hölderlin often joins his friends in outings to small cabins or garden houses in the hills surrounding Tübingen, especially on the Österberg, where Hölderlin raises his wine cup, extends it outside the open window, and proposes a toast to "the great spirit!" He also regularly makes the long hike and steep climb to the famous Wurmlingen Chapel southwest of Tübingen (see once again photo 4). It is a favorite goal of his walks, often in the society of his roommates at the Stift, Schelling and Hegel. He writes to his sister of his plan to walk there with Hegel, "where the beautiful prospect is well known" (CHV 2:462). As always, these outings offer relief from the otherwise relentless pressure of his university studies and the "destiny" imposed on him to be a pastor. It seems certain that in his December journey southward to Horb he would have visited the chapel once again or at least gazed up toward it with some nostalgia.

Tübingen, one must remember, will also be the site of Hölderlin's long declining years, the thirty-five years spent in the tower of Ernst Zimmer's house on the Neckar. A narrow street leads from the main gate of the Stift down toward the Neckar; following it, we have a first view of Zimmer's house and its position on the river (see photo 64). Here, Hölderlin spent more than half of his life—from 1807 to 1843, that is, from his thirty-seventh to his seventy-third year. A plaque on the tower wall reads: "1807–1843: Here lived, and passed away, Hölderlin"—but our journey to Bordeaux has only just begun.

From Tübingen, after passing through Wurmlingen, Hölderlin would have continued south to Rottenburg, where he rejoins the Neckar River. Now he walks upriver in a west-southwesterly direction to Horb-am-Neckar, some thirty-five kilometers distant. A long but beautiful day alongside his river, one may imagine. Perhaps we can pause for a moment to contemplate the Neckar. One of Hölderlin's river poems is dedicated to it. Oddly, the first draft of the Neckar poem has the title *Der Main*, even though he would hardly have confused that Mannheim-Frankfurt River with the stream of his home village. "The Main" (CHV 1:229–30) is an odd poem at that. Its original title is "The Neckar," making the circular fusion or confusion

The Journey to Bordeaux / 53

complete, but whether Neckar or Main, the poem is about something else altogether: of its ten stanzas, the first seven are about Greece, and the Main River, in stanzas eight to ten, seems but an afterthought. Indeed, in the seventh stanza Hölderlin calls himself "a singer without a homeland," *ein heimatloser Sänger*, so that the river poem—and perhaps the later river hymns as well—arguably have little to do with a celebration of national geography.

Knaupp, one of Hölderlin's editors, presents five different versions of this "homeless" stanza in the manuscripts (CHV 3:114), only one of which I will present here. The islands mentioned are, to repeat, the Greek isles, which, because Greece was part of the Ottoman Empire, Hölderlin can visit only in his mind's eye:

> To you perhaps, O islands, there once arrived
>   A singer without a homeland; for his wandering
>   There had to serve, in place of a fatherland,
>   The Earth, the free . . .

Two years before his departure for Bordeaux, then, this feeling of being an outcast from the land of his birth is already very strong in Hölderlin. If he tries to rein in his wanderlust in the later poem that is dedicated to his "home" river, "The Neckar" (CHV 1:253–54), something foreign, something distant in space and time, still calls him. The first three of the poem's nine stanzas, along with the last, do focus on the Neckar. Here is the first stanza:

> In your valleys my heart awakened
>   To life, your wavelets played all around me,
>   And of all your lovely hills, hills that know you,
>   Wanderer! none is a stranger to me.

Yet the middle five stanzas, to repeat, find themselves called elsewhere—to the river Pactolus, rich in gold and silver, which flows from Mount Tmolus in the region of Homer's Troy to the shores of Aeolian and Ionian Smyrna; the poet envisages the woods around Troy, the temple of Poseidon at Sounion in Attica, and the temple of Zeus Olympios at Syracuse, Sicily. If all of Europe's roads lead to Rome, then all its rivers, at least in Hölderlin's vision of them, lead to Troy and Athens. And yet, these are places of the past, locales inaccessible to a contemporary river wanderer. Hölderlin would have longed to visit these sites before "stormwind and age" reduced the Parthenon and its images of the gods to ashes. "For a long time now you stand in solitude, O pride of the world, / A world that is no more" (*Der*

Neckar, ll. 22–23). No river, then, but only the sea of memory, can take him to that vanished world.

These are the faraway things that Hölderlin may be thinking about as he abandons the river of his homeland at Horb-am-Neckar. From Horb, he heads almost due west into the northern region of the Black Forest. He knows well the eastern slopes of the forest near Lake Constance, which he has hiked recently on his way to and from Hauptwil, Switzerland. If earlier on in his life he hiked westward to the Rhine, that was farther north, in the Palatinate near Speyer. The northern Black Forest is therefore uncharted territory for him, even if landscape is everywhere continuous, so that the designations Swabian Alps and Black Forest cannot be as sharply distinguished in life as they are on a map.

Yet there did seem to Joe and me to be a notable difference in the landscape. It had snowed during the night we camped on our way from Horb to Freudenstadt (photo 9). Prior to this, the evenings and nights had been rainy and chilly, but in the area west of Horb, spotted with small villages and farms, and throughout the Black Forest, the first major snowfall of December had begun. It was one of those wet snows that come early in the season, but it covered the houses and barns, fields and forests, all the way to the horizon. Joe and I began to realize, really for the first time, how

Photo 9. On the way from Horb-on-Neckar to Freudenstadt in the Black Forest, under the first December snowfall.

The Journey to Bordeaux / 55

strenuous such a journey on foot could well have been during the month of December 1801. By the time we arrived in Freudenstadt, the largest town of the northern Black Forest, where Hölderlin must have spent the night, snow was universal. We walked across the main square, visited the impressive church, and enjoyed the graceful arched porticoes around the square. We then learned at the local museum that the center of the town had been completely rebuilt after World War II. Virtually only one old house, a house with a steep four-sided roof, had been left standing after the shelling of the town and the resulting conflagration in April 1945. For the rest, the town square was all new—even though the red sandstone thresholds that led into the shops and restaurants around the square themselves were ancient. The town had used the rubble to rebuild, and the result tricked us into thinking that the town square was something Hölderlin himself could have seen. Freudenstadt today is filled with arts and crafts shops; above all, it continues to be famous as a *Kurort*, renowned for its invigorating air. (Mark Twain was among its many famous guests during the nineteenth century.) We spent the morning here, but then drove on toward the Kniebis, the highest mountain of the northern Schwarzwald. Hölderlin had to cross it to reach Kehl and Strasbourg.

There was more than one way to ascend the Kniebis, and we could not be sure which route Hölderlin had followed. He may have walked west-northwest from Freudenstadt, beginning to climb what is today called the Schwarzwald Hochstrasse, passing through Engelmann's Forest to the Kniebis Hut near the top, moving on then to Rotenbach. Joe and I, made cautious by the snow that continued to fall and by the thickening fog, decided on a slightly different route. We headed due north to the Schwarzwald Täler-strasse, the "valley road," which took us through the town of Baiersbronn. By the time we turned left and began the steep climb up the Kniebis, snow was falling heavily. It made us realize how decisive the weather is for any hiker, especially one who is in unknown territory. We drove through fog and snow, ascending the Kniebis, passing from the lower to the middle and upper valleys, running parallel to a hiking path that bore the strange name, "Stones Tell Stories," *Steine Erzählen Geschichten*. This day the voluble stones were suffocated by white silence. If the weather had been like this on the day of Hölderlin's climb, he could not have made much progress. He would have needed the entire day to climb the Kniebis, and he would have had to seek refuge on the top before proceeding the following morning down the other side. For the first time, Joe and I thought hard about Hölderlin's shoes and his cloak—both hopefully well-impregnated with linseed oil against the heavy snow. Wet feet and a sudden chill could have ended the journey before it really began (see photo 10.)

Photo 10. Atop the Kniebis in the northern Black Forest in early December, the snow already knee deep.

From Freudenstadt to the top of the Kniebis is a distance of only seventeen kilometers—as the crow flies, but not as the hiker struggles uphill through the snow. And the fog? It grew thicker as we climbed. How many times in the past have I drifted off the path in the Black Forest snow and fog! Allow me to tell two stories among the many possible ones.

I used to teach my classes at the University of Freiburg at midday during the winter semester, making certain I would finish by about two o'clock. I would then take the tram and then a bus to the village closest to the cabin and climb about ninety minutes up to it. One afternoon I was late starting for home, and the fog blanketed the hill as evening fell. The snow was up to my knees, so it was slow going. I was sure of my path, however, having climbed it for years in all sorts of weather. I could have done it blindfolded. Or so I thought. I trudged through the snow in the fog as night came down, until I wound up on someone's doorstep—a farmhouse I had never seen before. I had drifted off the path to my left, walking slightly downhill for about thirty minutes, even though I felt as though I were climbing. The farmer was able to explain to me where I was

The Journey to Bordeaux / 57

and how I might find my path again. I clambered across his field, heading straight up the slope until I found the pines lining the path, making my way home without further incident.

Some years later, while cross-country skiing, the same thing happened in perfect daylight. The fog was so thick and the snowstorm so intense that once I left the forest, where the path was relatively clear because of the thick pines guarding either side, I glided off to a place I had never seen before. Once again, a farmhouse enabled me to guess—after a period of confusion—where I must be. I estimated the correct direction homeward by skiing directly into the wind-driven snow, which I knew must be coming out of the west, until, after an hour or so, I recognized where I was. The following summer, on a bright afternoon, I was completely unable to determine where I might have been on that winter's day.

The point of these stories is this: without trying to dramatize, it is simply the case that had conditions on the Kniebis been as they were when Joe and I ascended it, Hölderlin could have gotten hopelessly lost. Even today, when the area is more settled than it was back then, a hiker would have to be well-informed about the path to follow, and he or she would need some good luck to be able to find and stay on that path. Nowadays one is likely to come across signs of civilization and to find one's way to safety. But there is no guarantee. And in the early nineteenth century there would have been many excellent chances to lose one's way in the forest. There were and still are few farmers up on the Kniebis. He would not have been in good shape when a hiker found him during the next spring thaw. In short, Hölderlin's trip to Bordeaux could have ended one week into the journey. *Steine Erzählen Geschichten* and many of these stories are tragic histories.

The top of the Kniebis, just short of a thousand meters high, was a wonderworld of fog and snow-laden, twisted trees. (Take a second look at photo 10, taken on the peak of the hill, just before the descent toward the Rhine Plain in the west.) The higher one ascends on the Kniebis, the more every trace of color disappears. The evergreens are now ever dark; there are only lines and contours of shapes. And the snow and fog work to ambiguate even those contours. In addition to the cold, there is a great deal of uncertainty up here. One feels a sense of growing relief as one follows the road that snakes its way down the western slope of the Kniebis toward Oppenau, Oberkirch, and Appenweier. The colors return, even if they are the drab colors of winter, the browns and faded greens and duns of meadows and plowed fields. Perhaps even a hint of blue sky, as the fog is left hanging on the mountain. It is some forty-six kilometers from the peak of the Kniebis to Kehl on the Rhine but, again, many more kilometers than

58 / Struck by Apollo

that for a person working his way down a forest path. It seems to me that Hölderlin could never have made his way either up or down the mountain in a single day, certainly not up *and* down. From Oppenau to Kehl, the forested hills flatten out to farmers' fields, and the going gets much easier.

From Kehl to Strasbourg, crossing the Rhine and the border between Germany and France, is a matter of some nine or ten kilometers, half a day's walk at most. Having descended the massive hill of the Kniebis, perhaps under snow, Hölderlin would have hiked across the flat and fertile fields of the broad Rhine Plain, passing through the villages of Legelshurst, Kork, Neumühl, Krimmeri-Meinau, and Kehl, some of them names that were beginning to sound strange. When he finally crossed the Rhine, either by ferry boat or by way of a pedestrian bridge, the Passerelle, he may have been struck by the fact that the Rhine is here only a modest-sized stream, nothing like the vast rivers he was later to confront in France or the Rhine he had visited on earlier journeys farther north near Speyer. Or it may well be that the alterations to the Rhine during the nineteenth century and the two huge canals that were built in the twentieth century have so depleted the river, altering and diminishing its course and its bed significantly, that it is impossible for us to imagine the force and breadth of the Rhine in earlier centuries.

Strasbourg and all of Alsace had become a part of France at the end of the Thirty Years War in 1648. To be sure, the prevailing language of Alsace remained German, or at least that strange form of southern Allemanic German that is the Alsatian *Dialekt* or *Elsässer Dütsch*. Today, only the older generations, especially in the rural areas, speak and understand it, whereas French otherwise dominates. Hölderlin would have been delighted by the similarities and differences between his own Swabian dialect and the Alsatian, already visible on the signs over the doors of the inns and on shopfronts. Yet an unpleasant surprise awaited him in Strasbourg—his stay would be much longer than he had anticipated.

Hölderlin is in Strasbourg by December 15. He applies for a travel visa to Bordeaux, intending to follow the normal route, which would take him due west to Paris and then south to Bordeaux. He has to wait two weeks for the visa, however, and when it arrives, the police tell him that he must travel by way of Lyon, not Paris, and that he must register periodically with the local gendarmeries as he makes his way south. We have to recall that these are the years of the Second Coalition War and that more than technically speaking the German lands (the Holy Roman Empire of Austro-Hungary and Brandenburg-Prussia), along with England, Russia, and a number of smaller nations, are all at war with France. By this time

Napoleon is well on his way to seizing absolute power and is conducting war all across Europe for Revolutionary France. During the year 1801, a number of attempts have been made on the First Consul's life, some of them by disgruntled Jacobins, and the Strasbourg authorities have been instructed to worry about spies and assassins infiltrating France from abroad. As unlikely a candidate as Hölderlin may have appeared to be, the authorities send him south.

An alternative explanation of the delay and the altered route—what I would call the Francophile explanation, since French commentators seem to favor it—is that Hölderlin himself chose to travel by way of Lyon, hoping to cross Napoleon's path there. For the First Consul had convened the so-called *Consulta* in Lyon, at which representatives of the north Italian states, recently overwhelmed by the French armies, were to choose their administrative head. There is little doubt that Hölderlin was still cautiously optimistic about Napoleon, seeing in him the only real hope that republicanism and the rights of humankind could be extended to his benighted homeland. Without foreign intervention, the princes and pastors of Württemberg would never relinquish power—that much he knew. Even as late as 1807, Hölderlin's friend Hegel would thrill to the sight of the Corsican version of the World Spirit passing through Jena on horseback.

Yet is it likely that Hölderlin would have voluntarily altered his route? His letters make it clear that he had planned to travel by way of Paris, so that the change of route was not his own wish but that of the police, even if he was able to make his peace with the alteration. Had he known at the outset that he would be heading toward Lyon, one can well imagine that he would have chosen to travel to Switzerland, heading due south from Stuttgart, crossing Lake Constance by ferry, then continuing on to Berne and Rousseau's Geneva. From there he would have passed through Annecy and proceeded on to Lyon. As it turned out, he had to follow the valley of the Doubs River to its confluence with the Saône, only then heading south to Lyon. In any case, as it turned out, the date of Napoleon's arrival at Lyon had been pushed back, so that Hölderlin in fact missed his dubious hero by a week or so. "Dubious" because it was not yet entirely clear that the *Consulta* would turn out to be a *Dictata* and that Napoleon would choose his own man to lead the new Italian government. That man would be himself.

What did Hölderlin do during those two weeks of waiting in Strasbourg? We do not know. Nor do we know where he stayed, or what his mood was, although we can imagine his impatience. More than one French commentator, beginning with Pierre Bertaux, believes that he crossed the Rhine back into Germany and headed north to see Susette one last time. Romance does

60 / Struck by Apollo

thrill to the possibility of such a visit, but the desires of the interpreters in this case make little sense. It is unlikely that Hölderlin knew how long the visa would take; probably he visited the prefecture every day, or in any case quite often. The idea that he would cross the border and then try to re-enter France seems to me highly unlikely: it would have made him look like the spy or assassin for which the French authorities were on the alert.

My own answer to the question as to what he did during those two weeks is that he *worked*. In August 1801 a friend had informed him that the Tübingen publisher Cotta would produce a volume of his poems for Easter 1802, so that Hölderlin prepared a clean copy of many of these poems. The various editors of Hölderlin's works list well over a dozen poems that they believe Hölderlin was working on during this period—even if a precise chronology is very difficult, since the poet reworked his poems over and over again. (It is reported that Schelling's wife Caroline once remarked that Hölderlin's retouchings indicated that he had no talent, a judgment that recoils on the judge, alas, with considerable force.) Among the poems he may have been working on are the following: "Dichterberuf," "Stimme des Volks," "Nachtgesänge" (including "Hälfte des Lebens"), "Ermunter-ung," "Natur und Kunst—oder Saturn und Jupiter," "Heimkunft," "Am Quell der Donau," "Friedensfeier," "Die Wanderung," "Der Rhein," and "Germanien." These are the suggestions made by Beck. Sattler adds "Brot und Wein" and "Stuttgart" to the list. Knaupp adds "Der Weingott," "Die Heimat" (second version), "Die Liebe," "Lebenslauf" (second version, first stanza), "Der Abschied," "Diotima" (third version), "Die Mutter Erde," and the sketch for the "Donau" poem.[2] Finally, Schmidt adds "Der Einzige." In addition to these twenty-two poems, it is quite possible that Hölderlin was already thinking about his translations of Sophocles' *Oedipus the Tyrant* and *Antigone*, both of which he would be working on intensely in Bordeaux. Because we have no diary or notebook from the Bordeaux trip, however,

---

2. When Sattler adds "Bread and Wine" and Knaupp "The Wine God" to the list of poems Hölderlin may have been working on or reworking during the trip to Bordeaux and back, they are referring basically to the same poem. It is Hölderlin's longest elegy, begun as early as the summer of 1800 and more or less completed by the winter of that year. Hoping that it might appear in that ill-fated volume of his poems promised for the spring of 1802, Hölderlin prepared a good copy during the second half of 1801, before his departure for Bordeaux. After he returned to Germany, he reworked the poem over the next two years, changing the title now to "Bread and Wine" but keeping the dedication to Wilhelm Heinse. For reasons that I cannot account for, the initial form of this poem became Joe's and my companion as our journey through France began. I will reproduce, in translation, the nine stanzas of "The Wine God" in the pages that follow.

we cannot be certain about what he may have been working on. Yet it is unlikely that those two weeks in Strasbourg were "time off" for the poet.

On days when the weather was clear, however, he would surely have walked about the city of Strasbourg, one of the jewels of Europe both then and now. It is likely that he had lodgings somewhere on the Grand Île, the "large island" that is the heart of the old city today. Two branches of the river Ill surround the island and make Strasbourg a city of quais. He would have visited the neighborhood of "the mills," with its many bridges, at the western end of the island; he would have enjoyed the swans that still thrive on the river; the *Fachwerk* houses (their exposed beams structuring the plaster walls) would have been familiar to him, but there were more flower boxes on the windows of these houses—even in winter!—than he had ever seen before. And many of the structures were ancient already in 1801, especially the ornate guild houses, such as the Maison des Tanneurs, the Tanners' House (photo 11).

Photo 11. The Maison des Tanneurs, one of the oldest and most ornate of the medieval guild houses in Strasbourg.

62 / Struck by Apollo

The many churches of Strasbourg would have intrigued him, and for a special reason—apart from their remarkable architecture. Almost all of them went back to the early or high Middle Ages and so were Roman Catholic in origin. Yet many of them were converted to Protestantism during the first third of the sixteenth century and then, a century or so later, became Catholic once again, eventually becoming ecumenical churches holding both Catholic and Protestant services. Particularly graceful is the church of St. Pierre-le-Jeune (Saint Peter the Younger), in the northeastern quadrant of the island. Constructed between 1250 and 1320 in the grand High Gothic style, the church has a cloister built during the eleventh century and a crypt dating from the seventh century; whereas the cloister might remind Hölderlin of his unhappy days at Denkendorf and Maulbronn, I suspect that he would have been fascinated by the crypt and its graves (photo 12).

The Protestant church of St. Thomas, in the southern portion of the "grand island" of Strasbourg, would have drawn Hölderlin's attention, if only for very ambivalent reasons. Attached to the church, which is fortress-like in its sturdy Romanesque construction, is the Strasbourger Stift that performed precisely the same function that the Tübinger Stift in Württemberg did. Hölderlin had come to despise the Stift as a bastion of oppression. The Stift at St. Thomas was founded in 1544 as the Collegium Wilhelmitanum, and it may well have reminded Hölderlin of his worst experiences in the Evangelical church, which he felt was not only reactionary but also fundamentally sterile and joyless, incapable of love.

As Joe and I visited church after church on our own trip, for the simple reason that the old towns where his post-coach may have stopped were invariably built around them, so that we could be reasonably certain that Hölderlin had seen them during his many layovers, we always looked for the most ancient parts of the building. Crypts, being the remains of earlier Christian churches, were almost invariably constructed on the sites of ancient pagan temples, whether Gallo-Roman or Celtic. Hölderlin would surely have made an effort to find out which of the ancient gods or goddesses had been worshipped there. Actually, he was already convinced, as his friend Schelling came to be convinced, that the polytheism of the ancients was to be admired rather than scorned. The ancient cult sites were always sites where nature invited both *cult* and *culture* to itself, and I suspect that this process always intrigued him. He would at least have heard of Santa Maria sopra Minerva in Rome, whose very name says it all, and during his trip through France he would have experienced this *sopra* over and over again, the superstructure of the Christian constructions of the Middle Ages having been superimposed over a hidden depth of religious history.

Photo 12. A monk's grave in the seventh-century crypt of St. Pierre-le-Jeune church, Strasbourg.

64 / Struck by Apollo

Photo 13. Notre-Dame-de-Strasbourg, at the main portal of the Strasburger Münster.

A particularly intriguing—and more controversial—aspect of the many churches he may have visited on his journey, especially when he had to spend considerable time at the rest stops and towns where he overnighted, is the omnipresent cult of Mary in French Catholicism (photo 13). I found myself photographing statues of the Virgin over and over again, principally, I suspect, for two reasons. First, Hölderlin was interested not only in the fraternity of Dionysos, Herakles, and Christ but also in the maternity of Demeter and the virtual sisterhood of Demeter and Persephone; his poems show that he was struck by the grandeur not only of Zeus Pater (Jupiter) but also of Athena, Artemis, and above all, Venus Aphrodite. In antiquity, the latter was mirrored in the mortals Niobe, Danaë, Semele, Io, Europa, Helen, and many

The Journey to Bordeaux / 65

others, all of whom had gripping stories to tell. Many of these stories were recounted in Sophocles' tragedies, on which Hölderlin may have been working. Second, whether for reasons of piety or desperation, Hölderlin would never have spurned the chance to find and gaze upon a loving mother. This is not to psychologize him, I hope, but merely to affirm that the nature he loved seemed to have more to do with Demeter than with a calculating Demiurge. Hölderlin's friend Schelling was convinced that the first rung on the ladder of deity was Demeter, with Persephone as the second rung. Schelling was also convinced that throughout nature it is the female gender that prevails, with the masculine entering on the scene only as an afterthought. When Jean-Pierre Lefebvre speaks of Hölderlin's "Catholic temptation," therefore, presumably referring to Waiblinger's report that the aging Hölderlin expressed a desire to convert, I suspect that the cult of Mary is what he means.[3] Three pages of the *Homburger Folioheft*, filled after Hölderlin's return from Bordeaux, contain a fragment that earlier editors of Hölderlin's works did not hesitate to call *An die Madonna*, "To the Madonna," a title that does not appear in the notebook as such but that nonetheless captures much of the sense of the long fragment. It begins like this (CHV 1:408):

Much have I suffered on your
Account and on that of your Son,
O Madonna,
Since hearing of him
In my sweet youth
For not only the seer stands
Under a destiny but also those
Who merely serve. Because I was

Determined to sing
Many a hymn
To the highest one, the Father,
Melancholy wore me down.

Yet, Celestial One, still I want
To celebrate you, and no one should

---

3. See Jean-Pierre Lefebvre, "Rhône et Garonne (La France de Hölderlin)," in *Bordeaux au temps de Hölderlin*, eds. Gilbert Merlio and Nicole Pelletier (Bern: Peter Lang, Gallogermanica no. 20, 1997), 203–27.

66 / Struck by Apollo

Rail against the radiance of my words,
Spoken in my native tongue,
While I walk alone
In the fields, where wild
The lily grows, fearless,
Stretching toward the unreachable,
Primeval vault
Of the wood,
        the western world,

        and has ruled over
Humankind, instead of some other deity,
She, the love that forgets every offense.

My translation of the last line is a bit of a cheat, for the line invokes *die allvergessende Liebe*, "the love that forgets everything," all-oblivious love. In what sense, however, does love forget everything? My answer is that whereas Hölderlin's mother and the Pietist church in which both she and her son grew up never forgot anything, certainly not an offense or a fault, Hölderlin is dreaming of a mother more generous, a mother less punishing and more forgiving, a mother born of the generous sea—one might dare to call her the Madonna of Sea Spume—but let me curb my polytheism and return to Strasbourg.

To the northeast of the Protestant Stiftskirche, St. Thomas, the towering Catholic cathedral of Strasbourg, dedicated to Notre-Dame de Strasbourg, would surely have astonished Hölderlin (photo 14). The entire edifice, designed by Erwin von Steinbach and built between 1176 and 1439 in a mix of Romanesque and Gothic styles, stands on the site of a Roman temple, an early Christian church, and a Carolingian Basilica. It is constructed of red sandstone, its main lacework tower the tallest structure in Europe until far into the nineteenth century. Goethe had helped make the cathedral and its architect famous by writing about them not many years before, and Hölderlin would certainly have read Goethe's essay. The Strasbourg Liebfrauenmünster is dedicated to Mary, "Our Beloved Lady," and its statuary, in the naturalist style of the Gothic renaissance, would surely have impressed him. Likewise the windows of the cathedral, which light up the gloom of the interior. The Liebfrauenmünster may have offered Hölderlin an aspect of a more forgiving god and a more loving goddess than the ones to which he was accustomed. Recall that some years later, Goethe, at the apotheosis of his hymn to the eternal feminine at the end

Photo 14. The *Liebfrauenmünster*, the Strasbourg Cathedral.

of *Faust II*, would not shy from addressing the mortal mother of God as *Göttin*, "goddess," and such she appears to be at the main portal of the cathedral dedicated to her.

All this is not to say that the secular buildings of Strasbourg would have failed to attract Hölderlin's attention. The Renaissance Maison Kammerzell, or *Kammerzellhüs*, built in 1427, was august already at the time of Hölderlin's visit. The more recently built Palais Rohan, where the bishop lived and where many municipal officials had their quarters, would no doubt have become familiar to him as he waited for his travel visa. As I mentioned earlier, the guild houses too, among them the Tanners' House, which were medieval or Renaissance in origin, would have delighted him. Scattered among these buildings on the Grande Île were the inns that he may have visited. One may venture the guess that even if he lived quite frugally here, as he had all his life, he still would have eaten better in Strasbourg than ever before in his life, indeed in any *Winstub* he may have entered, not necessarily the more expensive ones. True, we may be sure that he would have sought out the least expensive room and board over those two weeks, since frugality was customary with him, no matter how generous Consul Meyer's travel allowance had been.

68 / Struck by Apollo

The Second Leg: From Strasbourg to Lyon

Hölderlin leaves Strasbourg with visa in hand on or around December 30. If he arrives at Lyon on January 9, as the letter to his mother tells us, then he must have traveled some fifty-three kilometers per day. Obviously, this would have to have been done by coach or by riverboat. (If Sattler is right, and Hölderlin arrives in Lyon by January 6, then he would have to have traveled some sixty-eight kilometers per day, which seems well-nigh impossible.) Consul Meyer had sent Hölderlin twenty-five *Louis d'Ors*, for the voyage, some 550 Gulden or 625 French pounds, difficult to calculate in today's currencies but in any case a very generous provision, and with it Hölderlin was able to send his luggage directly to Bordeaux from Germany and to take the post-coach whenever he pleased. He traveled only with a *Nachtsack*, presumably a rucksack with the bare necessaries for overnighting. The post-coach route was dotted with relay stations, *relais de poste*, where the horses could be changed and the passengers (normally four to six in each coach) could take their meals and overnight. Hölderlin's travel funds were sufficient for all that, and, if only because of the long, frustrating wait in Strasbourg, he most likely traveled principally by coach to Lyon.

Joe and I felt certain as we made our own trip that Hölderlin would have kept at least a modest travel journal, making daily notes about what he was seeing and experiencing. Yet, as I have mentioned, no trace of such a diary has ever been found, and as far as I know there has never been any mention of its possible existence in the literature. The result is that we are forced to speculate about the precise route and all things else. One of things we do know about the month of December 1801 is that there was considerable flooding of the rivers, as there is almost every year, including the year Joe and I made our own trip. The roadbeds, which often ran alongside the banks of the major rivers, were in parlous condition. It is difficult to imagine the progress a post-coach could have made on such roads or what sorts of detours must have been necessary. Some suggest that Hölderlin could have made equal or better progress on foot. That he would have been happy to walk and thrilled to accept a boat ride along the Doubs and the Saône seems clear. As I also mentioned, by avoiding the post-coaches, he would also have been better able to evade the risk of robbery, far more common among post-coach passengers than among solitary wayfarers. Yet because of the long delay waiting for the visa, Hölderlin in all likelihood traveled most of the way to Lyon by coach. In any case, the modern departmental highways that Joe and I took (though not the autoroutes, which cut through the countryside, bridging the rivers

The Journey to Bordeaux / 69

and tunneling through the hills), like the old post roads, generally follow the contours of these major rivers.

How many kilometers could the coach travel in a day, provided the weather was clement and the roadbed solid? To repeat, surely little more than fifty, something perhaps closer to forty. We also have to remember that the December days are remarkably short this far north, with first light at eight in the morning and dark setting in by four or five in the afternoon—eight to nine hours of clear daylight. True, one reads of some post-coaches starting out at four in the morning, finding their way by torch or lamplight; yet one has to be skeptical. If one adds to the infelicities of weather and the dark December days what Laurence Sterne indicates about the inefficiency of the French post-coaches, or "post-chaises," as he calls them, Hölderlin's progress may have been as arduous as Tristram Shandy's—if only because Tristram is fleeing Death. The French *diligences*, Laurence Sterne complains, seem incapable of due diligence—they are perpetually breaking down. In volume VII, chapter 8, of *The Life and Opinions of Tristram Shandy, Gentleman*, Tristram tells us that there is *something* about the French coaches that displeases him, namely, the fact "*That something is always wrong in a French post-chaise upon first setting out. Or the proposition may stand thus. A French postillion has always to alight before he has got three hundred yards out of town.* What's wrong now?—Diable!—a rope's broke!—a knot has slipt!—a staple's drawn!—a bolt's to whittle!—a tag, a rag, a jag, a strap, a buckle, or a buckle's tongue, wants altering.——" [4] It could readily be that Hölderlin, like the weary Tristram, would "rather go a-foot ten thousand times—or that I will be damned, if I ever get into another" post-coach (Sterne 468). As for walking, however, readers who have hiked a thirty-kilometer day will admit, I think, that on the next day they were inclined to rest. Week after week of such days seems beyond the capacity of even the heartiest walker, although Hölderlin was every bit of that. He had hiked all his life, and only six months earlier, as we heard, he had thought nothing of walking from his home to Hauptwil in Switzerland and back. Yet the trip to Bordeaux was another matter: a thousand kilometers as the crow flies and much longer as the man walks. And how straight can a man walk? As I have argued, one may accept as a reasonable parallel the distances traversed by Roman aqueducts: their actual length was often double that of the direct distance from mountain source to city served. There is something about walking that is reminiscent of the meander.

---

4. Laurence Sterne, *The Life and Opinions of Tristram Shandy, Gentleman*, VII, 8 (Harmondsworth: Penguin, 1967), 467. Cited from hence by volume and chapter or by the page number of the Penguin edition.

70 / Struck by Apollo

The most likely route from Strasbourg to Besançon seemed to Joe and me to pass through Benfeld, Colmar, Isenheim, Aspach-la-Chapelle, Belfort, Tavey, Isle-sur-le-Doubs, Clerval, Baume-les-Dames, and Roulans. Some researchers profess that one of Hölderlin's relay-station stops would have been at Isenheim, where just possibly he could have seen the now famous Matthias Grünewald altar triptych. What makes this unlikely is the fact that the triptych became famous—for art historians today it is one of the great treasures of late Medieval art, housed now in Colmar quite splendidly in its own museum—only much later. But this raises a problem that Joe and I faced constantly: whoever retraces Hölderlin's (presumed) steps sees so many things that he or she *insists* Hölderlin must have seen. How *could* he have passed such things by? Every traveler, ignoring the danger of retrospective illusion, no doubt projects an entire itinerary of experiences onto poor Hölderlin, and the possibilities are infinite because the screen is so blank. Joe and I tried to restrain ourselves, asking ourselves where he might have overnighted, how much time he would have had before continuing on, and what sorts of things were closest to the centers of the "old town" in every city and village he may have passed through. One does not have to be a skeptic to see how impossible the task is. Yet in spite of all the uncertainties, except for the certainty of temptation, it is difficult to refuse the challenge, especially as one gets to know the poet better by reading his work—I mean the challenge of speculating what might have been of irresistible interest to him, what would have called to him imperiously had he had the time to look about.

One example. It is impossible to think that the great river poet Hölderlin would have been immune to the serene beauty of the Doubs River Valley or that he would not have been thrilled by the wider and wilder Saône and Rhône rivers as they flow through Lyon; impossible to think that the chain of volcanoes above Clermont-Ferrand, even in a snowstorm, would not have gripped him or that the hillside city of Périgueux would not have delighted him. True, the only direct statement we have from him, in *Andenken*, tells of his excitement when he sees the confluence of the Garonne and Dordogne rivers and their wide flow, as the Gironde, into the Atlantic. Yet Joe and I were not ashamed to speculate about earlier excitements, even if such speculation is forbidden to historians who think of themselves as scientists and archivists.

Again, there were two post-coach routes heading south from Strasbourg that Hölderlin could have taken, one following the Rhine closely, the river route taking him through Marckolsheim and Neufbrisach, then sharply west

The Journey to Bordeaux / 71

to Colmar, the more westerly route taking him through Benfeld, Sélestat (Schlettstadt), and thus more directly to Colmar. Joe and I selected the Benfeld route, primarily because we wanted to see the relay station there, which is known to be one of the oldest and best preserved in France. Some thirty-three kilometers south of Strasbourg, the Benfeld relay post bears the date 1784. The typical structure of these relay stations can be described as follows: the post-coach enters through a large arched portal at the side or in the rear of the walled compound; the stable and the inn and its kitchen form one large complex, with a generous courtyard separating the two main wings. Unfortunately, the relais at Benfeld is today under reconstruction, with much of the building now going to refurbished apartments, no doubt quite expensive ones. Historic landmarks too, even the "protected" ones, have their own fate.

From Benfeld the post-coach route passes through Sélestat and Colmar, heading southwest in the direction of Belfort and Besançon. The Vosges Mountains are on one's right as one drives south. The Vosges are wilder and less populated than the mountains of their twin chain across the Rhine, that is, those of the southern Schwarzwald. Joe and I stopped at Cernay to examine another surviving relais, today a restaurant but with few traces of its post-coach history. Hölderlin's route then takes him through the villages of Isenheim, Aspach la Chapelle, Tavey, and Isle-sur-le-Doubs. The names become increasingly French as one leaves the southern portion of Alsace behind and enters Franche-Comté. From now on, Hölderlin is in new linguistic territory. His French is good, Bertheau assures us (JB 13). Indeed, Bertheau argues strongly that all the evidence indicates that Hölderlin could speak French quite well, even if, as we will hear later, some native French speakers of his time demur. In the Gontard household during the late 1790s, he would have been tutoring young Henry in French language and literature among his other subjects. True, with Susette he more than likely spoke German; their entire correspondence is in that language. Yet we are told that he picked up enough of the Gascogne dialect while in Bordeaux, presumably from the sailors who frequented the wharves there, to curse very colorfully in that form of French during the years of his confinement and decline in the Tübingen Tower (JB 105).

One of Bertheau's oddest yet most compelling demonstrations of Hölderlin's abilities in the Gascogne dialect is his assertion (JB 119–20) that one of the poet's pseudonyms from the time of his internment in the tower, "Killalusimeno," is in fact an expression in the Gascognais dialect. Commentators have riddled over the word ever since Wilhelm Waiblinger mentioned it in

72 / Struck by Apollo

1827.[5] Some assert that it may be Tahitian in origin, and Hölderlin did know of Otahiti. However, Bertheau argues that it is merely a Germanized form of the expression—presumably common among the sailors Hölderlin spent time with on the wharves—*qu'il a lous y meno,* "that he's lost his mind." This would be important for two reasons: first, Hölderlin clearly had mastered at least a few French phrases from his sailor acquaintances, and second, during the period of his illness, Hölderlin seems to have known precisely what—at least in the eyes of the world—was wrong with him. Let us assume, then, that Hölderlin's French is good. Even so, it seems certain that he will be confronted every day of his journey through France with situations for which his vocabulary is inadequate, his ear insufficiently practiced, his tongue and his purse overtaxed—all the normal challenges and hazards of travel.

Joe and I faced some additional unexpected challenges, ones that made our effort to follow Hölderlin's exact route difficult if not impossible. In the days leading up to Christmas, virtually every German and French city or town of any size has its *Weihnachtsmarkt,* or, as I recall its being called during my own childhood days in Pennsylvania, a *Kris-Kringel-Markt.* Hordes of people descend on the city centers, entire school classes of children led by frazzled teachers, gangs of silly teens, and smaller groups of silly seniors, all flood the city center and block traffic, even the traffic of pedestrians. We often found it necessary to head for the hills to escape the consumer version of the Christmas season. This is the reason there are no photographs of Colmar and Belfort in this published version of our project. Even the photographs of Strasbourg and Lyon, which were both crucial cities for the project, had to be taken on a second visit to these cities in late January and early February, once the madness of Noël had passed. This leads me to remark that it was most often when we were enjoying *nature* rather than *culture* that we felt we were reliving things that Hölderlin himself might well have experienced. Crossing the Kniebis in deep snow, or later climbing the Massif Central west of Lyon in fog and snowstorm, or, finally, arriving at the Atlantic coast late on a sunny January afternoon—these were the telling experiences for us. And we could not help but feel that Hölderlin himself would have been most impressed by the offerings of nature that he confronted on his journey, the mountains and river valleys that have

---

5. For Wilhelm Waiblinger's account, see his 1827–1828 memoir of Hölderlin, *Friedrich Hölderlins Leben, Dichtung und Wahnsinn,* ed. Adolf Beck (Marbach am Neckar: Schiller-Nationalmuseum [Turmhahn-Bücherei 8/9], 1951), 35. I cite Waiblinger in the body of my text as WW with page number.

survived fairly intact from the eighteenth to our own century. When a blizzard on the Auvergne plateau caused our photos to show only gray on gray, we were consoled by the fact that at least they were "authentic," that we were seeing—or failing to see—things that Hölderlin himself would have met or missed. The distance between Hölderlin's and our own time, so vast when we entered cities and towns, diminished as we traversed stretches of the natural world, which was the "school" that Hölderlin himself preferred on the elliptical orbit of his life.

As we traveled south on the Rhine Plain, with the vast chain of the Vosges Mountains on our right and the mountains of the Black Forest farther away on our left, the green fields of winter wheat contrasted with the hills dusted in white. We passed Le Petit Ballon, familiar to us because we could see both it and our own Belchen every evening from our own hilltop homes in the Black Forest. Near Guebwiller, we passed Le Grand Ballon, wrapped as it so often is in clouds. Then, fearing the hordes of Christmas consumers, we drove on past Belfort to the area where the Doubs River Valley begins.

The course of the Doubs, 453 kilometers in length, traces the shape of an inverted horseshoe. It begins in the Swiss Jura and flows north before it descends into France near Montbéliard, south of Belfort. There it turns about and begins to flow south and west until it joins the Saône River near Chalon. This means that Hölderlin was able to follow it for a considerable portion of his journey toward Lyon. Knubben and Bertheau speculate that he may have traveled parts of the Doubs by boat, other parts by the post-coach road that hugs the river. Even if the river had flooded—Hölderlin's letter to his mother allows us to think that it was—it may have been just as easy to travel by flatboat as to walk or ride along the banks. Both forms of travel would doubtless have been made difficult by the winter flooding due to rainfall and snowmelt, particularly extreme in 1801–1802, but a constant feature of the Doubs down to our own time.

Bertheau notes that the more direct post-coach route from Besançon to Lyon would have taken Hölderlin through Lons-le-Saulnier and Bourg-en-Bresse (JB 95). Yet a traveler might instead have taken a boat on the Doubs—reduced flooding permitting—to Dôle and Chalon-sur-Saône. Joe and I elected to follow this perhaps less time-efficient route, taking Beck and *Tristram Shandy* as our guides, if only because Hölderlin was so dedicated to rivers, and the Doubs is one of Europe's most sinuously beautiful streams. And who knows, if the flooding of the river prevented his passage by boat, it might just as well be that the roadbeds too were flooded. That being the case, he may have made even better progress on foot. Weighing all these imponderables, we chose to follow Le Doubs, relatively unsung yet unostentatiously alluring even today.

After the Kniebis lay behind us, there were only patches of snow on our way from Strasbourg down through Belfort. For the rest, the fields of southern Alsace seemed as green as ever, especially during those hours or moments when the sun shone through the clouds. The departmental road we were on soon took us alongside the Doubs, which meanders all the way to Verdun-sur-le-Doubs, close to Chalon. Although less famous than the Loire and the Rhône, the Doubs is all the more inspiring because of the sparse population along its banks and the unspoiled countryside through which it flows. One of my most certain intuitions about Hölderlin is that he would have been captivated by its unspectacular beauty. The broad river, for the most part flowing sedately, would have offered some of that calm Hölderlin was desperately seeking in his life. Joe and I camped in a wooded area south of Belfort, not far from the curve of the Doubs, where it begins its journey southward. The evening was foggy and rainy, as the entire day had been, and the temperature was falling. By nightfall, and then in the morning, the rolling hills and thick woods were a portrait in black and white, the plowed fields overlaid by light snow and misty gray

Photo 15. A field near the Doubs River, on the way from Belfort to Besançon.

fog. The silence of our surroundings was that special sort of silence that snow brings, the silence that enables you to hear the *ping!* of each snowflake falling on the shoulder of your windbreaker, the silence that makes you reluctant to speak.

An unpaved road wound its way through the fields and into the woods, and Joe and I followed it that evening on foot (photo 15). The large, upturned clods of earth in the plowed fields now wore crowns of fresh snow. The woods, as Robert Frost says, were "lovely, dark, and deep." This was the sort of landscape that was quite familiar to Hölderlin, quite similar to the landscape of his home village. Yet we were so isolated here, so far away from any human habitation. It was strange to think of Hölderlin possibly walking along the same road in this atmosphere of absolute isolation. Yet the solitude and the intense quiet were more beautiful, or more quietly sublime, than any city or village could ever be, even if, come nightfall, Hölderlin must have been relieved to find refuge. Of course, he was most likely traveling by post-coach by that time, trying to regain the days he had lost in Strasbourg. In which case he would have been a mere spectator, as Joe and I for the most part were, Hölderlin gazing out the window of his *diligence* as we gazed through the windows of our Hymercar. After that evening walk, we returned to the camper, which at that point became a proper RV, which is to say, a truly "recreational vehicle": we cooked, ate well, drank well, then slept the sleep of the just. Not that we particularly deserved it. It was simply a gift of the thickly forested river valley and the snow-filtered air.

Along the banks of the Doubs a narrow road wended its way, sometimes paved, sometimes not. It was not difficult for us to picture Hölderlin walking or riding on such roads. There was something reassuring about the proximity of the river, in spite of the flooding: it seemed to know where it was going, even if Hölderlin's river poems often speak of the rivers' struggles early on in earth history to free themselves from their prison deep within the earth and to dispel the confusion about the route they eventually would take on its surface.

> I heard the youth crying out
> For rescue. . . .
> Deprived of light, he
> Writhed in his chains,
> The demigod raging.
> (*Der Rhein*, ll. 22–24, 29–31; CHV 1:342)

76 / Struck by Apollo

The youthful Rhine, for example, wanted to flow toward "Asia," as the Donau (or Ister) had done:

> Yet what one wishes
> Prevails not over destiny.
> But the blindest of all
> Are the sons of gods.
> (ll. 38–41; CHV 1:343)

The Doubs too had its problems, as we recall: somewhere near Montbéliard its northerly course was stymied, and the river turned about for the south. It was now flowing—*stillwandelnd*, "quietly wandering"—in Hölderlin's own direction, heading south and west as he was, toward Chalon and the Saône. It was not difficult to imagine Hölderlin here reflecting, as the Rhine hymn does, on the decisive destiny of one's birth and the "beam of light / That comes to meet the newborn" (*Der Rhein*, ll. 50–53; ibid.).

During the long journey to Bordeaux, following all the rivers to the sea, he must have been trying "To preserve the best things in memory" (*Der Rhein*, l. 201; CHV 1:347), even if he had suffered many reversals during the past few months, so that both good and bad fortune weighed heavily on him. No doubt he strove to be equal to every occasion, and like Socrates he wanted to remain wakeful at the *Symposium* when everyone else, even Aristophanes, was falling asleep. Yet his *Rhein* hymn ends darkly with a reference to noissome, hectic days followed by harrowing, restless nights,

> . . . when all is jumbled
> Devoid of order and what recurs is
> Primeval confusion.
> (ll. 219–21; CHV 1:348)

Perhaps his glimpses of the Doubs out of the corner of his eye were able to mollify his thoughts of chaos. The river flows wide, seems placid most of the time, as it makes its unhurried way to the southwest.

Joe and I were on the lookout for the post-coach relay stations on our route, not merely because the system of relais now serves as some of the finest country restaurants in France but also because we were looking for places where Hölderlin might have overnighted. I had found a list of all the inns and station stops on Hölderlin's route that are still functioning today as restaurants or hotels. "La Diligence" is a common name even nowadays of those relais at which post-coaches (*les diligences*) would stop, where horses were changed and passengers took refreshment and overnighted. Other telltale names for such former relais are *Cheval d'Or*, *Cheval Blanc* (indeed, horses of any color), and of course, *Relais de Poste*. Almost always, especially in the cities, we searched out these relais, but they invariably disappointed us. One could see what the intervening centuries had done to these old inns—the improvements, the urban growth, the disappearance of the post-coach system in the late nineteenth century, the wars of the twentieth. All these things made our dream unlikely if not impossible, the dream that we would find at least remnants of those shelters Hölderlin may have enjoyed. It was only when we were in the remote countryside or deep in the musty crypts of medieval churches that we could imagine we were seeing what Hölderlin himself might have seen. However, as I have said, it was always the hills and valleys, the woods and the rivers, that enabled us to dream with a better conscience.

As we entered Besançon, a picturesque city looped by the Doubs, we had hopes of finding the old relais that is called today the Hôtel de Paris. A fairly common name, one may assume. It is now in the center of the oldest part of town, but there is nothing like a courtyard, in spite of the preserved entryway for coaches. When we left Besançon, heading toward Dôle, we drove past a stately château and its park in the midst of wheat

Photo 16. The Pont de Navilly, one of the earliest flat-spanned bridges, across the Doubs River.

78 / Struck by Apollo

or corn fields and rolling hills of pastureland. Like any tourist, we stopped to examine the palatial residences, but we were mindful of the turmoil in which they would have been caught up during the early 1800s. The Terror had decimated aristocratic families throughout France in the mid-1790s, so that no such residence would have remained unscarred. As Hölderlin's coach passed by them, he would have had mixed feelings—horror in the face of all the bloodshed, the tens of thousands of guillotinings and shootings, many without trial, but also the strong feeling that the aristocrats and the higher bourgeoisie, the parvenus, which his letters often inveigh against, must finally cease their exploitation of society and their suppression of the rights of humankind. Hölderlin himself, as a man trained for the clergy that he hated, found himself somewhere between the stools of all the classes and castes, an outsider, a poet, a thinker. And now, on his way to Bordeaux, something like an outcast.

Joe and I then came across—and traveled across—the magnificent Pont de Navilly, reminiscent of the bridges of Paris (photo 16). It had been built over the Doubs River during the years 1782 to 1790, completed a decade before Hölderlin's journey. Designed by the architect and engineer Émiland Marie Gauthey, it was a flat rather than an arched bridge, with five large spans. (I wished that my father were still alive so that I could ask him about the Navilly Bridge: he was an engineer who designed bridges, and he taught his children most of the basics—but knowing whether the flat bridge was more challenging than an arched bridge, which was my intuition, far surpassed my inherited bridge-building skills.) The Doubs is quite wide here, just south of Seurre in the commune of Sermesse, on the way to Chalon. Near the bridge was a tired old inn called La Diligence, a reminder of the post-coach days.

We then drove past Verdun-sur-le-Doubs, where the river Doubs joins the great Saône, and continued on to nearby Chalon-sur-Saône. Here, once again, we sought out an old relais that still serves as a hotel. It was difficult to find, but when we finally located it, we were disappointed. Little remained of the eighteenth century structure, especially in the front of the building, which looked out onto a gutted pizza parlor, although a courtyard in the rear confirmed its age and its former purpose. While the city of Chalon is quite spectacular, principally because of the breadth of the Saône, enriched now by the Doubs, we were anxious to get back to the countryside. We were able to find a quiet, sheltered place to overnight before heading south the next day toward Mâcon.

Our route now took us alongside the wide Saône. Actually, we left the paved departmental road, turning onto a side road and passing a Do

Not Enter sign so that we could get closer to the river. We soon found ourselves on an unpaved, muddy road right on the riverbank, certain that this had been the old post-coach road. We looked across the wide river: there was something ghostly about the poplars on this misty day—thirteen of them, unless you counted their reflections (photo 17). Meanwhile, the Saône was even more flooded than the Doubs had been. Even when our side road was free of water, it was as muddy now as it would have been in Hölderlin's day. Ghostly or not, the wide Saône was flowing quietly along at its own pace, passing farms and châteaux, some of them with closed shutters, apparently abandoned.

A bit earlier I was bragging about Joe and me having conscientiously followed Hölderlin's route, avoiding every temptation to deviate. That is not entirely true. In all probability, Hölderlin was still traveling by post-coach; either that or he may have taken a flatboat south to Mâcon and on to Lyon. In either case, he most likely would not have had a chance to head those few kilometers farther to the west that would have taken him high into wine country. He was already in the south of Burgundy, entering now the region of Beaujolais. When it was time for Joe and me to seek out a place to overnight, we headed up into the vineyards. True, we had a guide that listed all the campsites of Europe, but even those that were listed as

Photo 17. The flooded yet placid Saône River not far from Chalon.

80 / Struck by Apollo

being open year-round were closed. During our entire trip of three weeks, we did not find a single campsite that was open. We were content to find a spot of our own, of course, even if there were no amenities apart from those offered by Dame Nature. We always looked for the highest point on the horizon, invariably in or at the edge of some wooded area and took roads there that otherwise had no traffic on them.

The vineyards themselves, even in winter, were sublime: the bare vines lined up like crosses on a battlefield cemetery, although come spring there would be a greening. While up on the Plâteau du Grille-Midi, we asked the permission of a young vintner, Thomas Jambon, to overnight on his property. He was more than forthcoming, and the next morning, before taking our departure for Lyon, we visited him and his father Alain and were invited into the cellar for a wine tasting—doubtless the tastiest breakfast of our trip. We hoped that at least during his overnights in the Burgundy and Beaujolais regions Hölderlin had had the chance to enjoy what we were enjoying.

Whereas I joke about "temptation," Hölderlin would remind me, I hope gently, that the particular temptation to which we were now surrendering was in fact the essence of religion. Yes, the very essence of religion. One of his most inspiring poems is "The Wine God," the initial form of his famous hymn, *Brot und Wein*. Without wishing to tire the reader, let me say one or two things about it, inasmuch as that poem to Dionysos was a sort of companion for Joe and me during our journey. "The Wine God" is Hölderlin's longest elegy, and even though it seems perfect in its initial form, he worked on it for some three or four more years. A reminder from M. H. Abrams's *Glossary of Literary Terms*, another one of my life's companions, about the elegiac form:

> In Greek and Roman literature, the term "elegy" was used to denote any poem written in elegiac meter (alternating *hexameter* and *pentameter* lines), and also to denote the subjects and moods frequently expressed in that verse form, especially complaints about love. In Europe and England the word continued to have a variable usage through the Renaissance. . . . In the course of the seventeenth century, however, the term began to be limited to its present usage: a formal and sustained lament (and usually consolation) for the death of a particular person.[6]

---

6. M. H. Abrams, *A Glossary of Literary Terms*, 5th ed. (Fort Worth: Holt, Rinehart and Winston, 1985), 47.

In the present case, Hölderlin's lament is not for the death of a friend or lover: both Heinse, the dedicatee, and Susette are alive and well when the poem is first written, even though the poet and his Diotima are no longer together. The lament involves perhaps the death of the ancient Greek gods, or the death of historical ages and entire cultures, especially the death of classical antiquity. And the consolation? That would be the *promise* of "The Wine God," the promise of either sleep or vigilance (the latter would be the positive side of insomnia, perhaps), which the god variously pledges for the night. For this elegy is also a nocturne.

Knaupp notes two strange ambiguities about the poem, one of form, the other of content (CHV 3:214–15). First, Hölderlin begins to allow the syntax of his sentences, and especially the grammatical cases of his subjects and objects, to become indeterminate, so that it is often impossible to say what is acting upon what, or who is performing and who is on the receiving end of an action; activity and passivity are therefore thrown into a kind fusion or confusion, in something close to what Hegel would have called a speculative proposition or, closer still, to what ancient Greek grammar knew as the middle voice. Knaupp's example involves a nominalized present participle, *die Erstaunende*, said of the rising moon: it sounds as though the moon *herself* (or himself, since even though *die Nacht* is feminine, *der Mond* is masculine in German, this indicating that genders too are often ambiguous) is astonished, and yet the sense appears to be that the moon astonishes the poet. Second, an increasingly common form of ambiguity in Hölderlin's poems involves the relationship between Christian monotheistic and Greek polytheistic themes: it is impossible to say whether bread and wine in Hölderlin's hymns have preeminently to do with the Last Supper or with Demeter and Dionysos, that is, with suppers that human beings, gods, and other forms of life have been sharing since time immemorial—at least up until the marriage of Cadmus and Harmony. In this second sense, Hölderlin's wavering between antiquity and Christianity seems to be a permanent condition, whereas the oscillation of his friend Schelling, who lectured on *Philosophy of Mythology* at about the time of his friend's death, sometimes pulls back from polytheism and at least tries to restore orthodoxy. Schelling shrinks from interpreting Christianity and Christendom as mere continuations of the history of polytheistic mythology—even though he knows that precisely this is the case. His friend Hölderlin, the poet and thinker, albeit not a professional or professorial philosopher, always seems to be more daring in his thinking than his erstwhile roommates and companions, Schelling and especially Hegel.

82 / Struck by Apollo

"The Wine God" begins with an invocation of the night and the moon. Precisely as a nocturne, it was the elegy that accompanied the evenings and the nights that Joe and I spent in the midwinter towns and villages—but preeminently in the countryside and the vineyards—of France:

> All around us the city is at rest; the lighted narrow streets grow still,
>   And carriages, sporting flaming torches, rush by.
> Well-satisfied, people head for home from the day's joys to rest,
>   And profit and loss are weighed by a head that can count,
> Happy now to be at home; empty now of its grapes and flowers
>   And all its handmade goods, the bustling market is hushed.
> Yet a thrum of strings sounds out there in someone's garden—perhaps
>   Some lover plays there, or a lonely man remembering
> Long lost friends and the time when he was young—and fountains
>   Gurgle endlessly on and lend their freshness to the fragrant
> Flowerbeds. Quietly in the air of dusk sound the tolling bells,
>   And, to honor the hours, a watchman cries their number.
> Now too a wind stirs in the grove of trees atop the hill.
>   But look! for the shadow image of our Earth, the moon,
> Also steals upon us; that enthusiast, the night, comes as well,
>   Full of stars and certainly not much concerned about us;
> The astonishing one shines, she who is a stranger to us humans
>   Comes in mourning and in splendor over mountain heights.
>   (CHV 1:314)

The second stanza expands this vision of the night and the moon, no doubt remembering that the night was sacred to Dionysos and his Maenad worshippers, perhaps because the name of the god's own mother, Semele, was a form of Selene, the Moon. Let us read the second stanza before we abandon the vineyards of Beaujolais for the metropolis of Lyon:

> Miraculous are the favors high sublimity grants, and no one
>   Knows whence she came and what she accomplishes.
> Thus she moves the world and the human soul so full of hope;
>   Not even wisemen understand what she prepares, for so
> Wills the uppermost god who loves you so much and whom,
>   As the bright shining day, you therefore love more than her.
> Yet from time to time even a luminous eye loves the shade
>   And tries to sleep for pleasure before sleep becomes need,

The Journey to Bordeaux / 83

Or a stalwart man is simply happy to gaze into the night;
　　Yes, it is fitting that we weave garlands and songs for her,
Because she is sacred to those who stray and sacred to the dead,
　　While she herself persists, eternally, in a spirit most free.
Yet she must also grant us who are in the dark a dawning,
　　So that something human remains for us in times of gloom,
She must bestow on us forgetfulness and sacred inebriation,
　　Must grant us the flowing word, the word that like lovers is
Sleepless, and the winecup full, and a keener life, and
Holy memory too, so that we may be wakeful by night.
　　　　　　　　　　　　　　　　　　　(CHV 1:314–15)

The wine cup full to overflowing—that we may remain vigilant by night. Clearly, Hölderlin is developing his own regimen for wakefulness and holy memory, and it is not the usual regimen. Vigilance has something to do with tragedy, but also with comedy, both of these dramatic arts sponsored by the wine god. Perhaps wakefulness also has something to do with anticipations of Lyon, which we are now approaching.

As soon as Tristram Shandy arrives at Lyon during the mid-1760s—or at "Lyons," as the English and Irish call it—he affirms two things about it: first, it is "the most opulent and flourishing city in France," let the Parisians sniff if they will, and they will; second, Lyon is "enriched with the most fragments of antiquity" (Sterne VII, 30; 494). This second characteristic would have been particularly important to Hölderlin. He says very little about the great city at the confluence of the Saône and the Rhône, except that it was "lively" during the two or three days he was there. It was no doubt politically lively, inasmuch as Napoleon had called for a *Consulta* at which the future of the northern Italian states was to be discussed. Bertheau (JB 96ff) thinks it likely that Hölderlin engaged in conversations with representatives from those states; indeed, they may have been staying in the hotel where he was residing, the Hôtel du Commerce on the rue St. Dominique, today the rue Émile-Zola. The hotel no longer exists as such, nor has it existed for a long time, even though most of the buildings on the rue Émile-Zola seem to be old enough to have been standing at the time of Hölderlin's visit.

A narrow street off the north side of the grand Place Bellecour, the rue Émile-Zola, runs parallel to the Saône and Rhône rivers. It is in that part of Old Lyon that seems to be a peninsula, a long stretch of land between the two broad rivers immediately before they converge. The street itself is closer to the Saône, hence to the oldest quarters of the city, which line both banks of that river. Hölderlin may have been able to see the towers of the cathedral St. Jean-le-Baptiste across the Saône from his hotel (photo 18). The street is now lined with fashion boutiques and exclusive shops. None of the shopkeepers I spoke to had ever heard the former name of the street, nor did the name Hôtel du Commerce mean anything to them. They were all too young, I thought to myself. And, in truth, who would be capable of remembering anything from the first years of the nineteenth century?

This ignorance or innocence was so different from my experiences with locals during the "Nietzsche trip" of 1994–1995 in preparation for *The Good European: Nietzsche's Work Sites in Word and Image*. More than a hundred years had passed since Nietzsche had frequented towns such as Recoaro or Sorrento or even Nietzsche's own Naumburg, and yet my colleague Don Bates and I found many people who knew about the philosopher's sojourns, often in impressive detail; some had heard it from their parents or grandparents, for there was almost universally a vibrant local culture and an oral history that preserved the memory of the famous German thinker. On more than one occasion, Don and I had local guides who were astonishingly well informed and who took us directly to the sites we were looking for. One century is not two, however, and the Hölderlin journey, for Joe

Photo 18. The Lyon cathedral, St. Jean-le-Baptiste, in the January sun.

The Journey to Bordeaux / 85

and me, was a far lonelier affair. No one I spoke with had any knowledge of the name Hölderlin, and so we were always left to our own resources.

Lyon had suffered terribly during the 1790s because of its Girondist— rather than Jacobin—leanings. Much of the city had been destroyed by General Kellermann's army, and there were endless executions, more by firing squad or massacre than by guillotine, which takes more time, until in 1795 the Jacobin radicals of Paris were themselves decapitated. The fact that Napoleon had chosen Lyon, a favorite city of his, to be the site of the *Consulta* that was to decide the fate of the north Italian states, now the Republic of Italy, may have bolstered Hölderlin's hopes that the First Consul was in fact a peacemaker and a paragon of the rights of humankind. As the various versions of *Friedensfeier* indicate, Hölderlin never separated his hopes for radical reform and even revolution in Württemberg from his equally intense desire for peace. Those hopes and desires were damaged when Napoleon summarily annulled the election of an Italian representative to head the new Republic, substituting himself instead. Although Hölderlin's stay in Lyon was limited to two or three days, there can be little doubt that he discussed the troubled recent history of the city with persons staying in his hotel or with others in the streets.

Yet there may also have been time for Hölderlin to visit the oldest parts of the city across the Saône, with the cathedral St. Jean-le-Baptiste at their center. Adjacent to the cathedral is the oldest of Lyon's buildings, the Manecanterie, "the Parish Choir School." The cathedral's interior is brightly lit by a sun that even in the dead of winter one does not hesitate to call "southern." That sun projects the colors of the stained-glass windows onto the light mustard-colored walls of the church. Remarkable among the objects in the cathedral is an astronomical clock built in the fifteenth century— Hölderlin may have seen a similar wonder in the cathedral at Strasbourg. The Lyon clock also drew the attention of Sterne's *Tristram* on his chaotic journey through France. The cathedral is at the heart of the so-called Renaissance quarter of the city, and it is true that even today one sees many signs of Tuscan influence in its architecture (see photo 19). Lyon is French and Burgundian, with a flavor all its own, but historically it is also Italian. And not only modern Italian, nor even only Renaissance or Medieval Italian. For Lyon was an important Roman city, Lugdunum by name, and the ruins of that city are but a half hour's stroll from Hölderlin's hotel.

For years now I have been struck by the oddness of Hölderlin's claim that the south of France had given him insight into the world of the ancient Greeks, even though Bordeaux is as far south as he ever got. He never saw Nîmes or Arles, Nice, Rome, Paestum, or Agrigentum, much less the grand

Photo 19. A Tuscan-style courtyard off the rue St. Georges in Vieux Lyon.

sites of western Anatolia or of Greece itself. And Bordeaux does not strike one as Roman, even though it too was indeed an important Roman city, much less as typically Greek. It was not until I visited the ruins of Lugdunum, high above the Saône Valley, that I began to understand.

It seems highly likely that Hölderlin, while in Lyon, would have found the time to mount the hill called Fourvière, where the ruins of Lugdunum are located, if only because the ancient theater on that hillside and the complex of buildings above it are nothing short of spectacular. Sterne is quite right: Lyon is "enriched with the most fragments of antiquity," at least if one excludes the Louvre collection in Paris. Could it be that Hölderlin attained from a visit to Lugdunum one of his most intense intimations of antiquity? As I walked through the new museum there, surely one of the most beautifully designed museums displaying finds from Gallo-Roman antiquity, it struck me that these objects would have held Hölderlin spellbound. True, many of the items exhibited were discovered only after the time of Hölderlin's visit: the nineteenth century is the grand century of archaeology there as elsewhere, and the twentieth century is the time when subway constructors and sewage system builders throughout Europe had to interrupt their work again and again over some find. Yet a number of the objects on display in the Lugdunum Museum were uncovered already during the Renaissance. I photographed many of these objects, not knowing for certain whether Hölderlin could have seen them but encouraged by the thought that any one of the items would have struck him with the force of lightning—fire from heaven, as it were. Scholars always attribute Hölderlin's sense of antiquity to his viewing of the Louvre holdings on his way back from Bordeaux to Stuttgart, and I would not challenge them in that respect; yet I could not help but think that more than one of Hölderlin's interlocutors in Lyon would have told him about Lugdunum and that the thirty-minute walk there would not have deterred him.

I restricted my own visit to two full days at Lyon. Lugdunum was available to me for the better part of a day, and the route to it took me through the most marvelous parts of Vieux Lyon. Is it conceivable that Hölderlin could have missed Lugdunum? I think not. As for the lack of written confirmation in Hölderlin's letters and notebooks, it is a lack that applies to almost everything else as well. To be sure, the walk up to Lugdunum is strenuous. The Roman city is perched on Fourvière, some three hundred meters above the Saône River and Vieux Lyon. One walks along the old Rue St. Georges in the direction of the cathedral, observing on the hillside to one's left the remnants of the medieval walls of the city.

88 / Struck by Apollo

Photo 20. The theater at Lugdunum, the Roman Lyon, built early in the first century of our era.

At the Maison du Soleil, one turns left and ascends the steep Montée du Gourgouillon to the ancient city.

The sheer sight of the theater and the upper precincts of the ancient city would have thrilled Hölderlin as it astonishes visitors today (photo 20). The Romans of Lugdunum built their theater in 15 BCE, some thirty years after the city's founding in 43 BCE by Lucius Plancus Munatius (87–15 BCE). The oldest Roman theater in Gaul, it is also one of the largest: its lower tier of seats holds 4,500 spectators, both tiers together between ten and eleven thousand. From the upper tier one has today a spectacular view of Lyon, although in antiquity, a thirty-meter wall blocked that view and forced the audience to concentrate on the scene being played out on the stage. And the scenes of antiquity were always on Hölderlin's mind: a friend of his in Tübingen once remarked that Hölderlin was so at home in the ancient world that he was a fish out of water in the world around him. These scenes of antiquity must have been particularly present during the days of his journeys to and from Bordeaux, since at the house of Consul Meyer he would be working on his translations of Sophocles. Here at Lugdunum he would have had his first inkling, I believe, of the performances such a grand ancient theater could house. Perhaps he might even have tested the theater's acoustics, as remarkable at Lugdunum as they are in the theater

The Journey to Bordeaux / 89

above Delphi or in any of the well-preserved ancient theaters, such as the Asklepieion at Epidaurus. And if any of the objects in the museum at Lugdunum today were available to his inspection, he would again have been thunderstruck by the creative force of antiquity.

Among the most impressive objects at Lugdunum are the sarcophagi, the engraved tombstones, and the funeral masks. These masks, expressing fright as well as grief, would have particularly impressed Hölderlin, I believe. Even if the Romans, like the late-born Christian Hesperians, were "carted off in a box" after death, it is clear that the Roman attitude toward death was different from that of Hölderlin's contemporaries. The funeral masks (see photo 21) seem to be apotropaic expressions of horror; there is certainly no lugubrious and delusional piety about them. The highly decorated sarcophagi often depict scenes from the life of Dionysos, the wine god who, at least according to Heraclitus, is also the god of the underworld. Two of the most remarkable sarcophagi at Lugdunum tell the stories of Silenos, the drunken tutor of Dionysos, and of Ariadne, his queen. The constantly repeated invocation on funeral plaques there, "To the *manes* of . . . ," would have reminded Hölderlin of his own dramatic personage, Manes, the ancient Egyptian priest who in the third version of *The Death of Empedocles* comes to unsettle the hero's conviction that his death by suicide will be both pious and heroic. Manes, it may be argued, causes the third and final version of Hölderlin's tragedy to end abruptly, so that the play remains but a fragment, or three fragments, never completed.[7]

Not only horror, however, but also grief and mournfulness are to be seen in these Roman monuments: the portrait of the deceased Pamilla, with the dedication "To the *manes* of Pamilla," expresses the deep sadness of mortal loss, one that no piety can assuage or obfuscate. Even if the most highly decorated sarcophagi have reliefs of a drunken Silenos or a victorious Dionysos with his Ariadne, as so many of them do, the intention does not seem to be delusion or distraction. To repeat, even if the Roman citizen too was carted off in a box, precisely as the Evangelical German is carted off in his or her Evangelical coffin, over which Evangelical words are spilled, the good news at Lugdunum is that the only news for mortals is bad news.

Hölderlin was no doubt long prepared for such news. His resistance to his mother's pleading that he become a pastor had to do with more than his distaste for preaching. Although he was familiar with death since his earliest years, he increasingly found that he had nothing to say about

---

7. See Friedrich Hölderlin, *The Death of Empedocles: A Mourning-Play*, trans. and ed. D. F. Krell (Albany: State University of New York Press, 2008).

Photo 21. A funeral mask at Lugdunum.

The Journey to Bordeaux / 91

it, certainly nothing by way of consolatory liturgical formulae. When his friend Neuffer's young wife died of tuberculosis in 1795, Hölderlin's letter to him is all about his inability to say anything comforting about human existence, which therefore remains in some sense "nameless." "Oh, my friend," he writes, "I do not grasp it, this nameless thing [*das Nahmenlose*] that gives us joy for a time and then rips our hearts to shreds; I have no thought that comprehends our passing away, where the heart, which is the best thing in us and the only thing worth listening to, has to beg for its very survival in the midst of so much pain—may the God to whom I prayed as a child forgive me, but I cannot conceive of death in the world that is His—" (CHV 2:585). Hölderlin confesses that he is no good at either counseling or consoling. Instead, he says, "I tap my way through the world like a blind man" (ibid.).

Perhaps Hölderlin is approaching another way to think about death as he goes out into the foreign, leaving all Pietist palaver behind him and venturing into the clearer skies of the antique south. If this is so, we may understand why a great deal of what the second letter to Böhlendorff tells us relates quite closely to things Hölderlin might have seen at Lugdunum. As one wanders slowly through the museum there, one sees an entire range of objects—some of which, to repeat, were discovered only after Hölderlin's visit—that reinforces the impression that the ancient world differed radically from Hesperian modernity. The series of statues, from Cybele, a late form of the Anatolian Mother goddess (see photo 22), to Zeus Serapis, whose name is a condensation of Osiris-Apis, the consort of Isis, the inscriptions, the mosaics of golden birds and fish and gods—it is too much to comment on any of these things in detail. Let me merely note that one of the constants of Hölderlin's theoretical work was his insistence on the *unity of life*, from the smallest plant to the greatest god, from dandelion to dove to Dionysos.

Before abandoning Lyon, let me add a word about food and drink. Why? Because Hölderlin never mentions them, except to say, as we heard earlier in his postscript to the Neuffer letter, that he eats only "mediocre" meals. His silence concerning food, albeit not about wine, first struck me at Strasbourg, which is famous for its Alsatian cuisine and its unsurpassed white wines; at Lyon, a heartier and more flavorful kitchen awaited both him and me. Is it not important to the modern traveler to notice—and to take note of—the striking differences from kitchen to kitchen as one travels? Is that not a significant aspect of "the foreign," one that alters at least for a time the very flesh of our flesh? To have been in Lyon and to say nothing about the chefs there—traditionally they are women, counter to the

92 / Struck by Apollo

Photo 22. Cybele, wearing the mural crown. The cult of the Anatolian mother goddess reaches far back into antiquity and endures well into the age of Rome.

custom in the rest of France—who work their daily miracles for the table? It is incomprehensible to me. There is so much that a German boy or girl would have to comment on: the andouillette, for example, is not exactly a sausage, since it has real meat in it; and if the contents of the quenelle remain a mystery, who can refrain from speculating on those savory contents? And the *Salade lyonnaise*? A three-course meal in itself. Savor, as Hölderlin surely knew, is *savoir*. And the red wines! Whether from the Rhône Valley itself or from farther north, that is, from the slopes of Burgundy and the rolling plains of Beaujolais—surely, Hölderlin must have said or written something about these phenomena?

But to whom? To his mother? She would have scolded him for having succumbed to the pleasures of the flesh. She was soon to discover that

The Journey to Bordeaux / 93

he had succumbed in other ways as well, at least in her imagination, when she opened his Bordeaux trunk and discovered the hidden cache of love letters from Susette.

At all events, not a word do we hear about the deliciousness of food. And precious little about the wines of France and Germany, even if, as we know, wine was an important part of the Hölderlin and Gock family traditions (presumably much of the wealth that accrued to Frau Gock came from the wine trade); furthermore, we know from the reports of others that Hölderlin from youth to old age, at least when he could afford something more than beer, savored his wines. It is not too much to say that he adored the wine god, the god who makes his epiphany in so many of Hölderlin's poems, including the one we have begun to read. I claimed earlier on, and I claim once again, that the wine god incorporates the essence of religion. Here is its third stanza, in which the invocation of the lunar night turns Hölderlin's thoughts to the joy he finds in ancient Greek lore in general:

In vain do we conceal the heart that beats in our breast, in vain
    Manacle our soul, we men and schoolboys, even now.
Who then can stop it and who can forbid us joy?
    Yes! The celestial ones by day and by night conspire
To emerge—so, then, come! That we may look to our own,
    May bless what is holy in what is our own.
One thing is certain: whether at noon or passing on to
    Midnight, always there prevails a measure,
Common to all, and yet each is granted his own,
    And by way of it each comes and goes as best he can.
Well, then! Jubilant madness will happily mock mockery
    When in holy night mania seizes the singers.
Well, then! Come to the isthmus, there where the open sea rushes
    Toward Parnassos and snow glistens on the cliffs of Delphi,
There in the land of Olympos, there on the heights of Cithaeron,
    There among the pines, among the grapes, where
The Ismenos rushes down to Thebes and to the source of Dirce,
    There runs my yearning, O there we shall look up and see gods.
                                                    (CHV 1:315)

Hölderlin's silence—at least in his letters—about the divine joys of food and drink, bread and wine, is therefore strange, and not even his Pietist upbringing can explain it entirely. I have given myself the assignment of searching Goethe's *Italienreise* to see if such silence about the palate is

94 / Struck by Apollo

universal in Germany. (So far, all I have heard from him are complaints.) Certainly, the English and French travel writers of the eighteenth century would not disappoint me in this respect. To be sure, at the end of the day one can be certain that Hölderlin would have sought out the least expensive relais and the least costly meals. Nevertheless, one hopes that neither his god Dionysos, of whom even Christ was but a younger brother, nor the great goddess Demeter failed him altogether—and one trusts that Hölderlin did not betray his deities.

The Third and Final Leg: From Lyon to Bordeaux

At this point, leaving Lyon in mid-January, Hölderlin heads west, crossing the Massif Central of France. The ascent begins directly outside of Lyon itself, and it does not stop for many miles. Remarkably, the route that Hölderlin takes early in the nineteenth century follows quite precisely the ancient Roman highways, from Lugdunum to Onemetum (Clermont), Augustoritum (Limoges), and Vesunna (Périgueux), a route still followed by today's national roads. The final phase, from Vesunna to Burdigala (Bordeaux), then as now, is rather more complicated.

In Hölderlin's day there were seventy-two post-coach stations between Lyon and Bordeaux, that is, on the route that took him to Clermont-Ferrand and then over the Auvergne, turning south at Limoges for Bordeaux (JB 97ff.). Bertheau estimates that the trip would have taken 144 hours, some eighteen days—and this is exactly what Hölderlin's correspondence from Lyon and Bordeaux tells us his trip took. During the final days of the journey, from either Périgueux or Libourne, it seems likely that Hölderlin traveled again by foot: his letter from Bordeaux speaks of "walking into the spring." January is hardly spring, but it is true that the contrast in the weather between Clermont and Périgueux can be remarkable. When Joe and I turned south at Limoges, we noticed that the skies were a bit more congenial, the temperature far less bitter than it had been up on the Auvergne plateau. By the time we arrived at Bordeaux, first making our way to the sea at Soulac-sur-Mer, it was possible to walk along the glistening strand in a light jacket, even though the wind off the Atlantic was gusty. It was an enormous contrast to the blizzards and windstorms we had experienced atop the Massif Central only a few days before. It seemed to us that we too had wandered into springtime.

Even nowadays the Auvergne is relatively sparsely populated. In Hölderlin's time it was a wilderness and a haven for outlaws. These were most often soldiers who had deserted—almost every able-bodied man was under arms at the time, since Napoleon's conquest of Europe was well underway—or men who had been part of civil uprisings, such as that of the Vendée in the 1790s. Attacks on post-coaches were fairly common on the Lyon-Clermont route, and even though the central government struggled to suppress them, they were still quite common in 1801–1802. Hölderlin writes of the snow-covered wilderness, the savage cold, and the pistol he kept under his pillow. (As far as I know, there is no mention anywhere, neither in Hölderlin's works and letters nor in the immense literature on him, concerning Hölderlin's familiarity with firearms, no mention of him hunting as a youth, and no mention of military service or of duels at university, so that the reference to the pistol is strange; no one, as far as I know, speculates where he got it and whether or how well he knew how to use it.) Bertheau argues that not very far along on Hölderlin's way from Bordeaux to Paris, that is, on his journey homeward, Hölderlin was in fact the victim of a coach robbery, and Bertheau supposes that on that occasion he wisely handed over his weapon to the brigands. The robbery was something Hölderlin had been fearing for some time, perhaps because he was carrying a good bit of money with him, money that Consul Meyer had generously provided. More on this later—for there are other theories about when, where, and how this robbery took place.

As I mentioned earlier, Joe and I approached Clermont from the south, since we had deviated from Hölderlin's route to spend the holidays with the Dasturs in the Ardèche, well south of Lyon. Hölderlin himself presumably headed due west from Lyon, following a segment of the main pilgrimage route to Santiago de Compostela, passing through the towns of Fenouilh, Feurs, Boën, S. Thurien, and Thiers (as the 1812 map indicates their names). As Joe and I approached Clermont, we stopped at Issoire, a town that Hölderlin may well have seen, even though it is a bit south of his probable westward route. We stopped to eat at a relais there and to see the town's magnificent Romanesque Basilica, dedicated to Saint Austremoine, an early bishop of the Auvergne region. The gaudy interior—at least its critics found it gaudy, but the architect who saw to the recent restoration of the church replied that it was decorated this way throughout the Middle Ages—was quite striking, something that Hölderlin would never have seen in the pallid churches of the austere Protestant north. And once again images of the Madonna haunted the interior of the church, silhouetted against the beautiful windows.

As we moved on toward Clermont, we passed below the mountain town of St. Yvoine. Near a site called La Ribeyre (clearly the "riviera" bordering the Couze River), we came across an old Roman bridge—today unused and hence reclaimed by nature's ivy, moss, and grasses. We climbed the road that led to St. Yvoine but then turned off onto a plateau from which we could see the hills and volcanoes of the Auvergne. It was our first sighting of this extraordinary landscape, and we spent two nights there, finding it difficult to leave the spot (photo 23).

During the first night a furious windstorm raged, and our camper rocked back and forth, with the two of us in and out of sleep. Rain pelted the roof. In the morning, which was unexpectedly bright and sunny, the wind having dispersed every cloud, we could see the mountains to the south, the highest peaks of the Auvergne, the Monts Dore dominated by the Sancy Massif, covered now with fresh snow, and the long chain of dormant volcanoes farther to the north and stretching west toward Limousin. In the distance, a bit farther to the north, was the fortress town of Montpeyroux. The sunset that night was spectacular, and I disobeyed Socrates' counsel and the instructions of the camera makers and stared right into it (see the cover photo of the book).

Yet it is important to remember the impression of the Auvergne that Hölderlin gives us—that of a frigid wilderness, barren but for the highway-

Photo 23. On the way westward from Lyon, not far from Clermont-Ferrand: the Monts-Dore, dominated by the Sancy Massif, in southwest Auvergne.

men who were hiding out there. Joe and I were reminded of this on the day we set out from Clermont: the blizzard we got caught in made every sighting of the volcanoes, including the famous Puy-de-Dôme that looms over Clermont, absolutely impossible.

A word about Clermont itself. It was cold and rainy when we walked along the cobblestone streets of the city, but the weather could not dampen the charm of the town. Once again, we visited the churches, thinking that if Hölderlin had overnighted here, as he almost certainly did, he would have found the time to see them—first of all, the cathedral, built out of black volcanic rock (Volvic) in the high Gothic style, with its two high towers dominating the main square (photo 24). The interior of the cathedral, dedicated to Our Lady of the Assumption, held a particular surprise, namely, "The Virgin with Over-Size Hands" (see photo 25), a depiction of Mary that was utterly new to the two of us. She seemed to have made the journey to Clermont from ancient Egypt or Phrygia. Viewed from certain vantage points, the head of the statue, at one time in its long history separated from the torso, seemed to be being restored to its rightful place by those huge hands. Hölderlin would surely have wondered what those hands of the Madonna were otherwise for, whether for comforting or chastising, for

Photo 24. The Cathedral of Clermont, Notre-Dame-de-l'Assomption, constructed from 1238 to 1355.

Photo 25. In the interior of the cathedral is *The Virgin with Over-Size Hands*.

The Journey to Bordeaux / 99

caressing or pummeling. All his life he had craved the former but usually received the latter.

After our visit to the cathedral, Joe and I went searching for a second church that we had heard about, a much older church in the Romanesque style, and it took some wandering through the hilly streets of Clermont to find it. It is tucked away in the so-called port region of the city, but it is a jewel worth uncovering. The pilgrimage basilica of Notre-Dame-du-Port has a much older and much more modest look than the cathedral. Constructed of motley stone, much less impressive than the black Volvic of the cathedral, it is hemmed in by other secular buildings on its tiny square. Yet as you climb down the stairs to enter it you have the feeling that the entire church is a kind of crypt, and in some sense, it is precisely that. It is one of those edifices built on top of former churches and temples stretching all the way back to the time before the arrival of Christianity in Gaul. The church of Notre-Dame-du-Port is a pilgrimage church (on the Santiago route), but the current edifice, completed in 1185, was itself built atop older structures dating from 946 and 571. The first church, for its part, was constructed on an ancient cult site, whether Celtic or Roman we were unable to determine.

The crypt is, as usual, the most interesting part of the church, partly because of the capitals of the sturdy ancient columns. One of the capitals appears to depict Saint Juliana, said to have thrown a rope around Satan's neck and, becoming the first recorded dominatrix of the Church, to have beaten him with a cudgel. One hopes, for piety's sake, that it is she. The crypt also contains one of the famous Black Virgins or Black Madonnas that are of particular interest to historians of religious art (see photo 26). There are said to be 180 such figures in France alone, and it is intriguing to think that they appear also at Montserrat and at Santiago de Compostela, the goal of the pilgrimage route on which the Clermont basilica is located. The austere yet not chilly style of the church and its crypt (warmer perhaps because of the pale mustard walls), along with the pre-Christian mythologies surrounding the Black Madonna, make one wonder whether such a Madonna would have crossed Hölderlin's mind when he was appreciating and then later recalling "the brown women" of Bordeaux who, as we will see, are mentioned in "Andenken."

As we climbed the high road that heads west out of Clermont (the departmental road D 941), the rain became snow. The flakes were driven on a high wind out of the west, a wind that did not disperse but rather donned the fog like a cloak. The horrific weather made for hours and hours

Photo 26. In the crypt of Notre-Dame-du-Port, in Clermont, one of Europe's many *Black Virgins*.

of difficult driving. We had seen the volcanoes and the mountain peaks of the Auvergne at a distance on that first morning, when we were perched on the plateau near St. Yvoine, in sight of Montpeyroux. Yet from now on the volcanoes were hidden to us, both on our way to Limoges and on our way back home weeks later, when fog, rain, and snowfall once again obscured the heights. We passed the famous Puy-de-Dôme twice without ever seeing it; we caught the barest glimpse of the volcano called Lampegny. Joe and I were reminded of the Kniebis back in the northern Black Forest. We did not have to wonder whether the Auvergne had been as forbidding to Hölderlin as it now was to us—his letter from Bordeaux certainly suggests that it was. Only when we left the Auvergne behind us, descending gradually into the region of Creuse, passing through Aubusson, then entering Haute Vienne and Limosin, did the snow and fog abate. We had been heading downhill quite gradually for hours, and as we stopped to enjoy the sight of the pastures of Limosin and its special breed of kine, the winter seemed to be relenting and giving way to spring. It was still January, and the fields were still frosted, at least those on the hills facing north, but suddenly there was sun. We stopped to photograph a lovely château at Quéret near St. Avit, where the sky was reassuringly back up there where it belonged and had its color restored. Even if the trees were bare, the sturdy Limosine cows were already out there on the pasture, and the pasture, at least on the slopes facing south, was green.

Our route (still the D 941) took us to the village of Pontarion, its old stone bridge crossing the river, Le Thaurion, which gives the village its name (photo 27). The nearby château, quite spectacular, the placid stream,

Photo 27. On the way to Périgueux lies idyllic Pontarion, "Bridge over Le Thaurion."

102 / Struck by Apollo

and the old bridge encouraged us to stop and do some walking. Perhaps we were feeling a bit euphoric, having escaped the wintry Auvergne and entering now into the friendlier atmosphere of the Creuse region. After our trip was over, we often talked about that particular spot, even though we had visited many beautiful locales, without knowing exactly why it had made such a strong impression on us.

At St.-Léonard-de-Noblat we stopped to admire an old mill, knowing that it was surely there when Hölderlin passed by or perhaps stopped (see photo 28). We then drove on to the town of Aixé-sur-Vienne. The Vienne River was much larger than the streams we had recently been crossing, and it was reminiscent of Le Doubs back in Franche-Conté or even the Saône and Rhône of Lyon. We were headed south on the N 21 to Périgueux, which is the probable post-coach route followed by Hölderlin during the first days of 1802, even if many commentators assert that he headed toward the city of Angoulême, west of Limoges, and only then turned south to Bordeaux. We passed the somber Château de Malaveix, then the more stately Château des Bories (see photo 29), near the village of Antonne. As we viewed all these remnants of the feudal past, we had to think once again about Hölderlin's ambivalent relation to the aristocracy. In one of his letters, written soon after his ejection from the Gontard household, he complains about the superciliousness of the "aristocrats," although what he is actually complaining about are the nouveaux riches, the parvenus or higher bourgeoisie whose children he is hired to tutor. He complains in that same letter that in the Gontard household he was treated like a servant rather than as an educator—at least by one-half of the Gontards. His political leanings made him feel closer to the working class, the farmers, and tradespeople—*le peuple*, if you will—than to the upper crust and the clergy. The clergy he had learned to hate, and neither the old nor the new nobility was ever a part of his life. Yet his education, his love of music and of classical literature and philosophy, and especially his dedication to poetry—these things made him closer to the aristocratic class than to any other. Perhaps as he drove or walked past these splendid residences he wondered if their families had survived the Terror. He may also have reflected on the sense of his own exclusion from the nobility and in effect from every class. He was *solitary* in so many different senses of the word.

Joe and I spent a wonderful morning wandering through the city of Périgueux. It was the first time either of us had seen it. Dominated by the Cathedral of Saint Front—an early Christian saint neither of us had ever heard of—the hillside city is a gem. (There is a portrait of Saint Front in

Photo 28. An old mill at St.-Léonard-de-Noblat on the Vienne River, on the way from Limousin to Périgueux.

Photo 29. Château des Bories, near Antonne, on the way to Périgueux.

104 / Struck by Apollo

one of the stained-glass windows that shows him baptizing the future Saint Exuperius, bishop of Toulouse, in the fifth century; however, legend says that Saint Front converted the Perigordians during the first century. One has to be a native of Périgueux to appreciate their patron's longevity.) As for the remarkable architecture of the church, one has to imagine that the five pineapple-topped bell towers of the cathedral are not there. They are constructions that make one think of the Kremlin or some other Eastern phenomenon, and they were added to the church, which itself is in the form of a Greek cross, in the second half of the nineteenth century, long after Hölderlin had visited the city. He would have been more impressed with the simple cloister behind the church, on the crest of the hill (photo 30). The relatively austere interior of the church may have pleased him too, however. And one should be kind to the memory of the long-lived Saint Front: in 1575 the Huguenots sacked the church and tossed the relics of the saint into the Dordogne River.

Departing Périgueux, Joe and I took route D 6089, which follows the Isle River, heading southwest toward our final destination. The Isle led us to a charming complex of buildings at Sourzac-sur-l'Isle, in the region of Pomarède (see photo 31). The old Romanesque church, like an abandoned fortress, was in ruins. We were able to learn its name (Saints Peter and Paul) but nothing about its history, other than the fact that it was sacked during the Hundred Years' War. We wondered whether it was still a ruin in Hölderlin's time, or whether, having been rebuilt, it succumbed once again during the Revolution.

We passed through the twin towns of Mompon-Ménestérol, and since night was coming on we looked for a place to overnight among the fields and forests of Perigord. It had been raining in the region for the past week, and many of the fields were flooded. We found an abandoned farm near such an inundated field and pulled off the small country road onto an even smaller dirt road at the edge of a fallow, sodden field. It was there that we had the first and only mishap of our trip. The dirt road we backed into was in fact a mud road. And instead of being perfectly level, it inclined slightly downward—enough to prevent our being able to move from the spot. Joe felt the Hymercar slowly sinking into the mire and immediately tried to liberate it. Yet he could not employ that rocking motion that usually enables one to escape from mud or a snow drift; automatic transmissions are too slow to rock and roll, and soon we were mid-hubcap deep in muck. Luckily, a forest ranger drove by on the larger, paved road and I rushed out to flag him down. I suppose we would

Photo 30. The cloister at the cathedral of Périgueux.

Photo 31. At Sourzac-sur-l'Isle, Nouvelle-Aquitaine, the ruins of a church destroyed during the Hundred Years' War.

call him a forest ranger; he was a *maître-de-chasse*, in charge of enforcing the hunting-free zone we were in. He explained that almost all the local farmers were off visiting relatives for the holiday season but that there was one farmer in the neighborhood who could pull us out. Because it was growing dark, he suggested that we simply settle down—the camper had already taken his advice—and enjoy the evening and the night. Meanwhile, he called the farmer to let him know that I would be coming by the next morning to guide him to our bog. The farmer, like the ranger, was a friendly and capable fellow, and his tractor gently extracted us from the muck.

We started off on our way to Bordeaux, but we stopped at a nearby farm that had been abandoned for at least a generation or two. It would have been in operation at the time Hölderlin passed by, and there was something photogenic about it and the nearby pond (photo 32). We then stopped at the next *Intermarché* service station and gave our RV a much-needed shower and foot bath, then set off for Bordeaux and the Atlantic Ocean.

Photo 32. An abandoned farmhouse in the commune of Pomarède, not far from Mompon-Ménestérol, on the way to Libourne.

Photo 33. An early January morning at Soulac-sur-Mer, near Bordeaux.

3

"Its Floor Is the Sea"

Even though many of Hölderlin's letters may be presumed lost, the paucity of letters from Bordeaux is still quite striking. The months of February, March, April, and May of 1802 see almost no correspondence at all, as though Hölderlin has indeed entered into a kind of caesura in his life, a period of uncustomary silence. Bertheau, in the fourth chapter of *Hölderlin's French Education* (JB 91ff.), emphasizes Hölderlin's remarkable declaration in the letters immediately prior to his departure for Bordeaux that his fellow Germans "have no use for" him (*sie können mich nicht brauchen*). The remark reflects his despair over the failed *Iduna* project, a journal of poetry and essays he had hoped to found and edit, believing that the journal might make a name for himself and provide an income. However, his most influential associates (Goethe and Schiller among them) refused to support it. Furthermore, he was unable to garner a lectureship in Greek literature at the University of Jena. Of course, there were his continued desperate attempts to convince his mother that he was not suited to the life of a Pietist pastor. Finally, and perhaps above all, he had failed to gain the future companionship—for he did possess the love—of Susette. If neither Jena and Weimar nor Nürtingen and Frankfurt had any use for him, he would seek a new beginning in France.

France is therefore not only the source and destination of his political hopes but also a personal goal; it is perhaps the last possible refuge for an *homme de lettres* who has been reduced to being an *instituteur* or household tutor. *Homme de lettres* is Hölderlin's self-description on his entry visa application in Strasbourg; on his exit visa application in Bordeaux he confesses himself to be an *instituteur*. Bertheau relates that there were precedents for impoverished Swabian authors making their way to France to pursue a

110 / Struck by Apollo

literary career. Yet one wonders whether Hölderlin continues to hope that his situation as a tutor is merely temporary and that things will improve for the man of letters in exile.

Because of the dearth of firsthand testimony concerning the Bordeaux stay, Bertheau looks for some evidence of Hölderlin's life in Bordeaux in "the three France poems" of his œuvre, the famous poem *Andenken* and two lesser-known fragments, *Vom Abgrund nemlich* and *Das Nächste Beste.*[1] In the next few pages I will follow Bertheau's readings, which, while quite speculative, manage to draw interesting conclusions about Hölderlin's life in Bordeaux. Bertheau attempts to elicit from the poems what he calls their "topographical aspect," assuming that Hölderlin's experiences in Bordeaux are important for our reading of the poems and fragments.

A caveat or two has to be entered here, however, not so much about the importance of Hölderlin's experiences, but about the poems and fragments of poems themselves. As T. W. Adorno emphasizes in his "Parataxis,"[2] Hölderlin's poetic thinking often defeats our efforts to read the poetry syntactically: the words and phrases often seem to line up, one after the other, for no apparent logical or grammatical reason; some critics refer to what they call the "laundry lists" of the *Folioheft*, even though laundry is not their subject; others call Hölderlin's poetry "eidetic," perhaps referring to his own notion of the "ideational" or "ideal"; it would perhaps be more fitting to say *eidoletic*, since it is often a matter of stark images rising off the page in apparent isolation from one another. Or, if *eidoletic* is too idolatrous,

---

1. See chap. 5, 101ff., of Bertheau's book. For Hölderlin's texts, see CHV 1:473–75 for "Remembrance," and 1:420–25 for "The Next Best." "From the abyss, namely . . ." does not appear as such in CHV (but see the edition by Jochen Schmidt at DKV 1:416–17), since Knaupp edits the notebook differently here; however, some of its lines do appear at CHV 1:422. The confusion about the "abyss" lines is that Hölderlin himself is often unclear in the *Homburger Folioheft* about where one poem ends and another begins. He also often fails to indicate whether the additional lines that he sketches into the margins are meant to be *added to* the poem or to *replace* other lines. Each editor makes his own best guess. There are five different recent editions of Hölderlin's works, all of them impeccable in terms of scholarship. Yet each one presents the poems differently (especially the late poems and the poems and sketches of the *Homburger Folioheft*, from the period immediately after the Bordeaux trip), sometimes in major ways. The serious student has no option but to compare all the editions.

2. Theodor W. Adorno, "Parataxis: Zur späten Lyrik Hölderlins," *Neue Rundschau* 75:1 (1964). The piece appears now in Adorno, *Noten zur Literatur*, ed. Rolf Tiedemann (Frankfurt am Main: Suhrkamp, 1981), 447–91. For an English translation, see Adorno, *Notes to Literature: Volume Two*, tr. Shierry Weber Nicholson (New York: Columbia University Press, 1992), 109–49, with endnotes at 338–41.

one might say that the poetry is *visional*, evoking sudden images that have enormous power for him and for us; they are numinous visions that we others have little trouble descrying but great difficulty ordering into some sort of proper sequence and significance. This will be plain enough in the discussion that follows—even if the topographical aspect does seem to offer us considerable help in understanding what excited the poet in and about Bordeaux. A second caveat comes from Heidegger's 1941–1942 lecture course on Hölderlin's *Andenken*.[3] Heidegger, fearful that a biographical reading of Hölderlin's poem will inevitably reduce its poetic quality, urges his listeners to consider that the poem and the poet alike are *überdichtet*, "hyperpoetized," as it were. What he means is that in a sense the poem sings the poet. Perhaps we should define our present task as an effort to think about what in and around Bordeaux might have so "worked" on Hölderlin that we could say it "poetized" him. I should not suppress the judgment of a whole range of psychiatrists, including notables such as Jean Laplanche, who see in these fragments of poetry signs of schizophrenia; yet one should also note that such psychiatrists—Laplanche being a notable exception—almost invariably betray the fact that they have never looked into any poet's notebook. Their sometimes elaborate, sometimes clumsy diagnoses cannot conceal the layman's dependably dumbfounded reaction to poetry—which often does seem to be singing the poet.

But let us back up a bit. What is it that Hölderlin expected to find in Bordeaux, and what did he hope to see during his journey to it? His letters tell of his excitement to see Paris—which in fact he saw only on his return voyage—and his desire to experience the sun of southern France and to see the Atlantic Ocean. As I mentioned earlier, Bertheau tries to gather evidence about what Hölderlin actually experienced during his Bordeaux stay by examining a number of poems: (1) the well-known poem *Andenken*, which contains Hölderlin's clearest statements about Bordeaux; (2) the incomplete poem *Das Nächste Beste*; (3) the fragment *Vom Abgrund nemlich*, all of these from the time immediately following Hölderlin's return to Germany; and, adding another later poem from the year 1808, if not considerably later, (4) the incomplete poem that Hölderlin places in the mouth of his beloved—and by that time departed—Diotima, which begins, *Wenn aus der Ferne*, "If, out of the remoteness." This last is surely

---

3. Martin Heidegger, *Hölderlins Hymne "Andenken,"* Gesamtausgabe vol. 52, ed. Curd Ochwadt (Frankfurt am Main: V. Klostermann, 1982), esp. 6–8, and 13 at midpage. Translation by William McNeill and Julia Ireland, *Hölderlin's Hymn "Remembrance"* (Bloomington: Indiana University Press, 2018).

112 / Struck by Apollo

Bertheau's most speculative source, whereas the first, *Andenken*, is his and our most reliable font of evidence.[4]

Andenken, "Remembrance," recalls Hölderlin's arrival at Bordeaux and his first look at the Gironde, the conjoined Dordogne and the Garonne rivers and flowing into the Atlantic northwest of Bordeaux. Here is an attempt at translation:

> A northeaster blows,
> Most beloved of winds
> To me, because it promises
> Mariners fiery spirit and good voyage.
> But go now and greet
> The lovely Garonne
> And the gardens of Bordeaux,
> Where along the sharp line of shore
> The narrow walkway winds, and into the stream
> Steeply plummets the brook, while above
> Gaze down a noble pair
> Of oaks and silver poplars;
>
> I still think of that, and of how
> The broad peaks and their elm wood
> Bend over the mill below, but also
> Where in the courtyard a fig tree grows.
> On holidays the brown women walk
> On silky soil there,
> In the month of March,
> When night and day are equal,
> And, crossing meandering walkways,
> Laden with golden dreams,
> Breezes sway and cradle.
>
> But hand me
> One of those fragrant cups
> Full of darkling light,
> That I may rest; for slumber
> Would be sweet among the shadows.

---

4. I offer a translation of *Wenn aus der Ferne* in the Epilogue at the end of my text.

"Its Floor Is the Sea" / 113

It is not good
Soullessly to ponder
Mortal thoughts. Good
Is a conversation, saying
Things the heart means, listening much
About days of love
And deeds that were done.

Yet where are my friends? Bellarmin
With his shipmates? Many are
Too full of awe to go to the source;
For treasures have their start
In the sea. These mariners,
Like painters, gather together
The beauties of the Earth, and they do
Not scorn the wings of war, nor
To dwell in solitude for years under
The leafless mast, where all through the night
The city's holidays cast no light,
And no thrum of strings and no folk dances.

But now to the Indies
The men are gone;
There on the windswept peak
Of mountain vineyards, plunging down,
The Dordogne comes,
And together with the splendid
Garonne, as broad as the sea,
Their stream spreads wide. But it takes
And gives memory, the sea,
And sedulous love engages our eyes,
But what remains the poets institute.
                    (CHV 1:473–75)

It has become an obsession of the French Hölderlinians to locate quite precisely that "windswept peak" from which Hölderlin seems to be singing his poem, if only in remembrance. Jean-Pierre Lefebvre is adamant that the peak—not so much a peak as a lookout point—is to be found high above Lormont, a small village across the Garonne north of Bordeaux. He is certain that Hölderlin frequents this place, if only because it is famous

114 / Struck by Apollo

for its evening entertainments. Waiblinger reports a rumor that Hölderlin frequented the ladies of the evening there and that his "debauches" were clearly the cause of his later madness; unfortunately, there appears to be no evidence that Waiblinger's rumor (WW 9, 20) has any substance to it.

Lefebvre begins his "situationist" interpretation of the poem with an exergue by Michel Deguy, which sets the stage for Lefebvre's own thesis— which is that local circumstances, such as Hölderlin's precise vantage point for what he describes in *Andenken*, his precise "situation," are determinative for poetry. Even if the search for geographical reference points soon seems futile and perhaps even capricious, to me at least, Deguy's statement is moving. In *Les Temps Modernes* for August-September 1990 (page 7), Deguy, himself a poet of considerable stature, writes:

> Every poem is circumstantial. Its obscurity resides there—its difficulty. In other words, a poem waits. It waits so that it might pass its "meridian," that is, recoup a circumstance; born of circumstance in its very nomination, vocative, transforming and encrypting in this metamorphosis where it loves to hide itself and its circumstance—the poem waits to be citable, waits to regain its verticality in an "analogous" circumstance, where it will be re-citable in its luminosity, illuminating a circumstance and illuminated by the circumstance, looping meaning, looping its sense, in this "loop of anniversary." The poem awaits anniversary and the anniversaries that give meaning to it once again.

The circumstance of *Andenken*, which is itself a celebration of anniversary or at least of memory, is, in Lefebvre's view, Hölderlin's occupying a site on that promontory above Lormont, on the northern bank of the Garonne—from which vantage point all the details of the poem ostensibly can be plainly seen. As far as Joe and I were able to determine, however, this is not the case: the confluence of the Garonne and the Dordogne lies several miles to the northwest of Lormont at the Bec d'Ambès. For his part, Bertheau is certain that the site on which *Andenken* is based is a high windswept sand dune on the Atlantic coast, either at Arcachon, which has the highest dunes in Europe or, more likely, at the windswept Pointe de Grave near Soulac, where, about a hundred kilometers northwest of Bordeaux, the Gironde empties into the sea. Joe and I found our way to this site as well, but we could not agree that Hölderlin would have been able to see all the details of *Andenken* from it. In the end, we decided to let the debate carry on without us. Deguy's "loop of anniversary" is a fitting phrase, one he borrows from Jacques Derrida, and Derrida is a thinker of "undecidability." In this case, as in many others, Joe and I felt we had to accept undecidability even as we searched eagerly for all the possible circumstances and loops of meaning. All treasures start in the sea, says Hölderlin, and poets are painters who gather rather than cut, divide, and decide. Their "situation" is mobile, and their circumstances shift. This is why poets rather than commentators institute what remains, while the rest of us simply have to wait for Deguy's "analogous" circumstance and Derrida's "loop of anniversary."

The sea takes memories as well as gives them, taking all the gifts offered it by the rivers and eventually returning them to the land. It sows considerable confusion on the shore, scattering sea wrack and sea spawn all over the strand, where sweet and brackish waters mix. What seems quite certain is Hölderlin's awe in the face of the Gironde, with the Garonne and Dordogne joining forces and moving on at last to the sea. And he is in awe of the sailors who are on their way to or from the West Indies during a time when England and France are warring to achieve supremacy on the Atlantic. Bertheau pictures Hölderlin spending a great deal of time on the wharves of the Garonne, listening to the mariners during weekend festivals there, festivals of music and folk dancing, as the sailors regale the poet and their mates with tales of love and songs that sing deeds of war. As I noted earlier, what little we know about Hölderlin's attitudes concerning class and social status tells us that he despised the bourgeoisie, the new rich, with all their arrogance and philistinism. A lover of nature, he was also a lover of the people who worked in and with nature, the farmers and shepherds, and in Bordeaux, the sailors. They were the artists of the sea, like painters gathering together on their canvas sails the beautiful things of the Earth and bringing them to the port and to the poet who will "institute" or "found" them, *stiften*, in his poetic remembrance of them.

But—and you will have noticed this—in *Andenken* as in so many other poems, Hölderlin's favorite conjunction is not "and" but "but," as though the singer wants us to notice always something new, something else, not only this *but* also that. But what about those "brown women"? (There is a famous dispute between Heidegger and Adorno about them, but I will let that pass.) In the past, I felt that they were simply the women who worked in the vineyards. For even in the high Swiss Alps I have seen young women in the hay fields who were toasted by the sun, blond, blue-eyed, and quite brown. Yet Bertheau speculates in a different direction. Bordeaux was famous not only for its wine exports but also, notoriously, for the slave trade. Many ships, replenishing themselves for the long Atlantic voyage, set off from Bordeaux for the plantations of the West Indies and the southern states of the United States. Over the years a large African population formed in and around Bordeaux. Many Black women—or Brown women—served as dressmakers and beauticians, some of them achieving relative wealth and status in the city, along with a certain measure of freedom. An American is reminded strongly of New Orleans. One can only imagine Hölderlin's astonishment in the face of such beautiful human beings—unlike any he had ever seen before. Scorched by the sun, perhaps, in some earlier time, but now graced by *einwiegende Lüfte*, breezes that sway and cradle.

Joe and I made the odd decision when approaching Bordeaux to head straight for the sea, stopping only at Blanquefort and Consul Meyer's country home there, Château Fongravey (photo 34). Consul Meyer spent many of the spring and fall months there—the heat was too intense in summer—and one can be sure that Hölderlin would have accompanied the family when it ventured out into wine country. Fongravey gives us an inkling of Consul Meyer's wealth and the importance of the wine trade in the acquisition of that wealth. As Joe and I approached Bordeaux we were entranced by the signs along the road, with names that sounded like a wine

Photo 34. Château Fongravey, the spring and fall residence of Consul Daniel Christoph Meyer at Blanquefort, in a vineyard northwest of Bordeaux. Hölderlin would have taken boat trips down the Garonne to Fongravey on weekends and holidays with the Meyer family.

"Its Floor Is the Sea" / 117

list—St. Émilion, Pomérol, Médoc. After our visit to the Meyer château, we decided to drive northwest through the Médoc region to reach the sea as quickly as possible.

Earlier I called it an odd decision, because it was something like an automatic reflex rather than a deliberate decision. We felt an urgent need to get to the sea as quickly as possible, and we were convinced, not only intellectually but also in our bodies, that Hölderlin had felt the same urgency. Our entire journey, like his, had been a meander toward the sea, and now we were anxious to follow the Gironde until it emptied into the Atlantic. I recalled that one of the isolated names that Hölderlin jots down into his *Homburger Folioheft* is "Soulaco," and I surmised this to be a form—perhaps the Gascognais form—of Soulac-sur-Mer. And that is where we headed. We paused briefly at a number of the châteaux of the Médoc region, some of which are truly Disney creations, others merely reflecting fabulous wealth. We stopped briefly at Paullac to observe the Gironde (the Garonne and Dordogne rivers, *meerbreit*, as Hölderlin says, "as wide as the sea") flowing together into the Atlantic. It was late afternoon, late at least by January standards, when we arrived at the coast. We stopped immediately before Soulac, parked the Hymercar beneath the umbrella pines, and walked through a breach in the Dune d'Amélie, where we had our first sighting of the sea (see once again the frontispiece of the book).

It seemed to us at that moment—with our first glimpse of the sea— that this was the entire point of Hölderlin's journey. He himself had written that he was looking forward to it, but neither Joe nor I, even though we have both spent a great deal of time at and in the sea, was prepared for this. The sheer breadth and length of the strand, with the sea then stretching out to the horizon, the winter wind whipping up great swells on the tide—we found ourselves quite alone on the beach, even though the late afternoon sky was suddenly clear, almost cloudless. We walked, Joe in one direction, I in another. I took an absurd number of photographs, entranced by everything I saw. It was a form of enchantment, and I could not stop snapping. When I turned away from the sea, just before sunset, I saw the moon, three-quarters full, rising over the dune, *traurig und prächtig herauf*, as Hölderlin says in "The Wine God." Splendidly, to be sure. But "mournfully"? Perhaps. The truth is that the Man in the Moon, or rather the Lunar Woman, wore a troubled expression that evening, as the moon sometimes does (see photo 35).

I once proposed a psychoanalysis of the moon, literally a psycholunalysis, precisely on account of its severe mood swings, but the idea has not yet caught on among astronomers. Back here on Earth, the wrack that had

Photo 35. At Soulac-sur-Mer, the moon rising "in mourning and in splendor."

been washed ashore, especially a tree with most of its branches still intact, caught my eye, and that tree, along with the foam and the filmy reach of the water on the sand, the *tain* of the mirror for the sky, reminded me of some lines from Hölderlin's *Homburger Folioheft*:

> As on seacoasts, when celestials begin to build,
> Shipping endless splendors ashore, the work
> Of the waves, one after another, and the Earth
> Puts on its array, so that one who is most joyous
> Gaily brings it together and breaks out
> Into song, with the wine god promising much. . . .
> And these things are from her, beloved as she is
> In all of Greece, from her who was
> Born of the sea and wearing the look of destiny,
> Overwhelming plenitude on the shore.
>   (CHV 1:416)

"Its Floor Is the Sea" / 119

These lines appear a few pages after Hölderlin began to sketch out the poem I mentioned earlier, one that might have been called, or dedicated, "To the Madonna," whom I prefer to call "The Madonna of Sea Spume." Clearly, Hölderlin's was an amalgam of madonnas that the world had not seen in quite a while, if ever. It is true that our first view of the sea after a period of absence from it is always, as Hölderlin writes, *gewaltig*—overpowering, overwhelming, or, as Herman Melville writes, simply "whelming." And those diurnal miracles, the setting of the sun into the sea and the rising of the moon into the sky, impossible (not) to photograph, do seem to have the look of destiny, that is, of the *schiklich blikenden* goddess, opening herself to our vision.

Joe and I awoke at sunrise on the following morning and walked over the dune to the edge of the Atlantic. Once again the surf was high, and the waves broke thunderously hundreds of yards out to sea. A large gull flew by (photo 36). The sound of the surging surf was unrelenting. And once again it was hard to stop taking pictures of treasures the celestials had shipped ashore. We walked—again separately, Joe slipping off into the horizon (photo 37), each of us lost in his own thoughts—for hours. The dunes had a fresh look and smell to them; the morning air was invigorating. The tide had left uncannily ornate designs around the assorted stones and shells that had been deposited there (photo 38). A number of small sea birds, quick on their feet, dashed across the sand, clearly looking for breakfast. Their mirror image scampered beneath them in the wet sand.

It is equally as likely, however, that Hölderlin's first view of the sea was not at Soulac but near the Bay of Arcachon, due west of Bordeaux. Soulac he may have seen only on his homeward journey, taking a ship from the port of Bordeaux on the Garonne and traveling downriver to the seaport at Soulac. He had probably already been to the seaside at Arcachon during his stay. Bertheau tells us that the entire area west of the city, the so-called Landes region, beginning with the Quartier St.-Seurin of Bordeaux itself, was marshland, humid and insect ridden, a place where only wild horses or shepherds and their flocks roamed or where refugees of the Revolution and fugitive slaves found shelter in a former Carthusian monastery (JB 122–24). He describes the Landes as a kind of bayou country. Yet he also insists that Hölderlin, against the advice of his host and all other sensible persons, would surely have made the long trek to the sea on more than one occasion—it would have taken him two days to get there on foot. And even in April or early May that wilderness was unbearably hot, at least for a northern European. At the Bay of Arcachon he would have climbed to

Photo 36. Soulac-sur-Mer. The gull too is heading south.

Photo 37. Early morning at Soulac, looking south toward Bordeaux.

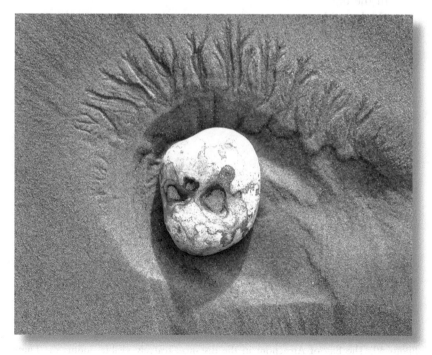

Photo 38. The tide creates a unique setting for every gem scattered on the strand.

the top of the highest sand dune on the European continent, the Dune du Pilat, welcoming the sea breeze and surveying the treasures that foam-born Aphrodite had shipped to the land below him (photo 39).

Bertheau traces many references in Hölderlin's poetry to Bordeaux and the Gascogne region, and even though we need not follow each reference, several of them are striking. In the fragment that some editors title *Vom Abgrund nemlich* (cf. CHV 1:422–25), we find the lines, here in translation:

> But to the very point of pain
> There wafts to my nose
> The scent of lemons and the oil of Provence and where in
>   gratitude
> And in the most natural way the land of Gascogne is given to
>   me.

Earlier lines of this fragment read:

> For human beings are more sensuous
> In the fire
> Of the wilderness

Photo 39. The Bay of Arcachon; in the distance, scarcely visible, looms the Dune du Pilat.

"Its Floor Is the Sea" / 123

Drunk with light, and the animal spirit is at rest
With them. Yet soon, like a dog, my voice
Will wander in the heat on garden paths
Where human beings dwell
In France.

These final words, telling us where human beings dwell, may seem jejune. But we have to remember that Hölderlin's *Hyperion* had found only shards of human beings in Germany, never complete and whole ones. If whole human beings dwell in France, that needs to be duly recorded. It is presumably part of the "test" that the German nation must pass.[5]

The many references to the *Wüste* in Hölderlin's fragments, which we naturally take to mean "the desert," Bertheau understands as referring to the moors of the Landes. Too humid to be a "desert," spotted with shallow pools of brackish water where fowl and foal play, the Landes is nevertheless a place where one can be "scorched" by the sun even in springtime. Perhaps because Hölderlin pictures the poet standing bareheaded beneath lightning bolts, opening himself to "fire from heaven," he is also sensitive to the mortal danger of being singed by too much solar fire. In "The Next Best" we find the following lines, where the syntax is difficult to establish and the context very difficult to surmise—the lines seeming simply to spill like sea spawn from Hölderlin's lips or pen onto the strand of his hyperpoetized page:

Thus like starlings
With joyous cries, when in Gascogne, in places
Where so many gardens are,

---

5. Earlier in the book I referred to Heidegger's view of Hölderlin as a "test" for the German nation. I should add a note on Heidegger's remarkable lecture course on *Andenken* during the winter semester of 1941–1942. The historical context could not be more stark: whereas Hölderlin's poem remembers the France of his political and personal hopes, Heidegger begins his lectures only a few months after the German *Wehrmacht* has overrun northern France. There are admirable moments in the lecture course, as when Heidegger stubbornly insists that poetry cannot be reduced to the psychological circumstances or historical conditions of its gestation, or when he insists that the poem is not what the poet opines but what the poem compels the poet to sing. Yet to treat France as nothing more than a pathetic substitute for ancient Greece, to consider "the foreign" as nothing more than a necessary but transitory part of the poet's education, to be quite certain that the important matter is to get the poet back to Germany so that he can found a new and festive beginning for Heidegger's history of *beyng*—all of this, in my view, is a reduction more damaging to the poem and the poet than the psychological or literary-critical reductions ever were.

124 / Struck by Apollo

When in the land of the olive, and
In foreign lands so worthy of love,
Leaping fountains on grassy paths
Trees unwitting in the wilderness
The sun scorching,
And the heart of the Earth
Opening up, where, circling
The hill of oak trees
From the burning land,
The rivers flow and where
Sundays there is dancing
And thresholds that welcome,
On streets garlanded with blossoms,
Quietly walking.
  (CHV 1:420)

Bertheau takes these lines—and he makes this convincing, even though here too there is much speculation—as meaning that Hölderlin especially on weekends frequents the wharves on the Garonne, the so-called *rivière* of Bordeaux, where sailors from all over the world gather (JB 116–29). It would have been a riot of nationalities, a colorful troupe of Melvillean mariners, the likes of which the landlubber Hölderlin would never have experienced beforehand. He may have confronted there nefarious slavers such as Jackson, the nemesis of Melville's *Redburn*; yet he seems to have met more hospitable types, say, the outspoken "Larry," who prefers "Madagasky" to "Ameriky." These are sailors who, at least in their ripe old age, actually might have crossed Melville's own path when he was on his way to or from Liverpool or was out adventuring in the South Seas. As for the garlanded streets and ships of Hölderlin's poems, Bertheau reports that every weekend during the clement months there were dances on the *rivière* and much music making. Sophie Laroche, a popular and ubiquitous novelist who had visited Bordeaux a dozen years earlier, confirms that these celebrations, with folk dances, folk music, and folk refreshments, were common on Sundays and holidays.

About those "folk refreshments." In Hölderlin's fragment *Vom Abgrund nemlich*, there is a reference to *Rappierlust*, which I and everyone else would normally translate as the pleasures of fencing, the desire to wield the rapier. As we know, Hölderlin possessed or at least borrowed a rapier from his friends during his university years, although we have no idea whether he ever used it. The context of the lines in which the word appears, however, would make the fencing reference quite strange. Bertheau comes up with

"Its Floor Is the Sea" / 125

a far more likely sense: *Rappierlust* is more likely a desire for *vin râpé*, the least expensive form of wine available to the sailors. Laroche reports that in Bordeaux there were (and in some places still are) four stages of wine pressing, with descending levels of quality and price: after the finest wine had been attained from the juice produced by the sheer weight of the grapes pressing and bursting the grapes at the bottom of the vat, a vintner gently trods the grapes; only then were the crushed grapes *gekeltert*, that is, pressed in a giant wooden press. Finally, after all the juice had been extracted for fermentation in barrels, water was poured over the crushed grape must and the diluted juice subjected to yet another fermentation. Because of the large amount of skins, stems, and seeds in the must, which today produce in *grappa* and in *Tresterschnaps* that woody-yeasty taste, this final concoction must have had a rough flavor and a texture other than velvety. It was called *vin râpé* because of the rasping effect it had on your throat on the way down. Not the favorite of the connoisseur or the *sommelier*, to be sure, but no doubt preferable to fencing.

This image of Hölderlin cavorting with the nationalities of the world—in the form of fairly rough sailor types—is so different from any other image of him that we have! He is usually pictured as the sober and somber Poet of Being who spends all his time lamenting the flight of the gods of Greece. And there is much to say for that forlorn image. The third stanza of *Der Weingott* left us on Greek shores, gazing upward in hopes of espying a deity or two. Yet the desire that drives Hölderlin's search is in fact the desire for celebration, even "jubilation," something not so so(m)ber. The fourth stanza, in search of celebration, reads:

> Blessed Greece! house of all the heavenly ones,
>   Is it true, then, what we once heard when we were young?
> Festive hall! its floor is the sea! and its tables the mountains,
>   Verily constructed for one use only in primeval times!
> But the thrones, where are they? the temples? where the vessels
>   Filled with nectar and where, for the gods' pleasure, the song?
> Where? where do they flash, the sayings that strike home from afar?
>   Delphi sleeps and where is the grand destiny intoned?
> Where the quick? where does it invade, all-present happiness,
>   Thundering mightily from clear skies over the heads of nations?
> Father Aither! thus it cries and flies from tongue to tongue
>   A thousand times. No one can bear life alone.
> Once they are given and distributed, such good things received
>   Are a jubilation, the force of the hoary word waxes strong

126 / Struck by Apollo

Father Aither and it echoes no matter how deep and eternal
     the night is,
No matter how vast our need, it descends victorious and
     invigorating.
For thus the heavenly ones come, the day climbing the night,
     preparing
Itself to descend on humankind.
                    (CHV 1:316)

Yet the advent of the dawn is long, and it is surely not yet time for jubilation, except perhaps on the wharves of Bordeaux. There can be no doubt that Hölderlin is plagued by worries, not only about the "grand destiny" that is missing from his own times, despite the Revolution, but also about something closer to home. He is worried that Schiller and the others may be right and that his ambition to be a great poet, a great among the greats, is a pipedream. We latecomers trust the power of Hölderlin's words, but Hölderlin himself certainly does not. The power he is waiting for may come as thunder and lightning, yet he suspects that the poet's words, if they are to institute what lasts, have to sing as naturally as wildflowers in rain-drenched springtime—just as William Wordsworth and Samuel Taylor Coleridge had recently insisted they must. What sort of pressure is that, the pressure that a poet must release a poem as winter releases the spring crocus? The fifth stanza says, concerning the coming of the gods:

Unwelcome they come at first; we children strive against
     Them; the happiness comes too blindingly bright
And humankind shies, even a demigod can scarcely call
     By name who they are that approach him now with gifts.
Yet their courage is great, they fill his heart with
     Their joys and he hardly knows how to use this good,
He labors, squanders, and the unholy seems almost holy to him,
     So that his blessing hand touches foolish and benevolent alike.
The heavenly ones are as patient as they can be; but then
     They themselves come, in truth, and humankind greets happiness
And daylight and the chance to see what has been revealed,
          the face
     Of those who long ago were named the One and All
In its depths the silent breast is filled with liberal contentment,
     And for the first and only time every yearning ends well—
Thus the human being; he can do nothing else; otherness alone

> Challenges the sacred deep in him with friendship and enmity;
> To the barren one it was concealed; now he calls it best beloved,
> Now, now the words for it must bloom like flowers.
>
> (CHV 1:316–17)

The carousing sailors, piping, dancing, and singing: are these the profane ones whom the poet foolishly confuses with the holy? Or is it precisely their kind of joy that has gone missing from the temples? Is the crude earthenware cup of *vin râpé* in fact the only surviving form of chalice? Is the sacred song now to be heard only in the doughty sailor's ditty? Is it the very *hospitality* of the thresholds in Bordeaux that reveals the sacred? And the scent of lemon that rises to astonish the poet's nostrils to the point of pain—what is that? Bertheau says it is the lemon juice squeezed over lamb meat that is being grilled with garlic and olive oil then sprinkled with sacred oregano, the same way it is cooked now not only in Bordeaux but throughout Greece and the eastern Mediterranean.

Speaking of that part of the world, it is intriguing that Hölderlin now finds Greece not only to the east of him but also to the west. The sailors themselves have all sailed for the Indies, says my translation of *Andenken*. This does not mean the India of the Indus and the Ganges, from which, it is true, the wine god initially advanced toward Greece, or at least not India alone; it also means the West Indies, both the Greater and the Lesser Antilles—Cuba, Jamaica, Barbados, Trinidad, Martinique, and all those dozens of other islands whose exotic names Hölderlin hears now for the first time.[6]

If spirit loves colonies, as *Brot und Wein* says, it is not for the sake of colonization. It is rather because the sailors, like Aphrodite's sea itself, carry so many gifts to the shore, above all, gifts of stories about things that have happened and loves that have been won and lost. It is the sailors—not the merchants, not the sea captains, not the wealthy and powerful, but the circus of motley human beings in diaspora—who tell the tales that lift the heart. It is reported that during Hölderlin's stay in Bordeaux one of the large ships docked on the Garonne for several months was the US ship *Columbus*. Hölderlin later sketches a poem by that name into the notebook he is using

---

6. Most commentators are certain that Hölderlin's reference to *Indiern*, following Herder's and Friedrich Schlegel's use of the word in that form, means India, taken by the Romantics to be the genuine source of what is to become Occidental culture. Bertheau tells us that the sailors at Bordeaux are headed west, however, and I have accepted his controversial reading—even if, to say the least, Hölderlin has nothing against the valleys of India and Asia, where the wine god is gathering strength.

128 / Struck by Apollo

at Homburg vor der Höhe. In the opening lines he says he wishes he could have been a "hero of the sea," learning how to practice nautical skills with mastery, gathering treasures "but despoiling nothing" (CHV 1:425). There are scattered phrases in French connected with that poem too, a poem that is dramatically charged but for the most part incomprehensible to us, seemingly incoherent. One of the few things that is evident about it is that Hölderlin is struck by Columbus's "hypostatization of the prior *orbis*" (CHV 1:429; 3:250–52), that is, the way in which the entire world of Christendom is shaken, reshaped, and vastly enlarged by his voyages to the West Indies and by the explorations of the buccaneers who preceded him. To put it minimally, whatever Hölderlin undergoes in Bordeaux reshapes his own world. To repeat, Greece, Hyperion's homeland, is no longer exclusively to the east of him or entirely behind him, historically speaking; or, alternatively, it is so much farther east, so far beyond India and Asia, that others will call it west. And it belongs to the future, not to the past.

Allow me now to scamper back to our camper and continue our own modest voyage, no Columbiad, this time to the city of Bordeaux itself. Let us start with Hölderlin's place of employment and the apartment where he dwelled during his four-month stay. The so-called Hôtel Meyer (see again photo 6 of the Prologue), where Hölderlin tutored his pupils, is a magnificent building, as are all the buildings on the splendid Allées de Tourny, which are the Champs-Élysées of Bordeaux. The opposite ends of the street open onto two of the largest squares of the city, that of the Grand Theater, which truly is grand, and the large oval Place de Tourny on which the Hôtel Meyer abuts. Concerning this magnificent residence, however, Bertheau mentions one important reservation (JB 112–13). Although the three-story house is undoubtedly grand, it does not have much living space; the building has little depth and hence much less interior space than one would think. The high-ceilinged ground floor was and still is dedicated to business offices and a reception area, the second to the living room and kitchen of the Meyer family, and the third to the bedrooms for the Meyers, their many children and step-children, along with perhaps a bonne or two. As a result, Hölderlin had his quarters not in that house but several blocks away. A plaque on the Hôtel Meyer wall—the name Meyer is still to be seen on the building—proudly proclaims that Hölderlin "lived" there in 1802 (photo 40). He did work there, but he lived elsewhere. Bertheau, with help from Lefebvre, has been able to decipher the handwriting on Hölderlin's departure visa and so has located the address of Hölderlin's residence (photo 41) for us: rue St.-Rémi, no. 2 (today renumbered 4, somewhat mysteriously, since

Photo 40. A plaque on the side of the Hôtel Meyer commemorating Hölderlin's stay with lines from *Andenken*, "Remembrance."

Photo 41. Hölderlin's apartment in Bordeaux is somewhere in this building at rue Saint-Rémi no. 2 (now no. 4), close to the Place de la Bourse.

130 / Struck by Apollo

it is still the second entrance on that street), near the Place de la Bourse (JB 114)[7].

That address is about a ten- or fifteen-minute walk from the Hôtel Meyer. Hölderlin would have walked down the splendid Allées de Tourny to the Grand Théâtre de Bordeaux. The Allées consist of a double avenue lined by splendid houses, the finest in Bordeaux even today, the Grand Theater being the most splendid edifice of them all. No doubt Hölderlin was able to attend performances at the theater. The nine muses, including Terpsichore, and three Greek goddesses who overlook the enormous square from the top of the building offered to the citizenry performances of comedy, tragedy, opera, symphonic music, and ballet. Molière, Racine, Mozart—these were the order of the day, even if Hölderlin himself has left us no hints about what he may have seen and heard there. After a normal working day, he would continue his walk past the theater, heading down the rue St. Catherine—so it is called today, but in post-Revolutionary France, the "Saint" would have been dropped—all the way to his own street, the rue (Saint) Rémi. Or he may have jogged left off of rue Catherine onto the rue du Pont-de-la-Mousque, then right onto the rue Courbin, then left again onto the rue Rémi. His own apartment, to repeat, was entered by way of the second entrance on this street. The rue St.-Rémi continues down to the enormous Place de la Bourse (photo 42). The Place de la Bourse was designed by Jacques-Ange Gabriel (1698–1782), the architect and bridge builder who later designed the Place de la Concorde in Paris. One can imagine that residing at a distance from the Meyer family allowed Hölderlin greater freedom in shaping his leisure time.

The Place de la Bourse abuts the quays, wharves, and promenades along the Garonne River. Hölderlin frequented the Quai de Salinières, the Quai des Chartrons, and some others that were close to his residence. He would on occasion have passed beneath the Porte Cailhau, perhaps on his way to the Place du Palais, both to the west of his residence. Close by, on the rue Neuve, is the Maison Jeanne de Lartigue, the former residence of Montesquieu, author of *L'esprit des lois*, a fundamental influence on Hölderlin's political views. From his riverside walks Hölderlin would have returned to the Place de la Bourse, turning up the rue Rémi to his build-

---

7. Knubben (169) suggests that Hölderlin's apartment may have been on the rue Jouannet, a side street off the rue Rémi, house number uncertain. It may be that some stationery Hölderlin used when writing home, bearing the letterhead "Gauthier et Compagnie," is the source of Knubben's surmise. I find Bertheau's suggestion more convincing.

Photo 42. Place de la Bourse. The rue Rémi is the street to the right. One can make out the wrought iron balcony of Hölderlin's residence.

ing, which adjoins its elegant neighboring houses in a Bordelaise version of the row house. The wrought iron railing that extends across the second floor of his building, matched by the wrought iron work on the front door, reminds one of buildings readers may have seen in the French Quarter of New Orleans—for obvious reasons. Today there are no apartments in that building, which is occupied by offices and storage spaces of a firm whose business Joe and I were unable to discover. Yet a worker there assured us that the façade of the building and its front door are precisely as they were in the eighteenth century. One touches the doorknob with one's writing hand in the hope that something will rub off.

It is likely that during the weekends Hölderlin had no teaching duties. He may have been invited out to Fongravey with the family on multiple occasions. From there he may have ventured by ferry across the Gironde to Bourg-sur-Gironde and a bit farther north to Blaye. The confluence of the Garonne and Dordogne rivers at Bec d'Ambès, a confluence celebrated in *Andenken*, occurs not far from Bourg, near the Corniche Girondine. From here, or a bit farther on, from the terraces and vineyards of the grand châteaux, one can see the Dordogne and the Garonne, the Dordogne no longer "plunging down" from the hillside, as *Andenken* suggests. Rather,

132 / Struck by Apollo

both rivers, joined now as the Gironde, are pushed back by the incoming tide from the sea, which is eighty kilometers away. That powerful tide, *Le Mascaret*, enacting the give and take of the sea, is famous in local folklore for endangering boats and ships on the otherwise placidly flowing Gironde.

Another likely excursion, already mentioned, one he probably made by himself, would have been across the Landes to the Bay of Arcachon and the Atlantic. Today the Landes is covered by a vast forest of spruce trees, but in Hölderlin's time it was moor and marsh. The Bay of Arcachon is about fifty kilometers southwest of Bordeaux, but there would have been post-coaches bringing the mail to the fishing villages and oyster farms on the coast and along the bayside; moreover, it seemed to Joe and me, there must have been wagons carrying precious loads of oysters to the wealthy households and fine restaurants of Bordeaux, and Hölderlin could easily have hitched a ride to and from the Bay with one of the drivers. Whether he ever enjoyed the oysters there, some of Europe's finest, we of course do not know. But he surely would have climbed the Dune du Pilat, of that we have no doubt, all one hundred fourteen meters of it. Bertheau speculates that he even had visions of Susette standing atop that dune as he gazed west and north to the Atlantic coast, as though Susette herself had been a fateful gift of Aphrodite. He would have been astonished to find the tide in the bay ebbing and flooding every five hours or so, such that boats were regularly left high and dry in a sea of mud. The fragrance of the bay, heady and delicious, would have challenged a man unaccustomed to the sea, but I suspect that Hölderlin—unlike Hegel, who complains about the "stench" of the sea—would have relished it. That fragrance too takes and gives memory.

All the more does the sea give and take when one travels a bit farther north to the town of Lège and its nearby shoreline on the open Atlantic, the Grand Crohot-Océan (photo 43). As in December, so in May, the sea is restless, sending wave after wave crashing onto the sandy beach. The sun is blinding, the roar constant, conversation difficult. One listens instead to the sea. Bordeaux, itself an exotic sea creature to Hölderlin, seems far away from Nürtingen. Yet perhaps not far enough. Hölderlin may not have been exaggerating when he heard the call of Otahiti out in that other even more vast ocean of the world. In his "Columbus" poem he dreams of sailing on the open ocean—what does Melville say? "Yes, as every one knows, meditation and water are wedded for ever."[8]

---

8. Herman Melville, *Moby-Dick, or The Whale*, eds. Harrison Hayford, Hershel Parker, and G. Thomas Tanselle (Evanston and Chicago: Northwestern University Press and the Newberry Library, 1988), 4.

Photo 43. The Atlantic coast near Lège, west of Bordeaux.

The wind at Lège seemed even sharper to Joe and me in May than it did in January at Soulac. Yet the sun was returning from its winter sojourn in the south, and it burned more intensely now. We were able to ride the waves (without surfboards) for a good part of the afternoon. The dunes we were facing as the waves hurried us to the shore were not nearly as high as the Dune du Pilat at Arcachon, but these more modest dunes had the cavalcade of waves and the roar of the open sea as their companions. Behind the sand dunes stretched the vast forest of spruce trees that extends all the way back to Bordeaux.

Before we abandon Bordeaux and the south, however, allow me to return to the question about what Hölderlin was working on during his four months there. There is good evidence that he borrowed a volume or two of Sophocles' tragedies from Consul Meyer's library—Hölderlin possessed an older and less reliable edition of his own back in Nürtingen—and that he worked on a translation of *Oedipus the King* (which he preferred to take literally as *Oedipus the Tyrant*, τύραννος, not for political but for psychological reasons, Oedipus being the man who is tyrannized by his need to know his origins) and *Antigone*. Translation of classic texts, especially from the Greek, had always been an important part of his life as a poet. He affirmed his friend Neuffer's fondness for translation by calling it "healthy calisthenics

134 / Struck by Apollo

for language," noting that translation, seeking as it does to capture "foreign beauty and grandeur" and even "making do with foreign caprices," makes one's own language more elastic, more flexible (CHV 2:538). Yet he cautions his friend that the so-called target language, the language *into which* one is translating, has to remain the focus: "Language is the organ of *our* head, *our* heart; it is a sign of *our* fancies, *our* ideas; it must hearken to *us*" (ibid.). Too much translating causes one's own spirit to forfeit its freedom of expression. It is therefore an activity to be engaged in only from time to time. *Es ist recht ein Geschäft zu seiner Zeit* (ibid.). Translation is therefore like philosophy and theoretical work in general, a kind of hospital stay for the poet, sometimes necessary, often salubrious. Yet one would not want to spend one's entire life in a hospital.

When in 1795 Schiller asked Hölderlin to do a verse translation of Ovid's *Phaëton*, Hölderlin was enthusiastic, even after the work was completed (CHV 2:583). When Schiller criticized the work and declined to publish it in his "almanac," however, Hölderlin was not only upset about the refusal but also reversed his own judgment concerning the quality of his work. It was a foolish project, he says, and the result is an embarrassment to him. By contrast, the Sophocles translation seems to be an apt activity for the Bordeaux stay, since he feels that the south of France is bringing him closer to Greece—closer to the very *physis* of Greece, one might say—than he has ever been before or ever will be again in his life.

Translations with commentary, principally from the Greek (Homer, Pindar, Sophocles), had also been a vital part of Hölderlin's plans for his illfated journal, *Iduna*, in 1799. Hölderlin scholars agree that during his four months in Bordeaux the translation of *Oedipus the Tyrant* was his principal occupation, once his tutoring obligations were fulfilled.[9] Sattler estimates that Hölderlin completed two-thirds of that play, along with all the choral odes of *Antigone*, by the time he left Bordeaux. We recall that before leaving for France, Hölderlin had confessed the need to find what is *lebendig*, "lively" or "vital," in poetry; this is the word he also uses some years later, in 1803, when describing the final stage of his work on the Sophocles translations. We may suppose that he is seeking "liveliness" in his translations so that his contemporaries might gain a "living" sense of the Sophoclean tragedies. Such vitality has something to do with his discovery in the south of France of what he called, perhaps unexpectedly, the Greek "heroic body." That "body"

---

9. For a detailed discussion, see David Farrell Krell, *The Tragic Absolute: German Idealism and the Languishing of God* (Bloomington: Indiana University Press, 2005), chapter 8, esp. 250–63.

"Its Floor Is the Sea" / 135

had to incorporate "fire from heaven," but it also needed to protect itself against excessive exposure to celestial fire. Perhaps we may anticipate here some strange words from the second letter to Böhlendorff, written after his return from Bordeaux, where he speaks of the particular beauty of the men and women that he met in southern France:

> The overwhelming element, fire from heaven, and the tranquillity of the human beings, their life in nature, their modest lives, their contentment, constantly gripped me, and I can very well say of myself what they say of heroes, namely, that Apollo struck me. . . .
>
> The athletic quality of southerly humanity, seen in the ruins of the spirit of antiquity, made me more familiar with the authentic essence of the Greeks; I came to know their nature and their wisdom, their bodies, the way they grew up in their climate and the rule by which they protected their enthusiastic genius from the overwhelming element.
>
> This is what constituted their sociability [*ihre Popularität*], the way they adapted themselves to foreign natures and communicated with them; that is why they have their peculiar individuality, which seems so full of life, inasmuch as supreme understanding in the Greek sense is a force of reflection, and this becomes comprehensible to us when we grasp the heroic body of the Greeks. It is tenderness, as in the quality of our own sociability. (CHV 2:921)

So much is odd and unexpected about these words! "Fire from heaven," which is the element in which every "tragic ode" originates and proceeds, does not make the southern peoples furious or even ardent, as we today always say it does. At least not preeminently. Hölderlin notes their *Stille*, the contentment they manifest in their life with nature, and their *Eingeschrenktheit* (*sic*), which normally would be an insult: the word suggests a phlegmatic or "narrow" or "limited" character, even a reduced intelligence, a simplicity to the point of simplemindedness. Yet this is clearly not what Hölderlin means, because he says that the "force of reflection" defines their intelligence, even if (or precisely because) their wisdom resides in their bodies, and their bodies know both how to receive illumination and when to protect themselves from the blaze. Thus he does not mean that the southern peoples are dull-witted; they are possessed, rather, of an enthusiastic genius—they are precisely *lively*. Their liveliness also seems to have to do with their ability to accept foreign

136 / Struck by Apollo

peoples, even quite alien natures, to communicate with them and adapt themselves to them. One might think of the Aeschylus who is capable of writing *The Persian Women*, or of the Homer who can sing the praises of Hector rather than hectoring him. This quality of openness and generosity, this hospitality, is their *Popularität*. And they owe it to their "heroic body." And when is a body "heroic"? The unexpected answer: when it is *tender*. The heroic body of the Greeks, and presumably of other athletic, southerly peoples, is *Zärtlichkeit*, "tenderness."

Tenderness? Does this not upset the applecart of every concept of heroism? Is not the first requirement of heroism that one suppress tender feelings? Anyone who loves to cite Nietzsche's "Become hard!" does not immediately add the command "Become tender!" How many steps, courageous steps, one would have to take to think the two together, "heroism" and "tenderness"! One is put in mind of Nietzsche's words in *Ecce Homo* about the human being who has turned out well. He says that such a man or woman is "carved from a single piece of wood, wood that is at the same time hard, tender, and fragrant."[10] *Hart* and *zart*, although they rhyme perfectly, seem to be in contradiction with one another. Oak and balsam wood, acacia and white pine, thought together as a single piece of wood? *Zart* is not "soft," however, but "tender," "delicate." Recall Hölderlin's letter to his family after his arrival in Bordeaux: he says that the dangers and exertions of his journey have "tempered" him, made him more able to confront the uncertainties of the future. This at least is his hope. It is Nietzsche's hope as well, even though he recognizes that only the rarest human beings achieve both hardness and tenderness. The two thinkers realize that such an achievement has more to do with the body than with brave talk and that the body is exposed to its own challenges, of which we clever folk know next to nothing.

Could it be that the "heroic body" Hölderlin is speaking of enjoys an essential intimacy with the sea, the sea he has so recently encountered? True, there are seas at both the North and South poles, so that the "southerly peoples" must be distinguished from the Vikings in some other way. Yet Hölderlin has no experience of the North Sea. For him the sea of his imagination is that of the Corinthian isthmus where the Mediterranean and the

---

10. Friedrich Nietzsche, *Ecce homo*, in *Kritische Studienausgabe der Werke*, 15 vols., ed. Giorgio Colli and Mazzino Montinari (Berlin and Munich: W. de Gruyter and Deutscher Taschenbuch Verlag, 1980), 6:267. Cited henceforth as KSW with volume and page. My thanks to Lauren Smith of Yale and Brown Universities for the reference and our conversation about it.

Aegean (almost) meet. And now the sea of his perception is the Atlantic. Yet the Atlantic, as one heads south along the coast of the European continent, has to do with Provence or Spain, or at least with Gascogne and Languedoc, even if Hölderlin goes no farther south than Bordeaux. The tenderness of the Greek heroic body and the sea? This would be Achilles weeping on the shore, lamenting to his mother the loss of his beloved Briseïs. So much could be thought and said about this, though all of it highly speculative.[11]

An instant ago I mentioned Corinth. The Corinthian ships are mentioned in "The Wine God," indeed in the stanza we have now to read, the sixth. Hölderlin has just mentioned the poet's crisis, the crisis that comes when words must be found to celebrate the coming gods, words that have to blossom as naturally as flowers in May. Yet how are those words to be nurtured in Hölderlin's own impoverished times? He says of the challenged poet:

And now he thinks to honor earnestly the blessed gods
    Everything must sing their praise truly and in deed.
Nothing dare come to light that does not please their majesty,
    In the face of Aither vain attempts will not avail.
To stand then worthy in the presence of the heavenly ones
    The nations found among themselves their splendid cults
And build their splendid cities and their temples on firm
    Foundations, and nobly these will rise on cliffsides at the sea—
But where? where bloom the ones we know as festive crowns?
    Thebes withers, and Athens; do weapons no more clash
In Olympia, no golden chariots run the race,
    And do garlands no longer deck the ships of Corinth?
Why have they too gone silent, the ancient holy theaters?
    Why does no one take joy in the sacred dance?
Why does no god mark the human brow as once they did,
    Impressing their seal, as once they did, on the one thus struck?
Or did he himself come and take on human form,
    Completing and closing consolingly the heavenly feast?

(CHV 1:317)

---

11. Allow me to mention two recent books of mine where the weeping Achilles is discussed: *The Sea: A Philosophical Encounter* (London: Bloomsbury Press, 2019), especially 210, 239–42, and 284–85; and *The Cudgel and the Caress: Reflections on Cruelty and Tenderness* (Albany: State University of New York Press, 2019), especially chapter 2, "Homer's *Iliad*, Hölderlin's *Briseiad*."

138 / Struck by Apollo

The answer to that startling final question remains suspended for Hölderlin's entire lifetime. In any case, the consolation does not work for him, has never worked for him. Like his youthful friend Schelling, Hölderlin insists on a *company* of gods—what Schelling calls the *socii* and the *dii consentes*, the panoply of deities who live and die together. And like his friend, Hölderlin finds the wine god, Dionysos, to be at the center of that greater mystery we call polytheism. In the seventh stanza there is specific mention of the wine god, even if the stanza begins with a sense of melancholy and irretrievable loss. The poet cries out to his old friend Wilhelm Heinse, to whom the poem is dedicated:

> But my friend! we come too late; true, the gods live,
> But over our heads, up there in another world.
> Endlessly they do their deeds and seem to heed us very little,
> Whether we live, though the heavenly ones do safeguard us.
> For a weak vessel cannot always contain them;
> Only now and then can humankind bear divine cornucopia.
> Then our life is but a dream of them. Yet our confusion now
> Helps us as sleep helps us, as need and night invigorate us
> Until heroes grow strong in their iron cradles, heroes
> Forceful of heart, as once they were, akin to heavenly ones.
> They come thunderingly. In the meantime, I often think,
> Better to sleep than to be this way, bereft of comrades,
> To hold out and what to do in the meantime and what to say
> I do not know, and why poets at all in a destitute time?
> But they are, you tell me, like the wine god's holy priests,
> Who wandered from land to land in holy night.
> (CHV 1:317–18)

It is perhaps important to add a word about the "friend" to whom the poem *Der Weingott* is addressed in this stanza and to whom the whole is dedicated, even in the later versions that bear the title *Brot und Wein*. "Heinze" is Johann Jakob Wilhelm Heinse (Heintze, Heinze), author of *Ardinghello and the Isles of the Blessed* (1787). He was twenty-five years Hölderlin's senior and doubtless a father figure to him. Their most important connection involved Susette. For when Hölderlin traveled with Susette and her children to Kassel and Bad Driburg, where Susette and the poet declared their love for one another, they were joined and accompanied by Heinse. Heinse himself, a disciple of Christoph Martin Wieland, surely encouraged—if one may put it this way—the erotic, sensual component

"Its Floor Is the Sea" / 139

of their love. He was therefore the ideal chaperon from the lovers' point of view, and it is safe to say that Hölderlin remembered Heinse with the most profound gratitude. In *Der Weingott* it is his friend Heinse who tells the despairing poet that the priests of Dionysos, like the poet himself, were for long periods of time nocturnal drifters, refugees wandering by night, carrying the message of the wine god from nation to nation and facing violent resistance and persecution everywhere. Where did they originate? In the Indus Valley, or perhaps farther east on the banks of the Ganges, Hölderlin tells us in other poems—although now he might add, after a pause and with a slight smile, perhaps also in the West Indies.

Before the wine god carried us off, we were talking about Hölderlin's translations of Sophocles, which the poet worked on during those four months in Bordeaux and for two more years after his homecoming. Are there remnants of Bordeaux in these translations and the notes appended to them? It is perhaps foolish to look for direct references or even allusions to places and persons in the translations. Perhaps our only strategy should be to highlight the liveliest of those lively translations that Hölderlin was seeking during these years, even though this too is highly speculative.

It may be that what is liveliest, as we arguably learn from Hölderlin's notes, is his decision to read Sophocles from the perspective of a theater director or dramaturge rather than that of a scholar, if one may put it this way. For Hölderlin becomes keenly alert to the pace and "velocity" of the scenes in *Oedipus the Tyrant* and *Antigone*. As he is translating, it seems he is also blocking off the scenes as a director does, trying to calculate the impact of their performance on the stage. Perhaps this is something that his own *Death of Empedocles* was missing; one very gifted reader of *Der Tod des Empedokles*, the late Philippe Lacoue-Labarthe, says that Hölderlin's earlier mourning play is more like an oratorio than a piece for the theater.[12] We know that Hölderlin dreamed of having Goethe produce the play for the stage at Weimar, although this never came to pass. Perhaps what Hölderlin was learning from Sophocles was what Lacoue calls *theatrality*—which is something other than "theatricality." If that is the case, then the liveliness of Sophocles' plays may not come through when we merely read their scripts—even in Hölderlin's lively translations. But let us try.

One of the last changes Hölderlin made to his translations, in 1803, many months after his return from Bordeaux, was his transformation of the names of the gods into epithets that he hoped his contemporaries might

---

12. Philippe Lacoue-Labarthe, *Métaphrasis* (Paris: Presses Universitaires de France, 1998), 52.

140 / Struck by Apollo

comprehend. He called Demeter "the Impenetrable," which seems strange, since, as the famous second choral ode of *Antigone* tells us, human beings scratch the surface of the earth constantly with their shovels and their plows. It may be that Hölderlin wants to caution the overconfident humans, however; no matter how much they displace and offend the earth of Earth, there is something about divine nature that resists penetration and mastery. Hölderlin called Zeus, known to the Romans as Zeus-Pater, literally "Jupiter," not merely "the father" and not simply "Aither" (the upper air) but "the father of Time or the Earth." Volumes could be written about the association of time with earth, or with planet Earth. As for time itself, Hölderlin's translation of *Antigone* transforms some lines of the fifth choral ode, which invokes Zeus's love of Danaë. Instead of having Zeus bathe her in a shower of gold, as the most familiar forms of the myth relate, Hölderlin reverses the situation and has Zeus himself submitting to the time that is marked by his passion for Danaë:

> Sie zählete dem Vater der Zeit
> Die Stundenschläge, die goldnen.

> She counted off for the father of time
> The strokes of the hours, the golden strokes.[13]

She counted off the hours for the father of time. Ask not, therefore, for whom the strokes of those hours toll a death knell. Heinrich von Kleist, in his *Amphitryon*, showed that he too understood this fragility of the enamored god. Victorious in his conquest of Amphitryon's wife Alkmene, but only because he transformed himself into a perfect replica of her husband, Zeus the victor finds himself ultimately defeated by the woman's love, since it is her love for her husband, not for him. The final word of Kleist's play is Zeus's sigh of defeat, "Ach!" Time, Hölderlin notes, is counted best in suffering or in passion, *im Leiden* (CHV 2:372), and that means in Zeus's final "Ah!" to both Alkmene and Danaë. Indeed, Hölderlin's translation of Sophocles' lines is one manifestation of his growing insight, from around the time he is in Bordeaux, that the gods are ineluctably drawn to the Earth—to the abyss, as "Die Nymphe" puts it—and thus to mortality.

---

13. CHV 2:353; ll. 987–88. Hölderlin himself, in his "Notes on *Antigone*," points to this "mistranslation" of his, explaining that it was intended to make Sophocles more comprehensible and more deeply *felt* by his Hesperian contemporaries: see CHV 2:372.

In the *Homburger Folioheft* a strange notation appears in French in the margin of a page devoted to "The Next Best": *apoll envers terre* (CHV 1:421). Here, it is Apollo, one of the sons of the father of Time or the Earth (Dionysos is the other son), who returns inexorably to Earth, as though the heavenly ones too must cling precisely to what is closest to the abyss, and as though the "next best," as Silenos taught, is mortality itself. Hölderlin's *Der Rhein* adds that the celestials feel nothing of themselves; apparently, as "The Nymph" says, the gods need what dwells close to the mortal abyss so that they may feel anything at all. Apollo's descent toward the neighborhood of the earth therefore echoes Hölderlin's notes on *Antigone*, in which the poet observes that "the more proper Zeus" is called back from his ascensional trajectory, diverted from any and every world "beyond." Zeus and his sons are instead "compelled more decisively to Earth" (CHV 2:374). Perhaps this forced descent of deities to the Earth, their submission to mortality, is what Hölderlin saw in those funeral masks at Lugdunum or in the reliefs of Silenos, Dionysos, and Ariadne that decorate the ancient sarcophagi. And perhaps something of that new mix of sensuality and mortality—something quite different from the usual Pietist Christian stories, even if the annointed one too is condemned like Dionysos to die on wood—was gaining force during his time in Bordeaux, which was time spent with Sophocles.

As for *Oedipus the Tyrant*, the story of this exceptional family, the story that in our time has arguably become the universal family story, let me mention only a few moments early in the play that must have struck Hölderlin with particularly lively force. He would have noticed that Tiresias occupies the position of Silenos: Midas and Oedipus compel Silenos and Tiresias to reveal the truth, even though the latter pair warn their inquisitors that it would be best for them not to know. The "wisdom of Silenos," as I mentioned earlier, had impressed Hölderlin enough that he made it the epigraph to the second volume of his *Hyperion*. It is Oedipus's "insane quest for consciousness" that intrigues Hölderlin throughout the play. One line in Tiresias's response to Oedipus is notable for its cryptic and clipped style, the style of so much of Hölderlin's work after Bordeaux (CHV 2:265, l. 420): "*Weisst du, woher du bist? du bist geheim. . . .*"—"Do you know where you come from? you are secretly. . . ." Now, this last word, *geheim*, through *enjambement* with the next line, connects directly with the word *verhasst*, "you are secretly hated." Oedipus is secretly hated by his own family members, both those still on the surface of the earth, his mother, and those below, his murdered father. That is the initial sense of the passage. Yet the German *geheim*, translating the Greek λέληθας, "concealed, hidden,

142 / Struck by Apollo

forgotten," has a mysterious relation to the "home," *Heim*, and even to what is unhomelike or unfamiliar and uncanny in and about the home. In this one line, under intense compression, Hölderlin's Sophocles enables Tiresias to tell the entire story. Hölderlin is expert at bringing all the Sophoclean ironies home in the most concise and compelling words.

Near the end of the third choral ode, the Theban elder who leads the chorus says something that Hölderlin himself had been saying to himself quite recently. Why poets at all in an impoverished time? The old man of Thebes says, τί δεῖ με χορεύειν; "*Was soll ich singen?*"—"What should I be singing?" (l. 918). Hölderlin's situation at this point in his life is uncannily close to that of an old man in plague-ridden Thebes. If Bordeaux is enhancing his own vitality after the bitterness and exhaustion of recent months in Germany, and it is, that enhancement comes in the midst of a long night. Why? The last line of the choral ode says it with incredible force: ἔρρει δὲ τὰ θέα, "God's service perishes," or "Faith grows cold," as some translate the Greek. Hölderlin is quite literal: "*Unglücklich aber gehet das Göttliche.*"— "Yet deity wanders in misfortune," or "Deity is unhappily adrift." That could be a line from one of Hölderlin's own late hymns.

Allow me one word more. At the midpoint of the play comes the decisive confrontation between Oedipus and Jocasta. The mother and wife of the king whose craving to know his origins tyrannizes him seems herself now to know what would be best for this mortal, her son and husband, not to know. Oedipus believes that Polybus, in reality his stepfather, has died of natural causes, so that Oedipus is blameless of his ostensible father's death. The Delphic oracle must have been mistaken—Oedipus has not slain his father. Yet his mother is still alive. Oedipus confesses that earlier on he was "seduced by fear," the fear that he might be a parricide. Only one thing now seduces him further, the frightening possibility that he will sleep with his mother. Jocasta tells him not to take that possibility—or reality—to heart. Oedipus: "What? should I not also fear my mother's bed?" Jocasta replies in words that will reverberate down through the ages all the way to the twentieth century and well beyond:

> For what does a human being have to fear if his luck
> Holds? There is no clear presentiment of anything at all.
> To live straight ahead, as well as you can,
> That is best. Do not fear wedding
> Your mother! For oftentimes
> In dreams a mortal has slept with

His own mother: yet when he takes this to be
Nothing at all, he can most readily bear life.
(CHV 2:287; ll. 1000–7)

After even the brief sketch I have given of Hölderlin's difficult mother, and his trying relationship with her—and even if she is now a thousand kilometers distant, out of sight if not out of mind—I dare not comment on Jocasta's words. Except perhaps to suggest that the mother—and it may be the mother who is Susette, the mother of her own four children but perhaps also of the interloper poet—is trying to seduce Oedipus away from his second and perhaps more crippling fear, trying, as Nietzsche would say, to seduce him back into life.

An infinite number of further things might be said about Hölderlin's translations of the tragedies of Sophocles as the main task of the Bordeaux months. Yet this is not the place to say anything more about them. It is time to get underway again, this time heading for home—no matter how unhomelike that homecoming may be for Hölderlin.

Photo 44. If Hölderlin indeed passed through Chartres and Versailles, then he surely saw this scrivener on the north side of Chartres cathedral.

4

The Journey Back

In a moment we will look at the maps, but here at the outset is a glance at Hölderlin's route homeward, as Bertheau calculates it—and he calculates it differently than every other commentator on Hölderlin's travels. From Bordeaux, Hölderlin journeys by ship down the Garonne and the Gironde to Soulac-sur-Mer and Pointe de Grave on the Atlantic coast. Then, by ferry, he crosses the wide mouth of the Gironde to the town of Royan on the mainland. At Royan he takes the post-coach heading northeast—once again it is the less expensive, economy class coach—to Saintes and then farther north to Niort. From there he travels, not east to Poitiers, as has always been assumed but, heading due north through the less populated Charente region, to Chinon.

To my astonishment, the 1812 map shows not a single post-coach route through the Charente territory, so that Joe and I were at first skeptical about Bertheau's calculation. However, it became clear that the map shows only the main postal routes, not all of them, so that we made our peace with Bertheau's itinerary and followed it. (After our journey, I discovered a post-coach map from 1783 that shows a new route opening up this relatively uncharted territory.) At some unknown point during Hölderlin's trip through the Charente and Vendée regions, according to Bertheau, Hölderlin's post-coach was robbed. Possibly, after the robbery, Hölderlin, without a sou to his name, traveled the rest of the way home by foot—yet the timeframe for journey back makes this seem unlikely.

From Chinon he travels northeast, following the Loire Valley to Tours, Blois, and Orléans; he then heads due north to Paris and its Louvre. After a visit of two or three days in the Louvre, he heads eastward, passing perhaps through St.-Dizier, Metz, and Nancy to Strasbourg. There we lose sight of him for two or three weeks, until suddenly he arrives in Stuttgart—where his friends do not recognize him.

146 / Struck by Apollo

Joe and I did not travel by ship down the Gironde, even though sightseeing boats now ply the river, but we drove along its northern bank through Bourg and Blaye, stopping to visit some of the magnificent châteaux along the river, all the way to Royan—the port city at which Hölderlin would have arrived by ferry (see map 11). We walked to the docks, where the ferry to Pointe de Grave and back to Royan still runs and looked across the stretch of bay to the Pointe. We then made our way north to Saintes, Niort, St. Jean d'Angelay, and Parthenay. It is somewhere along the later part of this segment that, according to Bertheau, highwaymen held up Hölderlin's post-coach. He would have lost not only his pistol but also his travel money and all his wages, unless he had been clever enough to stash some of it where the robbers could not find it. Upon reflection, it seems likely that they did not take everything, inasmuch as the twenty-eight-day timeframe for the homeward journey suggests that he must have continued taking coaches or at worst hitching rides—he could never have made the trip home by foot in that amount of time, it seemed to us, because it would have required him to walk well over thirty kilometers a day. In any case, at either Parthenay or Chinon, Hölderlin would have headed east toward

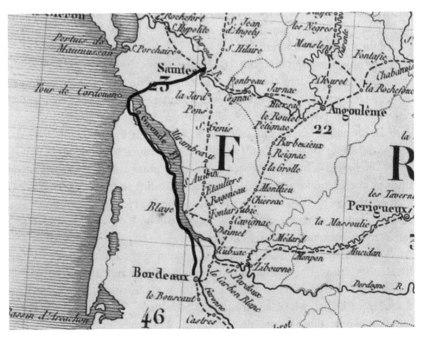

Map 11. Bordeaux-Saintes.

Tours. Joe and I did the same. We were eager to find Joué-les-Tours, now a suburb south of Tours, where Bertheau's most astonishing surmise about Hölderlin's trip home unfolds. That is a long story, and we will get to it after a few words about the earlier portion of the trip.

From Royan, Joe and I took the national road N 150 through St. Sulpice-de-Royan, Saujon, St. Romain-de-Benet, Pisany, Pessines, Luchat, Varzay, and Les Gonds, to Saintes. (The 1812 map does not show any routes connecting Royan and Saintes, but Bertheau assures us that there was such a route, albeit not an *express* one—and, to repeat, it is likely that the 1812 map shows only the major routes.) We were now in the Charente region of France, and the spruces of the Bordeaux forests and flatlands had given way to deciduous trees and rolling hills. We were leaving the region of Dionysos and entering that of Demeter.

At Saintes we found the magnificent church of the town, dedicated to Saint Eutrope, which has a history stretching back at least to the third, and perhaps to the first, century. Legend has it that Saint Peter himself dispatched Eutrope to southern France to convert the Gauls. There he lived in a hovel, and after his martyrdom in 122, there he was buried. A small wooden church was built over his grave; in the sixth century a Merovingian basilica replaced the church. After the Norman invaders destroyed the basilica in the ninth century, Cluny monks organized the construction of the present church between 1080 and 1096. There was something about the simplicity of the church's interior that reflected its legendary antiquity, which surely would have impressed the poet.

Yet the chief reason for Hölderlin's choosing to return home by way of Saintes was not St. Eutrope. One may be confident that Hölderlin visited the Roman ruins at Saintes. They lie not far from the Charente River: a large *circus*, that is, an amphitheater for gladiatorial games, with its grand entry gate, "the triumphal arch of Germanicus," and, at the opposite end of the oval-shaped arena, the exit through which the dead animals and humans—many more animals than humans—were removed. It is difficult to know how much of the site had been excavated by Hölderlin's time; certainly, a great deal of uncovering and restoration occurred in the nineteenth and twentieth centuries. Yet if indeed he did see it, this site would have been second only to Lugdunum as far as ancient Roman sites are concerned. Saintes itself was an active Roman town by 27 BCE. Its enormous arena, which held from twelve to fifteen thousand spectators, was built between 40 and 50 of the current era. It was strange to stand in the ancient Roman arena and to see the spire of the basilica of St. Eutrope, in reality hundreds of meters distant, seeming to emerge out of the ancient stones, as though two very different Occidental cultures were springing up simultaneously from the immemorial earth (photo 45).

From Saintes we drove due north on the N 150 and D 650 through St. Hilaire, St. Jean d'Angely, St. Denis du Pin, Loulay, and Villeneuve la Comtesse, three of these towns appearing also on the 1812 map, toward Niort (see map 12). At La Croix Comtesse we stopped to photograph a beautiful Romanesque church rising out of the endless wheat fields. The N 150 then became one of those straight roads lined on both sides by plane trees, the sort of road that used to be quite common in France; the boughs of the plane trees or, more rarely, lime trees, eventually meet at mid-road, their branches intertwining as a shady arcade or bower over the traffic below. We passed through the farm towns of Prissé and Beauvoir-sur-Niort, crossing the river that gives the larger town of Niort its name.

Photo 45. The cathedral at Saintes appears to be rising out of the ruins of the Roman arena.

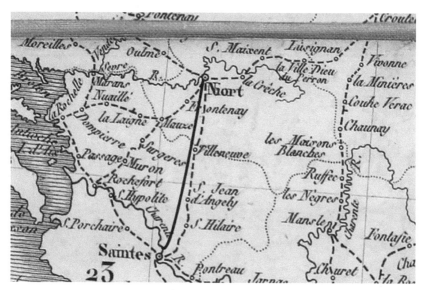

Map 12. Saintes-Niort.

The names of the towns were occasionally very strange, perhaps the result of shifting dialects—Granzay-Gript, Cherve, Niort. On this homeward journey the names generally seemed odder than the names we saw on our winter journey to Bordeaux, if that makes any sense at all; as we passed through the towns, the names themselves had a hypnotic effect on us. So many particular places there are in the world, so many of them peculiarly named, each name having its peculiar story, and each place containing particular people with their peculiar stories. One by one, either on foot or in the post-coach that Hölderlin may still have had access to, he passed through these villages and towns as we were passing through them now. I wondered whether Hölderlin experienced this same hypnotic effect of the succession of names. Certainly, when we read his lists of names of persons and places in the *Homburger Folioheft*, along with all the scattered words and phrases we find there, the parataxis seems to have this same mesmerizing effect. Whereas syntax weaves nouns and verbs together into propositions that make sense of our experience and enable us to move purposefully through the world, the names themselves, when isolated and insulated, one falling after another, reduce us to something like reverie, or perhaps childish babble.

From Niort we continued north on the D 743 and D 938, rather than heading east toward Poitiers (see map 13). As the emptiness of the

150 / Struck by Apollo

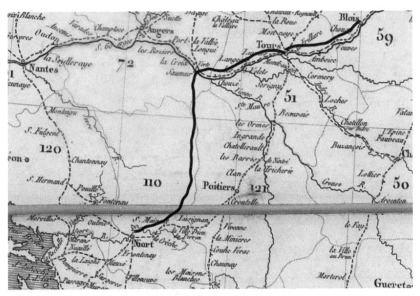

Map 13. Niort-Blois.

1812 map suggests, this region of farmland is one of the least populated areas of France. The reverie or hypnosis produced by the names, which were just short of nonsense syllables, did not stop until we reached the town of Parthenay, that is, Parthenay-sur-le-Thouet, a beautiful medieval village about a third of the way from Niort to Chinon (photo 46). The town boasts of its importance as a stopover on the "alternate route" to Santiago de Compostela. But that alternate route was not the secret of its charm for us. Rather, it was the old walls bursting with red flowers, the church tower high on the hill, and the lazy river, muddy brown, bridged by an old arch that seemed as old as Rome. Just outside the walls of the town we found a second pilgrimage church in the Romanesque style, St. Pierre, built in 1092. The church was locked—a note on the door told us that one had to ring at the sacristan's house to get the key—and so we merely walked about its exterior and enjoyed the weathered gray stones spotted with green and orange lichens. All was quiet except for the doves and crows that shared the tower. For reasons we could not fathom, the tranquil town of Parthenay remained in Joe's and my memories of the trip, if only for the peace and quiet of the place, the silence of its lazy river and its high hills. One could imagine Hölderlin charmed by the place (photo 47).

Photo 46. Parthenay-sur-le-Thouet, north of Niort in Nouvelle-Aquitaine, where the post-coach map of 1812 shows mostly empty space.

Photo 47. A Romanesque church dating from 1092, St. Pierre-de-Vieux-Parthenay, stands atop the oldest part of the town.

152 / Struck by Apollo

After Parthenay we continued north on the D 938 toward Thouars. The early June sun was already hot as we drove through the seemingly endless series of grain fields and farm hamlets. Again, the hypnotic effect of the names: Viennay, Lageon, St. Loup-sur-Thouet (a novena to Saint Wolf, anyone?), Lamaucarrière, Boullé, Soussigny, Airvault, St. Varent, St. Rouin de Marne, and St. Généroux, where we ate a generous lunch in the shade of a cemetery wall.

At St.-Jean-de-Thouars, the D 759 took us northeast to Chinon by way of even more wheat fields dotted with small villages. We traveled through Pas-de-Jeu, which means either there is no game in town or one can skip gaily through it, past the Château de Oiron, entering now the Department of the Vienne and driving through Curçay-sur-Dive, Loudun, and Beuxes. Beuxes has a lovely carp pond that mists over in the mornings, anticipating those haunting canvases by Claude Monet. We continued through Marçay and La Roche-Clermault, crossing the Vienne River once again and entering the fortified town of Chinon. To repeat, if the robbery story has merit, then Hölderlin by this time may have been on foot, wandering across the relatively flat terrain to Chinon and the Loire Valley, where the hills begin again.

After wandering about the walls of the impressive fortifications at Chinon, Joe and I followed the D 751 through rolling and thickly forested hills: St. Benoît-la-Forêt, Azay le Rideau, Ballan-Miré, to Joué-les-Tours. Bertheau devotes many pages to this last-named site, Joué, because it involves a story that most Hölderlin scholars have rejected as pure fiction. Bertheau himself tries to show, by way of a minute analysis, that the story may well be true. Here it is.

The poet and political activist Moritz Hartmann, banished from the German lands after the failed 1848 revolutions and finding asylum in France, recounts Hölderlin's supposed visit to Joué. In an article published in 1861, "A Surmise," *Eine Vermuthung*, he records a tale told him nine years earlier by a seventy-five-year-old woman. Hartmann, during his travels to Tours and Blois, south of Paris, came into contact with this elderly woman, an aristocrat from Joué, who married into a family from Blois. She tells him about an unnamed German wanderer's visit to her father's château in late spring 1802, when the old woman herself was a girl of fifteen.[1]

---

1. Moritz Hartmann's *Eine Vermuthung* appears in the first number of the beautifully illustrated and printed journal, *Freya: Illustrated Pages for Germany's Women and Girls* (Stuttgart: Krais und Hoffmann, 1861), 105–9. Bertheau (155–61) isolates no fewer than twenty preconditions for the truth of the story and, relying on his own archival detective work, which is truly impressive, he manages to convince us that the story could well be true. I will cite Hartmann by MH and page number of the journal *Freya* in what follows.

The Journey Back / 153

Madame Salaberry, for so she is called, begins by complimenting Hartmann, who is the first German she has ever met who is not somehow *odd*, not a creature of fancy and fantasy. Hartmann believes that she is confusing him with E. T. A. Hoffmann, whose fantastic *Night Tales* she may well have read in French translation, tales that may have convinced her that all Germans are simply strange. She replies that her lifelong impression concerning the oddness of the Germans was formed not by Hoffmann but by an uncanny and fascinating man, *einen merkwürdigen Deutschen*, whom she met when she was fifteen. Here is what the old woman tells Hartmann:

> It was at the beginning of this century, about fifty years ago. I lived here [rather, Hartmann corrects her, not "here" but at the Château la Rabière in Joué-les-Tours] with my father, when I was a child of fourteen or fifteen years. One day I was out on the balcony, and I noticed a man who appeared to be wandering aimlessly about in the fields down below, often abandoning the path and seeming to have no particular goal in mind. He returned repeatedly to the point from which he had started, without seeming to notice the fact. That afternoon, as I was taking a walk, our paths crossed. But he was deep in thought, and he passed me by without really seeing me. A few minutes later, at a turn in the path, we met again; he was gazing into the distance with a look of inexpressible longing. If I had encountered anyone else like this, I would have run home in terror and hid behind my father—I was a silly girl back then. But this stranger filled me with a kind of compassion that I could not explain to myself. It was not pity for some poor fellow in need of help, although his outer appearance showed that he well enough needed help, since his clothes were in disarray, soiled, and even torn here and there. Rather, his face bore a noble expression of pain; he looked as though his spirit was off somewhere else, lingering with persons far away whom he loved. That look filled the heart of a young girl with compassion and sympathy. Come evening, I told my father about the stranger. He said it must be one of the many prisoners of war or political prisoners that in those days were allowed to roam at least half free, as though out on bail, in the French provinces. (MH 106–7)

One begins to suspect that the tale may be a fiction after all, since it seems to project back onto an earlier period the confused state in which Hölderlin spent his final decades. Yet if we are to believe the account by Hölderlin's

154 / Struck by Apollo

friend Matthison, the poet was precisely in such a bedraggled and befuddled state when he arrived in Stuttgart a month later. What one cannot judge is whether the ostensible robbery had a jarring effect on his state of mind or whether such confusion began to prevail even during his days in Bordeaux. That might explain both his early departure from his post and Meyer's kindness and generosity toward him even as Hölderlin was leaving his employment. We may therefore hold our suspicions in check and allow Hartmann to continue with Madame Salaberry's story.

The disoriented stranger now enters the park that surrounds her father's château. He is drawn to a large pond bordered by a balustrade on which twenty-four statues of gods and goddesses from Greek and Roman antiquity have been placed. All are copies, to be sure, some of them large, some small, some from Roman workshops, others copies made in France during the sixteenth century. In the center of the pond stands a statue of Neptune by Giovanni da Bologna.[2] Hölderlin (presuming it is he) hurries now toward the statues, his arms raised high as though in benediction or supplication. He appears to be muttering something, but he is too far away to be heard. The girl and her father observe the stranger from the house, noting that he pauses for a long time in front of the most beautiful statue. He seems to be familiar with these deities. "He's quite an original!" murmurs the girl's father.

At that point a watchman tells the stranger that he is on private property and has to leave. The stranger smiles and ignores him, moving on to the next statue. The guard begins to shout—to no effect. He grabs the stranger by the arm, to escort him off the premises. At that point the girl's father, the master of Château la Rabière, rushes from the house. He tells the watchman to let the stranger be; he may spend as much time as he likes in the park. At all events, the stranger seems unaffected by the watchman's scoldings, as he turns and smiles at the owner. "The gods do not belong to any particular human being. They belong to the world. And when they smile upon us, we belong to them."

The owner, and presumably the daughter too, are standing close to the most striking statue, the one before which the stranger has paused a moment earlier. The stranger continues to speak. "Observe this Aglaia: see how she smiles at me and holds me captive. She does not smile upon her possessor alone."

---

2. Giambologna (1529–1608), actually the Frenchman Jean Boulogne, is known to have carved sea horses for a fountain of Neptune in Florence. Whether he himself carved a *Neptune*, I have been unable to determine. Yet such a statue could conceivably have wound up at La Rabière.

The Journey Back / 155

The stranger's words show that he knows the story of Aglaia, the "glowing" or "brilliant" nymph, one of the three Graces. The master of La Rabière tells the stranger that he is mistaken, the statue is actually of Pomona, the ancient Roman goddess of the orchards, not Aglaia. The stranger does not hesitate to correct him. "No, it is an Aglaia," replies the stranger with an air of certainty, and he goes on to register a complaint. "The water here should be clearer, like the water of the Cephissus or the stream of Erechtheus on the Acropolis. To see them reflected as they are here, in a turbid mirror, is not worthy of the gods' own clarity—but," he sighs, "we are not in Greece."

"Are you perhaps a Greek?" asks the girl's father, half in jest.

"No! On the contrary, I'm a German," sighs the stranger.

"On the contrary?" the father repeats. "Is the German the contrary of the Greek?"

"Yes," answers the stranger perfunctorily, adding after a moment's pause, "We are all contraries: you, a Frenchman, are also a contrary, and so is the Englishman, your enemy. We are all such contraries!" (MH 107).

The old woman, the storyteller, interjects a remark, telling Hartmann that Hölderlin's French pronunciation was execrable—the young woman had to struggle to understand what he was saying. One should not be concerned that her judgment contradicts Bertheau's assurance, which we heard earlier, that Hölderlin's French was excellent. My own French friends constantly lament the state of my French, which they claim is incomprehensible, even though I know my pronunciation to be impeccable. But to return to the story. "This quite original man pleased us all very much," continues Madame Salaberry, who forgives him for his bad French and for quite a few other things. "He was not handsome, and he had aged badly, even though he must have been not much more than thirty. [Hölderlin had recently turned thirty-two.] His eyes glowed ardently, yet gently; his mouth was lively, yet mild. One could also tell that his frayed and worn clothing did not correspond to his class or his education. I was very happy when my father invited him into our house" (MH 108).

The stranger—shall we agree now to call him Hölderlin?—follows them into the house, chatting freely and from time to time placing his hand in a friendly way on the girl's head. "That frightened me a bit, but actually I quite liked it," she says. The stranger marches straightway to a sofa in the parlor, announces that he is tired, reclines, and immediately falls asleep.

"He's crazy!" whispers the girl's aunt, who has entered on the scene, but the father replies, "He's an original. I like him. He's a German."

After Hölderlin wakes up, the girl's father invites "the German" to stay for supper. Hölderlin particularly enjoys the wine, and he becomes quite

156 / Struck by Apollo

cheerful and voluble. He talks of Germany and of southern France, which are worlds apart. He speaks in inflated tones of the sea near Bordeaux. Occasionally he lapses into silence, as though afraid that his stories will take him back to an unpleasant episode in his life. Even the aunt becomes convinced that this is not a madman but an exceptional human being, a man with great depth of spirit. The aunt, a pious woman, cites some verses from the Bible and invites the stranger to comment on the doctrine of the immortality of the soul, but he ignores her references to Scripture. Instead, he says some very strange things, such as the following, which the girl later records in her aunt's album:

> Immortality is this: every good thing, every thing we think to be beautiful, becomes a tutelary spirit [*ein Genius*] that never abandons us. Such a spirit is invisible to us, but in the most beautiful of forms it accompanies us throughout our life to the very grave. It takes flight from our gravemound and ascends to join the host of spirits that fill the world and work to achieve the world's perfection and transfiguration. These tutelary spirits are the births, or, if you will, the portions of our soul, and in these portions alone is the soul immortal. The great artists have bequeathed to us in their works the images of their own *genii*, but these images are not the *genii* themselves. They are merely their mirroring in the hazy atmosphere of our Earth, the way the sun is mirrored in the sea—no, in the fog. The lovely gods of Greece are such images, images of the most beautiful thoughts of an entire people.—That's how it is with immortality. (Ibid.)

The girl's aunt now asks Hölderlin—the mysterious German stranger—whether he believes himself to be immortal in this way.

"Me?" he says curtly. "I who am sitting here before you? No! I no longer think beautifully [*Ich denke nicht mehr schön*]. The self that was mine ten years ago, that one is immortal—to be sure!"

Ten years earlier, Hölderlin (if it is he) had begun to sketch out his *Hyperion*, the two-volume novel that he may have regarded as his one truly successful work. In 1797 he had dedicated the second volume, discreetly of course, on the final page of the volume, to Susette: "To whom else but you?" The rest of his literary production had been scattered verses, an incomplete drama on Empedocles, and a translation of Sophocles not yet finished. A meager harvest. Or so, on bad days, he must have adjudged it.

The girl's father and her aunt suddenly realize that they know nothing about their guest—not even his name. When the father inquires, the stranger buries his face in his hands.

"I will tell you tomorrow," he says. "Believe me, sometimes it is difficult for me to remember my name."

This once again sounds suspiciously like an anticipation of those later years, when Hölderlin hides behind various names, especially when unexpected visitors arrive at the Tübingen Tower. Scardanelli and Buonarroti, we recall, are the two most common pseudonyms during those years when, to all appearances at least, *killalusimeno*. Yet Hartmann, if he is making all this up, is providing his readers with a narrative containing so many details that the tale has at least some verisimilitude. There has been enough pain in Hölderlin's recent life to cause his name to slip away from him.

The father and the aunt, perhaps doubting the man's sanity but recognizing the profundity of his spirit and the breadth of his knowledge, offer him lodging for the night—when the strangest part of the tale unfolds, so strange that for all its fantasticality (and it is a genuine "night tale" by Hoffmann) it rings true. At about one in the morning the household is awakened by cries for help from a servant who has returned from a tryst and is sneaking back into the house by way of a mansard window. Hölderlin, hearing the noise and thinking it might be a second robbery being perpetrated on him, leaps from his bed and grabs an ornamental sword that is hanging on his wall. Because he has no bathrobe, he wraps a sheet around himself and lurches down the hall, candle in his left hand, sword in his right, toward the place where the noise came from. At the sight of the specter the servant falls to the floor near the stairwell. He cries out, begging for his life. The master of the house, the aunt, and the daughter rush to the scene and are shocked at the sight of the avenging revenant in white. To the girl he looks like a Greek statue, if not so fine a one as Aglaia. The servant blurts out his story, the vengeful ghost relents, things settle down, and they all go back to sleep.

When the family rises the next morning, they see Hölderlin once again wandering through the park. The father suggests that they let him be; if he returns to the house, they will try to be of help to him: several of his friends are physicians. He tells the girl and her aunt to stop gazing out the window, to leave the man in peace. The stranger drifts off and is never seen again. A bit later in the day, the father searches for him, scouring the neighborhood on horseback, but the stranger is nowhere to be found.

158 / Struck by Apollo

Hartmann tells us that at the conclusion of the old woman's tale he informs her who the stranger may have been. She does not recognize the name, but after hearing Hartmann's account of the poet's life she insists that it must have been Hölderlin. Hartmann closes by asking, "Could it really have been he?" (MH 109).

The majority of Hölderlin scholars, led by Beck, reject the story as pure legend—and it is certainly true that Hölderlin, "the mad poet," has always attracted such legends. A number of novelists, today forgotten, have woven Hartmann's story into their own tales, as novelists will. Bertheau replies that all the details fit: it really could have been Hölderlin.

Joe and I drifted off the main road from Chinon and approached Tours from the south, parking our Hymercar in the parking lot at the Lycée Rabière, the local high school. As luck would have it, we entered the park on the very path that Hölderlin would have followed, at least if Hartmann's tale is true. We were able to reconstruct the way the area must have looked until, at some point in the mid-to-late nineteenth century, the château disappeared. How, when, and why the grand house vanished we were unable to learn. Yet the layout of the park and its large pond, the empty lot where the house once stood, the brick-work stable and hayloft, the vine-covered dovecot, and the cistern—still supplying water to park visitors—were all visible, as were the gigantic lime trees, or *Lindenbäume*, that graced the double avenue connecting the château with the park and its pond. We walked past massive moss-covered rocks, a typical element of the Romantic garden, and found our way to the large pond (photo 48). Ducks had in the meantime replaced Neptune and all the nymphs. No statues anywhere. Aglaia vanished. We circled the pond then ascended the double avenue toward the cleared space at the top, now a large sand and gravel area, a children's playground off to the left, a flower nursery off to the right, but no memorial plaque to tell us about the fate of the château. The name *Rabière* survives only because of the park, the pond, and the high school.

As we stood on the site of the vanished château, we studied the gigantic lime trees and wondered whether Hölderlin might have gazed on younger versions of those same trees. There is an old folk wisdom that says the *Linde* waxes for 300 years, stands firm for 300 years, and then wanes for 300 more years. Folks exaggerate, of course. Even so, we had to believe that these were Hölderlin's trees—or at least the disoriented stranger's trees, still concealing Greek dryads among their boughs, even if the pond no longer offered their turbid reflection. The eighth stanza of *Der Weingott* says:

Photo 48. The pond, now deprived of its statuary, at the Château Rabière in Joué-les-Tours.

>   It is this way: some time ago, and it seems long ago to us now,
>   They all came into ascendancy who were a blessing to our life;
>   When the Father averted his face from humankind
>   And when mourning rightly began to o'erspread the Earth,
>   When at last a genial spirit calmly appeared, offering heavenly
>   Consolation, announced the end of days and then vanished,
>   Leaving as a sign that he once was there and again would
>   Come, the heavenly host left a spray of gifts behind,
>   That we could take joy in them in a human way, how otherwise,
>   For to enjoy in spirit something greater was too great
>   For us humans, and even now we lack those strong enough
>   To bear supreme joy, although some gratitude quietly survives.
>   Bread is the fruit of the Earth, but also a gift of the light,
>   And from the god of thunder comes the joy of wine.

> Thus we too ponder the heavenly ones who once
>   Were here and who will return when the time is right;
> Thus singers sing him earnestly, sing the wine god, and
>   It is not idly conceived, this praise to the ancient one.
>   (CHV 1:318)

Reluctantly, Joe and I abandoned the ghosts of the Château la Rabière at Joué-les-Tours. We crossed the Cher and Loire rivers at Tours, turned right at St. Cyr-sur-Loire, and headed up the northern bank of the Loire. We passed through Rochecorbon and Vouvray, stopping only to marvel at the spectacular Château d'Amboise on the other side of the river. Passing through Veuves, we arrived at the medieval city of Blois, divided into southern and northern precincts by the wide Loire (photo 49).

We walked along the river to the magnificent bridge built in 1724 by the seemingly ubiquitous Jacques-Ange Gabriel. We mounted the steep streets and ornamental stairways toward the Bishop's Rose Garden, admiring the houses along the way—one a Renaissance house that announced, "new uses for old things," *usu vetera nova*, another with a bridge of sighs, others with fine old oaken doors, and one with a poor chap carved in wood who had the job of supporting the upper stories of the house on his aching back.

Photo 49. Beautiful Blois occupies both sides of the Loire River.

We headed northeast toward Orléans on a small road, the D 2152, passing through Menars, Fleury, Suèvres, Mer, Beaugency, Meung-sur-Loire, and Saint-Ay, in the region of Le Loiret (see map 14). We overnighted on the thickly wooded banks of the wide Loire in the nature reserve of St. Mesmin. At Orléans we did not fail to visit the cathedral, many times destroyed and rebuilt over the centuries, most famous, no doubt, because of the maid of Orléans Jeanne d'Arc. The façade of the church is fairly recent (seventeenth century), but the older interior was grand, especially because of the royal banners that flanked the nave (photo 50). One coat of arms in particular gave us pause, for it celebrated "the bastard of Orléans." This hero of the history of French royalty, Jean de Dunois, a colleague in arms of Jeanne d'Arc, was unknown to me, but my research led me to the notable statement that the French army "was full of bastards." One of the many differences, obviously, between the French and the American armed forces. Even so, bastards apart, it was impossible to be entirely cynical about that young shepherdess from Lorraine who wound up leading the French army, even if the National Front has tarnished her memory by embracing her. Toward the end of her life, as a prisoner of the Inquisition, it became a life-and-death question for her whether she should wear trousers, as she had done when on horseback, or a dress, as a woman otherwise must. In a

Photo 50. The interior of the cathedral of Orléans reflects its importance for the kings of France and for the "Maid of Orléans."

162 / Struck by Apollo

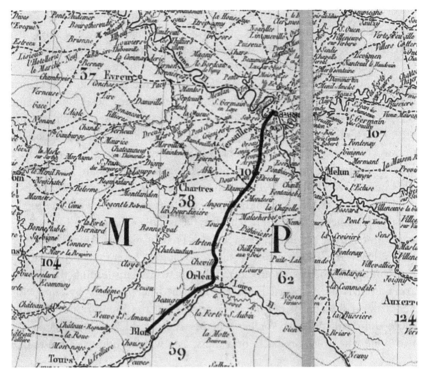

Map 14. Blois-Paris.

lecture course on the death penalty, Derrida names Joan alongside Socrates, Jesus, and the Muslim mystic El Hallâj as victims of the theological-political alliance that marks and mars so much of Western history.

Paris was now our goal. It had been one of Hölderlin's goals from the beginning. We drove north on the D 2020 and the N 20, through Cercottes, Chevilly, Artenay, Toury, and Angerville. We knew it was probable that Hölderlin, especially if he was in a hurry, would have continued through Estampes to Massy-Palaiseau and Paris. The 1812 map becomes difficult to read at this point, since so many towns cluster about Paris, the entire Île-de-France being magnetized by the Île-de-la-Cité. One can make out Etrechy and Arpaion, but then "Fromanteau" and "Longjumeau" are difficult to read, after which "Bernu" and "Denis" ("Louis"?) are virtually illegible. On a recent map one can make out his probable route: Longjumeau, Massy-Palaiseau, Antony, Villejuif, Montrouge, Denfert Rochereau, Boulevard

St. Michel, then across the Seine, heading left to the Vieux Louvre. In a recent short story, "Three Strolls down a Paris Lane," I picture him walking down the rue Vaugirard, farther west, and coming across a small street with the incredible name Impasse de l'Enfant-Jésus, "The Blind Alley of Baby Jesus." The name of that street—which actually exists—would have given Hölderlin and his friend Hegel considerable pause.

As Joe and I were approaching the larger cities of the north, especially Paris, the banlieues became increasingly depressing—monotonous consumer malls, cheaply constructed but of gigantic proportions, warehouses containing all the things you never wanted or needed to buy. Joe recalled having seen an inspirational message painted onto the back of a bench by a student in Tübingen, a message scrawled in American English: "Buy more shit."

We decided somewhere near Artenay to seek relief and to make a detour to Chartres on the way to Paris (see map 15). Our justification was that Chartres lay only fifty kilometers out of Hölderlin's way, and after seeing it, he would then have been able to pass through Versailles on the way to Paris—and Versailles would have fascinated Hölderlin. The lavish residence of Louis XIV was no doubt in a sorry state a dozen years after the Revolution: I recall the chaos there as reported in Stéphane Audeguy's

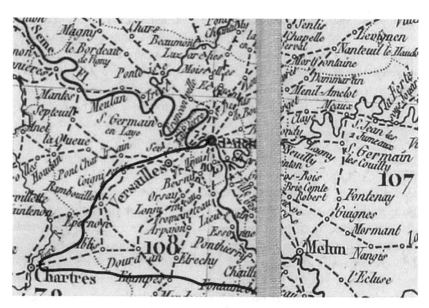

Map 15. Blois-Chartres-Paris.

164 / Struck by Apollo

History of the Lion 'Nobody.'[3] By contrast, one may suppose that the Chartres cathedral was not so radically affected by the Revolution, although historians might correct me here. In any case, today the cathedral is surely one of the glories of Gothic architecture, and Joe and I could easily imagine that Hölderlin was anxious to see it. We therefore decided that even if it was yet another sin on our part, we would veer some fifty kilometers to the northwest, taking the D 154 through the towns of Allaines, Allones, and Bonville to Chartres and Versailles.

We spent an entire day in the august cathedral square, walking endless rounds both outside and inside the church. Among the sculptures on the north side, we were drawn to a number of figures of the Old Testament, especially figures that were writing texts of some kind, royal psalmists perhaps (see again photo 44 at the outset of this chapter), with whom Hölderlin would have felt a kinship. In the interior of the cathedral Hölderlin would have seen the remarkable windows, some of the oldest and finest in all of Europe. We know that in Paris the Louvre, rather than Notre-Dame-de-Paris or La Sainte-Chapelle, was his objective, so that Chartres may have been the last of a long line of magnificent cathedrals that Hölderlin saw—this one too dedicated to the Madonna, if not specifically to Our Lady of Sea Spume.

As for Paris itself, one of our principal goals, an unpleasant surprise met us at Chartres. We planned to leave the RV there, well outside the metropolis, where traffic and parking are nightmares, and to take a train into the center, then make our way immediately to the Louvre. But a national train strike, threatening to last for several days, stopped us in our tracks, as it were. After mulling it over, we decided to reserve Paris and the Louvre for a later visit—it is only four hours distant from Freiburg by fast train.

It was difficult to decide which was the most likely route for Hölderlin's journey from Paris to Strasbourg (see map 16). Already by 1812 there were multiple routes to choose from, whether by post-coach or on foot. Saint-Dizier lay on a straight line due east, and so we determined on a route that would take us there, a route south of Châlons and Metz that would lead directly to Strasbourg. Once again, we preferred river routes, simply because the post-coaches so often followed them, as did our poet. After driving eastward from Chartres toward Estampes, we rejoined Hölderlin's supposed route at Nogent-sur-Seine. We drove along the departmental road D 169, lined with plane trees and cutting through endless fields of wheat and oats, from Nogent to Romilly. At the small village of St. Hilaire we stopped to visit yet another Romanesque church that loomed over the grain fields bordered by red poppies.

---

3. Stéphane Audeguy, *L'Histoire du lion Personne* (Paris: Gallimard Folio, 2016).

The Journey Back / 165

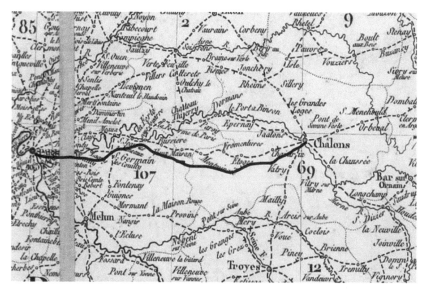

Map 16. Paris-Châlons.

On this final leg of our journey, the names of the villages again exercised their mesmerizing effect: Arcis-sur-Aube, Mesgrigny, Mery-sur-Seine where we crossed the Seine River, Pouan-les-Vallées, Villette-sur-Aube, Brienne-le-Château, Torey-le-Grand, Vaupoisson, Ortillon, Chaudray, Nogent-sur-Aube (not Nogent-sur-Seine, which we had left behind long ago), Coclois, Verricourt, Pougy, Molins-sur-Aube, Le Mont where we crossed the Aube River, St.-Léger-sur-Brienne—all these names so remarkably different, distinguishing villages that were seemingly identical, one after the other, at least to a stranger, as we passed through the bread basket of France. It was hard—no, really quite impossible—to imagine that a distraught and disoriented Hölderlin had trudged through all these towns and across all these fields in the heat of late spring of 1802 (see maps 17 and 18).

We took the D 400 now toward St. Dizier, planning to skirt also the large city of Nancy. We passed through Juzanvigny, Epothément, Louze, Ceffonds, Montier-en-Der, Planrupt, and Braucourt. At St. Dizier we took the N 4 in the direction of Nancy, crossing the Canal de la Marne, passing through Ligny-en-Barrois, Château Stanislas, and Void—successfully passing through the void—crossing the Meuse River before reaching Toul, where we crossed the wide Moselle. At La-Forêt-de-Haye, the hills began to loom higher than before. We followed the N 4, which circumvents Nancy, heading for Lunéville by way of St. Nicolas de Port. Hölderlin must have thought of the ephemeral Peace of Lunéville, signed in February 1801, which gave

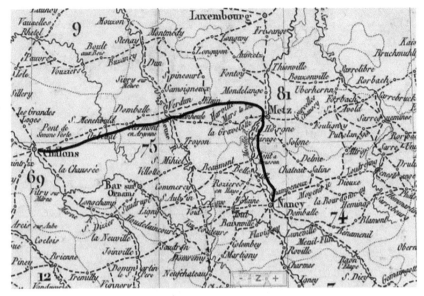

Map 17. Châlons-Metz-Nancy.

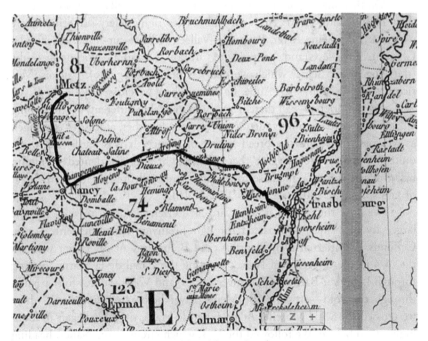

Map 18. Metz-Nancy-Strasbourg.

him so much hope: *Friedensfeier* was the long poem celebrating that brief interlude of peace in Napoleon's Europe.

Lothringen, or Lorraine, was hillier than any region we had seen for many days; it was a sign that we were nearing the Vosges Mountains and, beyond the Rhine, home. The names were now gradually changing, almost unnoticeably shifting toward the German: Blâmont, Sarrebourg, Phalsbourg, where a steep descent begins at the Col de Saverne, to Wasselonne down in the Rhine Plain. The names made us think of all the battles of the Franco-Prussian War, some thirty years after Hölderlin's death, the war that was as decisive for Nietzsche's life as the Coalition wars had been for Hölderlin's. After Ibigny and Richeval we passed through the towns of Héming, Bébing, Imling, Abreschviller, and Hesse, following the D 1004 into Strasbourg.

Hölderlin had arranged for his luggage to be sent ahead from Bordeaux to Strasbourg. Might he have been undecided about where to go from there? Having arrived in Strasbourg, he sent his trunk on to Nürtingen, where his mother would rummage through it, finding Susette's letters. Hölderlin's exit visa from France is dated June 7, 1802. Yet he did not arrive in Stuttgart until the end of the month, or perhaps even the early days of July. What did he do over the next three weeks? Both Pierre Bertaux and Jochen Bertheau have him traveling to Frankfurt to see Susette, either because he knows that she is gravely ill or quite simply because he wants to risk another visit with the love of his life. Sattler, astonishingly, has him traveling not to Frankfurt but down the Rhine to Basel and on to Lake Bienne, the *Bielersee*, where Rousseau once waxed ecstatic (see his fifth *Promenade*). Sattler then has the poet hiking east, through Berne and Thurn, to St. Gotthard, then farther on to the Lukmanier (Lucomagno) Pass and the Aduala mountain range. His goal, says Sattler, is Morea, as he heads down the Brenno Valley in Ticino to the mountain village of Aquila. Hölderlin, as Sattler imagines, then passes through the valley that lies between Rossetto and Sosto to Scaletta and over the Diesruth Pass to Glion. From there he heads toward Versam and the Rapusa and Rhine River valleys. There, on the last outcropping of the *Rheinwald*, on the hill called Scardanal—no doubt (in Sattler's view) the source of the name Scardanelli—not far from the confluence of the Anterior and Posterior Rhine, a travel companion robs and beats him. Only then, says Sattler, does Hölderlin make his way across Lake Constance and homeward.[4]

---

4. Sattler offers this astonishing account of the final days of Hölderlin's journey homeward in the opening pages of vol. 9 of the *Bremer Ausgabe*. I wish I could believe it. The broad sweep through Switzerland would have made such an extraordinary coda to the story! But I cannot find any evidence to support it.

168 / Struck by Apollo

Sattler's bizarre speculation is based on place names that are mentioned in Hölderlin's novel, his play, his poems, and his notebooks, as well as on the importance of the name Scardanal (Scardanelli) for him. It would have added hundreds of kilometers to Hölderlin's journey, however, most of them incredibly difficult kilometers cross the peaks and the valleys of the high Alps. It may well be that Sattler's account is no more than an ironic commentary on the fact that we know absolutely nothing about those final weeks of June. Whether after the disastrous confrontation with Susette's husband in September 1798 Hölderlin would have dared to travel the far more modest distance to Frankfurt is perhaps equally dubious, however, equally speculative. In either case, when Hölderlin finally does arrive home, passing through Stuttgart, he is clearly exhausted. And he is, as we say, dazed and confused.

The trip home took half the time of the trip to Bordeaux, both for Hölderlin and for Joe and me. And yet the homeward journey seemed much longer to us. Whereas the trip to Bordeaux was, roughly speaking, along the hypotenuse of a large triangle, the homeward journey, Bordeaux-Paris-Strasbourg, followed both long legs of that geometric figure. When Joe checked his odometer at the end of our voyage, he announced that we had traveled 2,700 kilometers since leaving Bordeaux. This seemed to me—and still seems—absolutely impossible. Odometers must have their own dream life. A calculation of the *minimum* distance, based on maps and digital information, in any case, and by stark contrast, is as follows in table 2.

This is of course a bare minimum. Recall that we calculated the minimum number of kilometers from Strasbourg to Bordeaux by way of

Table 2. Minimum distances between major stops from Bordeaux to Strasbourg.

Bordeaux to Soulac	113 kilometers
Soulac to Saintes	56 kilometers
Saintes to Chinon	228 kilometers
Chinon to Tours	47 kilometers
Tours to Orléans	28 kilometers
Orléans to Chartres	78 kilometers
Chartres to Paris	97 kilometers
Paris to Strasbourg:	475 kilometers
Total	1,222 kilometers

Lyon as between 1,087 and 1,234 kilometers. Obviously, the hypotenuse of that particular triangle was seriously sinuous. In any case, I hold to my earlier assertion that the walking or meandering distances would be roughly double the minimum, as with the Gier Aqueduct at Lyon, in which case Joe's odometer may not have been derelict or dreaming. If indeed Hölderlin was robbed of all his money before reaching Chinon, as Bertheau supposes, it would mean that he walked a minimum of some seven or eight hundred of those kilometers, perhaps even more. Assuming that the robbery occurred about a week into his travels, it would mean that, at a minimum, he walked some thirty-six kilometers per day over three weeks. An exhausting itinerary, truly, and all of it in the heat of France's wheat and oat fields, the fire from heaven already quite ardent by May and June.

Little wonder, then, that his friends and family find him much changed. The story of those changes takes us *beyond* Bordeaux and back, however. Before we head in that unhappy direction, let us take a brief look at the astonishing collection of Greek and Roman antiquities in the Louvre, which Hölderlin visited during the final days of May 1802 and which I was able to visit, once the trains were running again, some weeks (plus two centuries) later, that is, during the summer of 2018.

Photo 51. *Bacchus*, the Wine God, from the second century of our era. The statue, once in the possession of Cardinal Richelieu, was severely damaged when seized by the Revolution in 1793 and received significant restoration in 1797.

5

Heroic Tenderness in the Louvre

The date of Hölderlin's visit to the Louvre, late May 1802, is important, inasmuch as the museum, to be renamed in the autumn of that year the Musée Napoléon, may well have been adding new gains, especially spoils of war, during the many months of the Coalition Wars. With the help of the Louvre staff, I researched the 1800 catalogue of the collection so that I could be relatively sure about what was available for Hölderlin's inspection.[1]

I counted some 130 sculptures in the collection that Hölderlin could have seen, most of them high-quality Roman copies of Greek originals, among them some of the most prized works of Western art. My focus, as I examined the collection, was Hölderlin's meditation on "the heroic body" of the Greeks, the body characterized by "tenderness," *Zärtlichkeit*. Again, I succumbed to the temptation to pursue the impossible project of seeing through Hölderlin's eyes and recording the results with my camera. Because Hölderlin's deepening appreciation of ancient Greek culture is in many ways the legacy of his journey to Bordeaux and back, I took hundreds of photographs at the Louvre then reduced that number to a bare minimum for display and discussion here. I also restricted my Louvre visit for the most part to the statuary collection, ignoring—as Hölderlin may not have—the large collection of Greek vases, coins, and other objects. It seemed likely to me that the monumental sculptures would have particularly captivated him

---

1. *Notice des statues, bustes et bas-reliefs de la Galerie des Antiques du Musée Central des Arts, ouverte pour la première fois le 18 Brumaire an 9* [Handwritten addition: 9 Nov 1800]. Paris: Imprimerie des Sciences et Arts, rue Ventadour, No. 474. This edition of the *Notice* may have been published first of all in 1802, it seems, and I am uncertain of the exact date of publication. In any case, its listings are the most relevant ones we have for the period of Hölderlin's visit.

172 / Struck by Apollo

and that those were the works to which his second letter to Böhlendorff was most likely referring. It is strange to think that Hölderlin would not have known that the Greek originals were almost always painted, so that my camera, capturing all the images with little or no color, presented the aesthetic of purity that he would have expected was original in them.

In May 1802, when a bedraggled Hölderlin visited the Central Art Museum of the Louvre Palace, his energies and powers were no doubt depleted, but they were surely not exhausted. In addition to his study of the expanding collection of Greek antiquities at the Louvre, we may assume that he made at least a brief visit to Michelangelo's *The Slaves* and perhaps also with Leonardo's *Madonna of the Rocks*, which were displayed not far away.[2]

Which sculptures would he have been able to see, and which ones would have stirred him in the way that visions of the sea and the gardens of Bordeaux had recently stirred him? These were my questions as I visited the galleries of the Louvre with the 1800 catalogue in hand. As I soon learned, however, almost everything had changed since Hölderlin's visit: the names of exhibition rooms, the titles, attributions, descriptions, and even catalogue numbers of the objects exhibited—none of these jibed with much of the material in the 1800 catalogue. The bulk of the items in that catalogue were objects in the Royal Collection, which had expanded dramatically during the sixteenth century, augmented especially during the reigns of Henri IV and Louis XIV. After the Revolution, first in 1792 and then in 1798, many of those works were seized from the various royal and noble residences and added to the Louvre collection: by November 1800 the Louvre contained a Musée Central des Arts, which, to repeat, two years later—that is, not many months after Hölderlin's visit—became the Musée Napoléon. After the Revolution, the Louvre was to be a museum for the people rather than a private collection for the royal residence. Furthermore, hundreds of new objects had come to the Louvre as a result of Napoleon's Italian campaigns

---

2. Because it is under glass, da Vinci's *Madonna [or Virgin] of the Rocks* photographed poorly, so poorly that I will not reproduce my photographs here. Intriguingly, there are two versions of the painting, one in the National Gallery of London, the other in the Paris Louvre. The significant difference between the two is in the brighter lighting (or reduced sfumato) of the Louvre version, along with the bright red color of the angel's cloak and his pointing gesture. Not much about the creation of the two paintings is known. In any case, I find the argument—developed by Lefebvre—that Hölderlin may have based his lines in the *Homburger Folioheft* dedicated to the Madonna on this specific painting quite tenuous. Far more convincing to me is the claim that Michelangelo's *Slaves* had a strong and lasting impact on him—an impact so strong that he may have identified with their sculptor.

Heroic Tenderness in the Louvre / 173

in and after 1796, the most famous of these being the Hellenistic sculptures of *Laocoön and His Sons*, celebrated by Gotthold Ephraim Lessing, and the *Apollo Belvedere*, celebrated by Johann Joachim Winckelmann. After Waterloo and the Vienna Congress of 1815, to be sure, dozens of these artworks, including the two just mentioned, had to be returned to their countries of origin.[3] Yet Hölderlin surely saw both of these at the Louvre. No doubt he had discussed Lessing's *Laokoön* essay with Heinse, so that a study of the Laocoön Group at the Louvre would have been important for him.

I realized that to do justice to the complicated history of the Royal Collection, accrued over centuries, and to the confusions caused by the Revolution, the Napoleonic conquests, and the Restoration, one would have to be an enterprising and energetic student of art history—a student with excellent training not only in Greek art and its Roman imitators but also in the French artisan shops of the seventeenth and eighteenth centuries, which restored and sometimes altered many of the ancient Roman pieces. Indeed, such a student would have to possess a dozen other skills of whose existence I am not even aware. In what follows I offer a series of mere impressions and speculations on a number of works I believe Hölderlin saw. I try to provide at least some technical information concerning the pieces. Obviously, it is virtually impossible to say what Hölderlin actually examined; nor is it always certain which objects he *could* have seen—the catalogues, while impressive in their detail, are sometimes befuddling. One of the great disappointments turned out to be that a large number of magnificent sculptures from the Borghese Collection in Rome, on display now in the Louvre, were not yet available to Hölderlin: Napoleon "purchased" them in 1807, acquiring them at a very low price—some would say it was actually a "steal." In any case, these splendid works arrived five years too late for Hölderlin to have seen them, and I have largely excluded them from my discussion and from the gallery of photographs. Even so, the objects that remain are striking enough.

The Revolution altered almost everything in and about Paris, but in 1802 the splendor of the Louvre Palace was still intact. No matter which entry portal Hölderlin may have passed through or which exhibition hall he entered, the first impression must have been one of magnificence. As for me, I entered the Vieux Louvre from the rue de Rivoli. Once inside, I

---

3. The *Laocoön Group*, now in the Vatican Museum, is item no. 108 in the 1800 catalogue, which contains a long and glowing description on pages 43–45; the *Apollo Belvedere*, or *Pythian Apollo*, is item no. 145 in the 1800 catalogue, discussed at greater length than any other piece (pages 73–77); it too was returned to the Vatican during the Restoration.

174 / Struck by Apollo

tried to restrict myself to the objects that I knew Hölderlin could have seen, but it was impossible not to wish that he had seen objects much older than those from Classical Athens, ancient objects from the Cyclades, for example, that have so impressed modern artists. The torsos and heads of the Cycladic representations of the Great Goddess, who was no doubt related to the one we call the Great Mother of Asia or the Anatolian Kybele, would perhaps have struck him as primeval Madonnas. Her Cycladic name, used on those isles north of Crete during the Bronze Age, we do not know, but these statues are as impressive in their own way as those of Praxiteles millennia later. These archaic pieces would have delighted Hölderlin, if only because toward the end of his active life he became more and more convinced that the panoply of Titans was to be taken as seriously as that of the Olympians. He also became convinced that "Asia" or the "Orient" had been decisive for the development of Greece—today this is a commonplace in Greek studies, but Hölderlin and Schelling, along with Friedrich Creuzer, were among the first to realize how indebted Classical Greece was to much older cultures, including the ones we now refer to as the Ancient Near Eastern cultures.

Among the objects I could be relatively certain were available for his inspection, I was first struck by visions of Venus Aphrodite. The famous *Venus de Milo* was not yet there for Hölderlin to see, but other statues, most of them Roman copies (carved out of Greek marble, however) of much older works, would have spoken eloquently to him. When during the years 1802–1804 he was revising his translations of Sophocles, he translated the name Aphrodite simply as "divine beauty." It would have been difficult for Hölderlin to resist the goddesses sculpted by Praxiteles, just as it was difficult for Praxiteles to resist Mnesarete, or Phryne, who posed for his statues of the goddess. There is a nobility in the profile of these faces, reflecting a serene and luminous personality that accompanies—with apparent ease—the voluptuosity of the torsos. It would have been difficult for anyone raised in the way Hölderlin was raised to comprehend this ease, this naturalness. He might have remembered that when Michelangelo painted the saints of his *Last Judgment*, they were all nude—until the Pope and the Cardinals decided to paint them some clothing. This was the "school of destiny" at work, obfuscating the "school of nature." Here in the Louvre, to be sure, the school of destiny in Hölderlin's own background could not entirely obliterate the school of nature, as it had sought to do throughout Hölderlin's life. The statues of the Greek gods and goddesses resisted such obfuscation with overwhelming force.

Not that the struggle between these schools has ended in our time, if I may say so. Recall Sigmund Freud's remark concerning the most common form of degradation in (modern) love life, namely, the need to denigrate and disrespect the desired object. One of the most comical aspects of contemporary US-American culture is that many people believe that such degradation has been overcome, whereas an Eros that can show genuine respect and tenderness has arguably never been more rare: observe the behavior of the recent national political leadership.

An Aphrodite that Hölderlin surely had the opportunity to contemplate (see photo 52) is the *Aphrodite of Arles*, discovered in that city of Provence. Dating from the time of Augustus (27 BCE to 14 CE), it was in the collection of Louis XIV, whose court sculptor, François Girardon, added an apple to the right hand and a mirror to the left in an allusion to the judgment of Paris. The statue may be a copy of the *Thespian Aphrodite* by Praxiteles, named after the Boeotian city of Thespiai. Thespiai was the home of Phryne, one of the wealthiest and most famous courtesans of Late Classical Greece. An entire literature surrounds her, from the fourth century of the earlier era down to the present day. Around 360 BCE she commissioned the statue from her lover Praxiteles, who presumably used her as his model. Phryne was later brought to trial on charges of "godlessness," precisely as Socrates had been. She is said to have exposed her breasts to her judges, earning immediate acquittal, a ploy presumably not available to the gadfly of Athens. In 1798, the *Aphrodite of Arles*, long a part of the royal collection, was seized from Versailles by Revolutionaries and brought to the Louvre, making it available to the entire populace of the city. In the 1800 catalogue it is item no. 146, and it is said to have been carved from Hymettus marble. The catalogue also describes her a *Vénus victorieuse*, that is, an Aphrodite victorious not only in the beauty contest judged by Paris but also in the much later rise of the Caesars in Rome. Perhaps surprisingly, Venus—neither Diana nor Minerva nor even Juno—was the patroness of the Caesars.

To be sure, Athena was made of sterner stuff than Aphrodite, and Hölderlin would have been impressed by the archaic statues of Pallas clothed in her aegis of Gorgon and serpent. However, I confess that while I was gazing on the severe virgin goddess, after having dallied with the *Aphrodite of Arles*, I recalled the words of the moon, Selene, in John Keats's *Endymion* (ll. 800–1), words that would be blasphemous were they to come out of my mouth instead of hers. Selene, who descends from the night sky every night of every day to make love to Endymion, says of Virgin Athena, "Now I swear at once / That I am wise, that Pallas is a dunce—."

Although I have made considerable fuss about the notion of tenderness as the principal quality of the heroic body, as if such a combination were incomprehensible to us, nothing seems more natural than this combination

Photo 52. *The Aphrodite of Arles*, presumably a copy of the *Thespian Aphrodite* by Praxiteles.

of qualities in so many of the Louvre statues from antiquity. The representations of Hermes are especially notable in this regard, especially the *Hermes Richelieu* (see photo 53). Hermes (the Roman Mercury) holds a fragment of the caduceus in his left hand; on his head we see the indentations where small wings were once fastened. He carries the chlamys, a traveler's cloak, over his left arm. This second-century Roman copy is based on an original by Naucydes, which is dated about 370–360 BCE. The Revolution seized the statue from Richelieu's château in 1800. Unfortunately, the equally magnificent *Ares* (Mars) seen to the rear of the Hermes in this photograph was not in the collection when Hölderlin visited the Louvre in 1802. The *Hermes Richelieu* has about it a certain solemnity, especially in the almost mournful facial expression—perhaps a classic illustration of the *uncanniness* that Schelling analyzed for Freud and for posterity.

The image of Diomedes (see photo 54) would have surprised Hölderlin: here the Achaean warrior, perhaps the most ambitious killer among all the Greek heroes, shows a certain reserve, if not tenderness. Homer's *Iliad*, in song ten, recounts the daring mission of Diomedes and Odysseus to steal the Trojans' "Palladion," which had magical powers that protected their city from the onslaught of the Achaeans. It is as though Diomedes is reflecting on the possibility that his own and Odysseus's exploit was an act of sacrilege, one that might open up a new possibility of victory for the Achaeans but was nonetheless a bold theft that would offend Pallas Athena. This Roman copy of Diomedes, from the second or third century of our era, is said to be a copy of a statue by either Naucydes or Kresilas, both of the school of Polycletus, circa 440–430 BCE. The statue was seized in 1792 from Cardinal Richelieu's collection.

The Louvre's four busts or statues depicting Emperor Hadrian's favorite, Antinous, may have been among the most convincing exemplars of the heroism of tenderness and the tenderness of heroes. Only one of them is pictured here, item no. 105 in the 1800 catalogue, the so-called *Antinous of Écouen* (see photo 55). In our own time, heads of state pay hush money to those they love or pretend to love; the Romans commissioned statues of them to be venerated by all the world as gods. The bust, made in France during the eighteenth century on the basis of ancient models, has something of a movie-star quality in the face and coiffure. The Emperor Hadrian (117–138 CE) memorialized him in many statues and on many coins. Nevertheless, no matter how venerated the youth may have been, the 1800 catalogue notes that all the ancient portraits of Antinous betray the identical mood of melancholy, perhaps even dejection. Whether that applies to the *Antinous of Écouen* I am uncertain. Is it not rather a look of intelligence and

Photo 53. The *Hermes Richelieu*, based on an original by Naucydes, ca. 370–360 BCE.

Photo 54. *Diomedes*, a hero of the Trojan War, capturing the Palladion from Troy.

180 / Struck by Apollo

Photo 55. The *Antinous of Écouen*, from the second century of our era.

sensitivity? Undoubtedly virile, yet free of boisterous vulgarity? It does seem, at least to one or other glance at it, as though a slight smile is beginning to play uncannily across those lips. Perhaps the authors of the 1800 catalogue were searching for the word *tenderness*, which understandably eluded them, as it does most of us.

The horrific-sounding *Apollo Sauroctonus*, or *Apollo the Lizard Slayer*, which is listed as such in the 1800 catalogue, sounds like an Apollo for Jurassic Park. Here the luminous god is reduced to a scene from Tom Sawyer's boyhood: like any other scamp who would torture a helpless animal, Apollo is about to scoop up a small lizard in his left hand. The statue, of Parian marble, is said to be a first-century copy of a statue by the prolific Praxiteles dating from about 350–340 BCE. It is reported to be a part of the 1807 Borghese purchase, and yet the 1800 catalogue lists an *Apollo Sauroctonus* (item no. 127), which Hölderlin may therefore have seen. The theme it depicts, to repeat, is very odd, as though reducing Apollo's battle with the serpent Python to an adolescent prank—it seems as though the poor lizard, like our Hölderlin, is about to be struck by Apollo. Yet the face of the god, one has to say, is divine, perhaps precisely because it is not readable (photo 56). The expression on the face reflects a kind of dignity, perhaps even a tenderness that would not hurt a fly or even a fly-eating lizard. It is the expression on that face that perhaps has elicited the cry heard from antiquity through Keats and Benjamin Britten, "Apollo! young Apollo!" As beautiful as that divine face may be, however, *Apollo Sauroctonus* might well have struck Hölderlin as utterly uncanny.

Since I continue to mention Schelling and Freud on "the uncanny," allow me a brief digression. Schelling speaks about the uncanny in his lectures on the *Philosophy of Mythology* during the early 1840s, at about the time his friend Hölderlin's life is drawing to a close. Freud in turn accepts Schelling's words as the very definition of the uncanny, *das Unheimliche*, in his famous eponymous essay of 1917. Schelling invokes the uncanny twice, first declaring that the brilliant aither (the deep blue sky of the upper air) that stretches across Homer's Olympian panoply can come to shine in Greek art and literature only after the darker insights of mythology have

Photo 56. *Apollo the Lizard Slayer*, based on a statue by Praxiteles, ca. 350–340 BCE.

182 / Struck by Apollo

been preserved in the mystery cults. Schelling is thinking preeminently, I believe, of the cult of the Cabiri or the Great Gods on ancient Samothrace. Those darker insights preserved in the mysteries involve an "uncanny principle," according to Schelling. He cites "the dark and darkening force of that uncanny principle," defining it in a parenthetical phrase: "(one calls *unheimlich* everything that was supposed to remain in latency, in secret [*im Geheimnis*], in concealment, and yet has come to the fore). . . ."[4] Nine pages later, Schelling, reflecting on the figures of the Aegina temple frieze, which he has seen in Munich, observes that the ancient Greek sculptors were able to reveal something about the nature of the gods by fashioning for them human forms. Yet these forms always depict the divine—whether deceptively or for the sake of some hidden truth—by introducing a "nonhuman" or "extra-human" trait into their figures, thus cloaking the deity "in a certain *Unheimlichkeit*."[5]

Keats, on seeing the *Elgin Marbles*, invoked what he called "a shadow of a magnitude." The uncanny would perhaps be such a shadow. Might it be possible to think the uncanny magnitude here, as Schelling employs it, neither in terms of the Gothic—a tale by Hoffmann, for example—nor at all in terms of shadows and shades but in and through the figure of an inexplicable, unaccountable tenderness, a tenderness in which power is shown in restraint, a strength in which a certain vulnerability or fragility, or at least a certain delicateness and reflective sensibility come to the fore? This thought or question may have occurred to Hölderlin as he was gazing on faces such as those of Apollo the Lizard Slayer, Hermes the Messenger, Diomedes the killer, or even Ares, god of war.

Tender serenity appears unexpectedly in yet another set of figures, to wit, those of the Maenads or Bacchants and their god Dionysos. These particular worshipers of Dionysos, the ones in the Louvre, were apparently inspired by Euripides' *The Bacchae*: whereas the usual image of the women worshipers, mad for their god, is of a wild and bloody chase across forested mountaintops in the dead of winter, the Louvre Maenads betray a different

---

4. F. W. J. Schelling, *Sämmtliche Werke*, ed. Karl Schelling (Stuttgart and Augsburg: J. G. Cotta'scher Verlag, 1856–1861), II/2:649. Freud's references to Schelling in his essay "The Uncanny" appear in vol. 12 of Sigmund Freud, *Gesammelte Werke*, 17 vols., ed. Anna Freud et al. (London: Imago Publishing, 1952), 12:235–36, 254. In what follows I will cite Freud's *Gesammelte Werke* as SF with volume and page. For Schelling's account of the Cabirian cult, see his *On the Deities of Samothrace*, trans. and ed. by Alexander Bilda, Jason Wirth, and D. F. Krell, forthcoming from Indiana University Press in 2024.

5. Schelling, II/2:658.

aspect. Their posture is erect, their breasts and their sex are modestly covered, their hair is in perfect order, their gaze is calm, their composure unruffled. They are the very picture of sanity and sobriety—shades of Hölderlin's Juno! Only the decorative grapes woven into their hair give them away (photo 57). Euripides' messenger reports, here in Nietzsche's words:

> A messenger [in Euripides' *The Bacchae,* lines 690–714] recounts how in the noonday heat he drove his herds up to the mountain peaks: it is the right moment and the right place to see things as yet unseen. Now Pan sleeps, now the sky is the undisturbed backdrop to a *gloria*, now the day *blossoms*. The messenger espies

Photo 57. A *Maenad,* or *Bacchante,* copy from the second century of a statue from the fourth century BCE.

184 / Struck by Apollo

three bands of women scattered across an Alpine meadow, reclining, but the very picture of dignity. Many of the women are leaning against the trunks of pines. All sleep. Suddenly, Pentheus's mother begins to cry out with joy, sleep is cast off, all leap up, models of noble form. The young girls and women let their hair fall to their shoulders; those whose fawn skins have become undone at the strap or pin fasten them. They gird themselves with snakes that lovingly lick their cheeks. Some of the women take young wolves and fawns into their arms and suckle them. All bedeck themselves with garlands of ivy. One stroke of the thyrsus, and water bubbles forth from the rocks; one stroke of the staff upon the earth, and a fountain of wine wells forth. Sweet honey drips from their staffs, and if anyone so much as grazes the ground with the tips of her fingers, snow-white milk flows from it.—It is an utterly enchanted world; nature celebrates her feast of reconciliation with humanity.[6]

The appearances in the Louvre of Dionysos himself, the wine god who accompanied Hölderlin, and not only him, to Bordeaux and back, are equally uncanny. Some of them show a bearded figure, the beard being a common feature among the archaic images of Dionysos that are preserved in the many figures of Papposilenos, who is more satyr than god. More familiar is the figure of Dionysos or Bacchus as an adolescent, his posture entirely languorous, his head and gaze slightly raised, as though in dreams of his mother Semele or of Ariadne (see again photo 51). Here is an adolescent body only mildly athletic in its thighs, midriff, and arms and with remarkable hermaphroditic traits. Tender, no doubt, and yet a god—displaying another facet of uncanniness. Hölderlin would have recalled Pentheus's remark, delivered as an insult, that Aphrodite herself shines out of the eyes of the wine god. The priest of Dionysos, who in Euripides' play (l. 811) is in fact the god himself, asks Pentheus, "Would you like to *see* the women at their revels?" The instant that question is posed, the aggressive young king, who has pledged to bring the women back to the city and to get them under control, metamorphoses into a languid figure of the languorous god himself. Although up until now he has led an army against the women, he now replies to the god (l. 812), "I would give anything to see that sight!" He is from that point on a figure who is bound to meet his

---

6. Nietzsche, "The Dionysian Worldview," written in the High Alps of Switzerland's Maderandertal in summer 1870; KSW 1:558–59.

death as a sacrificial offering to the god. Tender as a lamb, and dressed as a woman, he dies by his own mother's hand. Not by chance is the languid Dionysos, even when he smiles, accompanied by panthers. Born, murdered, and ingested, then reborn again and again, Dionysos is always, Schelling tells us, at the very center of the mysteries.

Hölderlin must have continued thinking about this god, the wine god, who is so important to him. For example, he may have thought of the following problem. If Semele, the mother of Dionysos, was a mortal, then it is difficult to explain how her son by Zeus was a god. Usually, the offspring of gods and mortals remained a mortal. Dionysos, like Herakles, was a rare exception to the rule. The plethora of Greek heroes and demigods spawned by immortals with mortals poses a complicated "theological" problem. W. K. C. Guthrie comments quite soberly on the truth that dazzled Hölderlin from his high school years to the end of his life: "The gods were captivated by mortal beauty."[7] And once a god was captivated by a beautiful mortal woman, she was certain to become pregnant—but pregnant with a mortal, not with a god. Guthrie notes: "Yet the children of these mixed marriages . . . had blood, not ichor, in their veins. Curiously enough, this conception of the gods, linking them morally and physically so closely to mankind, is the one which bars the way most effectively to any aspirations after divinity in man" (ibid.). Herakles and Dionysos, to repeat, are among the few exceptions to the rule. Yet the rule itself must have inspired ancient casuists to inquire closely into Zeus's "golden rain," Aphrodite's golden rooms, and Leda's golden egg: how could the gods have failed to transmit to their progeny the ichor that was the elixir of their own life? Surely, divine ichor would overpower mere mortal blood? Surely, golden rain would wash away mere mortal seed? Or does mortality somehow come to infect the immortals themselves? Is the secret of the mystery cults the fact that the immortals have to be understood as genuinely vulnerable companions of us mortals? For the immortals, if such a thing dare be said, do seem to *need* the mortals. This mystery dominated Hölderlin's great hymns. The Rhine hymn says (CHV 1:345; ll. 105–14):

> But the gods have enough of their own
> Immortality, and if the celestial ones
> Need one thing, then it is
> Heroes and human beings and other

---

7. W. K. C. Guthrie, *The Greeks and Their Gods* (Boston: Beacon Press, 1950), 120.

186 / Struck by Apollo

Mortals. For inasmuch as
The most blessed ones feel nothing
Of themselves, it must be—
If such a thing dare be said—
That in the gods' name another
Feels for them. They need this other.

In the final pages of the *Homburger Folioheft*, in a poem called "The Nymph," and then once again in a sketch toward the poem "Mnemosyne" (CHV 1:434, 436), Hölderlin tries to say why deities need mortals: "Not everything is possible / For the celestials. Namely, mortals are sooner / Able to reach the abyss. / That is how matters turn / With them" ("The Nymph," ll. 13–16). The abyss, *der Abgrund*, surely has to do with death, but it may also involve the abysses of love and tenderness, the abysses of life itself. Long before Hölderlin lived and wrote, Michel de Montaigne invoked the humane notion of the *commourans*, "those who are dying with us," our "fellow mortals," meaning by that much more than the human animal. Schelling's notion of the divine *socii* and *consentes*, the "companions" who "are born and die together," an idea he developed in *The Deities of Samothrace*, modestly expanded that humane notion to include the gods. Hölderlin thought about this greater unity and ubiquitous vulnerability of life more and more as his life went on, especially after he returned from Bordeaux.

Dionysos is one of the central figures of the Greek myths and mystery cults, for it is he—with his Maenads—who promises that a human being can, at least for a time, be filled with deity (photo 58). Dionysiac experience "rests on the possibility of obliterating the line between human and divine, and, whether for a long period or for a brief moment of ecstasy, blending the two natures in one."[8] Thus Dionysos is the test case for the central question of Guthrie's entire inquiry: did the Greeks believe in an absolute split between god and mortal, such that the mortal desire to become godlike would be sheer delusion, or did they in fact believe that divinity served as the ideal and even as the end and goal of human being? To become godlike—is this the highest purpose of humankind, as Plato and Aristotle suggest, or the most heinous hubris, as the tragedians warn? And in either case does deity have to do with deathlessness or with the unquenchable desire to approach the abyss of mortality? Hölderlin may have been asking himself these questions as he gazed on the languorous wine god and his apparently tranquil women worshipers.

---

8. Guthrie, 49.

Photo 58. *Bacchus*, a detail of photo 51, the god ecstatic and utterly uncanny.

In today's Louvre, only a few steps separate the statues of antiquity from Michelangelo's *Slaves*. I cannot be certain where these statues stood in Hölderlin's day. Yet as I made my way to the works of the great Mannerist artist, I passed by one last remarkable image in the ancient Greek and Roman collection. I gasped. It was from the Borghese Collection, acquired in 1807, so that I knew Hölderlin could not have seen it. Even so, I photographed it obsessively (see photo 59). Its title, *Silenos carrying Dionysos (Bacchus), son of Zeus*, reflected the familiar story of Silenos, charged by Zeus with the task of protecting the infant, his bastard son, from Hera's wrath. But as I looked up into the face of the life-size Silenos, I realized that it was the most faithful portrait of Michelangelo ever executed—with the possible exception of Michelangelo's self-portrait in *The Last Judgment*—a thousand years before Buonarroti was born. I leave it to my readers to contemplate that face, even if our poet could not have seen it.

Hölderlin was familiar with the story of the capture of Silenos by King Midas. The man with the golden touch wanted to know what was best for a human being like himself. He possessed limitless wealth and all the power that money could buy but, perhaps sensing that these things

Photo 59. *Silenos Carrying Dionysos (Bacchus), Son of Zeus*, from the Borghese Collection of the Louvre. A portrait of Michelangelo?

were vacuous, or at least not enough, never enough, he netted Silenos in a wood and refused to release him until the tutor of Dionysos revealed what he craved to know. The "wisdom of Silenos" may be one of the things we have been tracking throughout Hölderlin's journey to Bordeaux and back, but perhaps now at the Louvre we can pause to quote Silenos's own words, once again from the pen of Nietzsche.

> There is an ancient saga that tells how King Midas for many years tried to hunt down the wise Silenos, the companion of Dionysos, who roamed the forests. Yet he was unable to capture him. When Silenos finally fell into his hands, the king asked him what was best and most advantageous for a human being. The daimon, who would not be moved, was as silent and as impenetrable as stone. Finally, compelled by the king, he laughed his shrill laugh and burst out with these words: "You wretched, ephemeral brood, you children of accident and toil, why do

you do me violence so that I might tell you what it is most propitious for you not to know? The most excellent thing for you lies altogether beyond your reach: not to have been born, not to be. To be nothing. The second best for you, however, is—to die soon."[9]

As I noted in an earlier chapter, Hölderlin chose the final three lines of this text—not from Nietzsche, of course, but from their source, Sophocles—as the epigraph for the second volume of his *Hyperion*, the volume dedicated to Susette. As I looked up into the smiling face of Silenos, here a perfect foster-father to the smiling infant, I thought about Hölderlin's nostalgia for "Father Aither" and, in sharp contrast, the statue I had seen a few moments earlier of Zeus wielding the thunderbolt, the *Jupiter of Smyrna*. True, the thunderbolt had been added to the figure's right hand by the court sculptor of Louis XIV, Pierre Granier, transforming a probable Asclepius into a weaponized Zeus. In any case, the statue cast an eerie shadow on the Louvre wall (see photo 60).

I could not help but think of Nietzsche's reflection on "the shadow of the dead god," or, once again, Keats's "shadow of a magnitude." I could imagine Hölderlin asking himself whether the father god, whose Roman name, Jupiter, derives precisely from the words *deus-pater*, could be said to mirror anything like either vulnerability or tenderness. This had been Aeschylus's question in *Prometheus Bound*, as Hölderlin also knew well. Fire from heaven scorches and singes—that is something Hölderlin had learned on his long journey. The shadow cast by Zeus, Father Aither, is a phantom of power, power seemingly invincible and yet spectral, the power of thunderbolt and storm, both of which, however, pass. If power itself is a phantom, the flitting shadow of a shade, then the flesh of the father god—once Danaë has taught him how to count the hours in passion—may be more vulnerable and more tender than we suppose. Indeed, that is the lesson of the mysteries, the ultimate mystery being the mortality of the gods, their need to be close to the abyss. Their need to *feel* compels them more decisively to Earth. No matter how imposing the shade of Zeus may be, no matter how darkly cast and long-lasting, it is but the shade of the now vanished Father Aither. It may be that the brightest light for Hölderlin turned out to be a gentle, graceful, and gracious figure of the Earth, one that he could see as a fitting companion to the wine god. Our poet may

---

9. See Nietzsche, *The Birth of Tragedy from the Spirit of Music*, KSW 1:35.

Photo 60. The *Jupiter of Smyrna*, originally an Aesclepius, now wielding the thunderbolt and casting a long shadow.

Heroic Tenderness in the Louvre / 191

Photo 61. Detail from *The Three Graces*, perhaps an Aglaia. Roman copy of a second-century BCE statue in the Hellenistic style.

have bathed in that light as he drifted past a glorious group of *The Three Graces*, one of whom was Aglaia, the nymph he had seen at the Château la Rabière in Joué-les-Tours (photo 61).[10]

---

10. Because I have been unkind to Heidegger's lecture course on Hölderlin's *Andenken*, let me mention a bright moment in the course that touches on the figure of Aglaia and the gracious tenderness of the earth. Heidegger refers to the women who walk on the "silky soil" of Bordeaux in March, and he adds the following remark on tenderness (*Zarte*): "is not the ground itself 'silky,' that is, as tender and as quietly shining as silk, which is to say, carrying within itself but also yielding a splendid and concealed richness? Does not the silky ground mean the earth that breathes forth and yet retains that indeterminate tenderness that stirs with the appearance of the first buds of early spring?" (52:82–83).

I was thinking of all these things as I took the few steps from *Silenos carrying Dionysos (Bacchus), son of Zeus*, the impossible portrait of Buonarroti, to the neighboring hall containing Michelangelo's famous statues. As far as I know, Hölderlin does not anywhere refer directly to *The Slaves*. In the end, it is only a conjecture that he saw them in the Louvre. And yet the greater mystery would be why, if he did not see them, he chose the name Buonarroti as one of his pseudonyms—or as what he perhaps felt was one of his *true* names. I follow Bertheau's and Lefebvre's surmise that Michelangelo was the intended reference. At all events, it is true to say that these extraordinary works, *The Slaves*, destined for the tomb of Pope Julius II and carved during the years 1513 to 1515 but then abandoned and left unfinished, doubtless because of flaws in the marble, strike every visitor to the Louvre with enormous force (photos 62 and 63). Here,

Photo 62. Michelangelo Buonarroti, *The Slaves*, here the "rebellious" slave.

Heroic Tenderness in the Louvre / 193

Photo 63. Michelangelo Buonarroti, *The Slaves*, here the "expiring" slave.

arguably, every bit as much as in the statues from classical antiquity, the athletic-heroic body as tenderness is displayed in unforgettable contours. Above all, one may say, in the *Dying Slave*, although the expression on the face of the *Rebellious Slave* is every bit as plaintive. We know from Michelangelo's poems—poems in the form of prayers—that he begged to be flayed, as though being stripped of his skin would release his self from itself. The fact that the flayed skin of Bartolomeo in *The Last Judgment* is a self-portrait of the artist speaks to this.

The poet's identification with Buonarroti appears to be quite intense. May we not speak of Hölderlin "in rebellion"? And perhaps even of Hölderlin "expiring"? One can imagine the poet circling these monumental works, lost in admiration, gradually realizing that a shocking identification with them is taking place. If the name Scardanelli is the memento of a robbery and beating, and Killalusimeno the memento of a distracted poet wandering on a wharf of the Garonne in search of his wits, then Buonarroti is a

194 / Struck by Apollo

name for a torture from which there appears to be no release—other than withdrawal to a tower, to slumber and a slow death.

A final word for this chapter, if I may, on the heroic body as tenderness. Having spent several days in the presence of these "old marbles ever beautiful" (Keats, *Endymion*, 1:319) and trying to imagine the impact they would have had on Hölderlin, I began to notice the impact they were having on me. Even if I was busy with my catalogues and to-do lists and camera lenses, these works were working on me in a way I had not anticipated. I noticed it when I sat down at the end of the day for a wonderful meal at Le Bouquet d'Alésia not far from Denfert Rochereau. Hölderlin's seemingly odd attribution of *Zärtlichkeit*, "tenderness," to the athletic and heroic body of the southerly peoples began to appear quite "natural" to me, quite "logical," I might have said. Tenderness was reflected in the shoulders and thighs, the feet and the faces, the hands and the buttocks of one statue after another, whether god or goddess or mortal hero. Over and over again, sexual and gender identities yielded to a tender erotic ambiguity, an Eros of *femasculous* and *mascuminine* intersections, fusions, and confusions, a tenderness in polished stone that no words of mine could capture, although the camera had better luck. There they were, before my eyes, an Apollo and a Dionysos who seemed as much an Aphrodite and a Maenad, a Diomedes who could have been a fourth Grace. The mystery was not why Hölderlin saw tenderness in the Greek heroic body; the mystery was why this obvious truth has been obfuscated for centuries—or, more modestly, for my own entire lifetime. It astonished me, me trying to see through Hölderlin's eyes, to observe that the Greek and Roman antiquities at the Louvre offer us intimate glimpses of a "liveliness" that has slipped away from us. These are the "flown gods" whom Hölderlin mourns, the eminently mortal gods who are also his only hope.

As I was examining the photographs weeks later, a second wave of this mystery whelmed me, and I remembered a conversation I recently had with a young and beautiful person whom I have loved for a long time. This person has gone through, and continues to go through, a wide spectrum of gender identifications and misidentifications, transformations and retransformations, vigorous rejections and tremulous acceptances, with all the accompanying celebrations and dejections, all the ups and downs of a bewildering love life. Over glasses of the wine god's very best, we talked and laughed and agreed that what seemed called for was this: less decisiveness about identities of any kind and a greater openness to persons of any and every stripe or style, persons whom we have come to respect and befriend and love and who, with great good luck, might respect and befriend and love us. The only requirement would be a certain heroic tenderness.

Photo 64. The Tübingen Tower viewed from the willow-lined banks of the Neckar. Hölderlin lived on the second floor, behind the middle window, from his thirty-seventh to his seventy-third year.

6

Beyond Bordeaux and Back

One of the reasons the journeys to Bordeaux and back are so important is that, after them, Hölderlin is never the same. When he arrives at his friend Matthison's house in Stuttgart in late June or early July 1802, he is so emaciated and unkempt—long straggly hair, fingernails zombie length, his frame bone thin, and a wild look in his eye—he has to murmur his name, "Hölderlin," before his friend recognizes him. They had known one another since their university years in the Stift, and they had been together that past December as Hölderlin was departing for Bordeaux. Now, only six months later, Hölderlin is unrecognizable.

It is true that many of the great hymns for which Hölderlin is remembered were sketched out or revised during the years 1802 to 1806, after his return from Bordeaux: the fragments of the *Homburger Folioheft* and the poems *Andenken*, *Brot und Wein*, *Der Ister*, *Der Einzige*, *Patmos*, and many others—these are his supreme poetic achievements. Yet during those same years, Hölderlin's friends and family notice remarkable changes taking place in him: by nature and upbringing a man of peace, reserved and unfailingly courteous, he now has outbreaks of rage, a fury that has been simmering over decades but that only now explodes. At one point he drives his mother and his siblings out of the Nürtingen house. To help him avoid Nürtingen entirely, his friend Sinclair arranges various apartments for the poet in Homburg vor der Höhe, near Frankfurt. Hölderlin's landlords, who seem to be serving more as guardians, complain that he insists on playing in the middle of the night the Hammerklavier that he had been given, playing it raucously, oddly, repetitively—performing a kind of nerve-jarring minimalism, perhaps. Particularly jarring would have been the click-clacking sound of the keys whose strings he—in some sort of confusion or rage—had snipped. After his disastrous nine-month forced confinement in the Autenrieth Psychiatric Clinic in 1806, and throughout the subsequent

198 / Struck by Apollo

years in the Tübingen Tower, he greets his visitors (though not his hosts and guardians, the Zimmer family) with a deep bow, saluting them as "Your Highness" or "Your Majesty." Almost everyone, both then and now, agrees that he had crossed the line or the no man's land that divides eccentricity from illness. Yet that is virtually all that the experts can agree on; the rest is in dispute, now as then.

Pierre Bertaux famously argues that Hölderlin is merely feigning madness during the final thirty-five years of his life, and there is some evidence for this.[1] Hölderlin's caretaker, Ernst Zimmer, affirms that Hölderlin's effusive handling of visitors is merely a ploy to keep them at a distance. Hölderlin has no need to treat the benevolent Zimmer or his kind daughter this way. And if Hölderlin signs the poems he writes for visitors with imagined dates and with the names Scardanelli and Buonarroti, he nevertheless signs his periodic letters to his mother with "Your most obedient son, Hölderlin." Is there anything that is safe to say about the illness of this "benighted genius"? Probably not, and I will seek refuge by merely reporting a few things about two very different books on the subject, two studies that I have found fascinating reading, namely, Laplanche's *Hölderlin and the Question of the Father* and Reinhard Horowski's *Hölderlin Was NOT Crazy: A Polemic*.[2]

A good place to begin—even if it means a certain amount of repetition—is that second letter to Böhlendorff, written in November 1802 in Nürtingen, not long after Hölderlin's return from Bordeaux (CHV 2:920–22). He had been in Regensburg with Sinclair for the first two weeks of October, recovering from the exhaustion of his voyage and the disastrous news of Susette's death. He was now, in Sinclair's estimation at least, intellectually and emotionally restored, indeed, at the peak of his powers. The phrase that I have taken as the title for my own project, *Struck by Apollo*, appears in this letter to Böhlendorff, as do other decisive hints about Hölderlin's experiences in France. Here is the letter, which I will cite now in its entirety

---

1. See Pierre Bertaux, *Friedrich Hölderlin: Eine Biographie* (Frankfurt am Main: Insel Taschenbuch, 2000 [originally published in 1978]), throughout, for such evidence.

2. Jean Laplanche, *Hölderlin et la question du père* (Paris: Presses Universitaires de France, 1961), cited as JL with page number in the body of my text, and Richard Horowski, *Hölderlin war NICHT verrückt: Eine Streitschrift* (Tübingen: Klöpfer und Meyer, 2017), cited as RH with page number. As for more recent discussions of Hölderlin's illness, I find myself in complete sympathy with the recently published study by Uwe Gonther and Jann E. Schlimme, *Hölderlin: Das Klischee vom umnachteten Genie im Turm* (Cologne: Psychiatrie Verlag, 2020), which contains harrowing accounts of Hölderlin's treatment in the Autenrieth Clinic and, more generally, of psychiatry's long history of obsession with Hölderlin. Even so, in my own view, Laplanche's psychoanalytic study is suggestive and at times convincing.

but which I will interrupt after each paragraph. And the articulation of the letter into brief, incisive paragraphs is itself noteworthy: the abrupt changes of paragraph seem to be signs of *parataxis*. As a whole, the letter seems by turns both sober and euphoric; it seems also to be, in a sense that is hard to define, "visionary" or "visional."

My dear friend!

> I have not written you for a long time. In the meantime I have been in France and I have seen the sad, lonely Earth; the shepherds of southern France and particular beauties there, men and women who have grown up in anxiety concerning the dubious fate of their country [*in der Angst des patriotischen Zweifels*] and in hunger.

Why sad and lonely, why *die traurige einsame Erde*? One will be tempted to say that after Susette's death the entire planet is bereft and in mourning. Yet there may be some thought here also of the devastation France suffered in the 1790s, the destruction of Lyon by warring factions, the bloody suppression of the Vendée uprising, the shattered nerves of Consul Meyer, who only barely managed to survive the Revolution—he was arrested, apparently to be put to death, but eventually released. Yet the very next words of the letter are about beauty, beautiful people. Not "the" beautiful people of high society, but the shepherds, the peasants, and even the brigands, all of them people of the south. And, above all, as Bertheau speculates, the sailors who roamed the wharves and the streets of Bordeaux. The letter continues:

> The overwhelming element, fire from heaven, and the tranquillity of the human beings, their life in nature, their modest lives, their contentment, constantly gripped me, and I can very well say of myself what they say of heroes, namely, that Apollo struck me.

"Apollo struck me." The god Apollo appears often in Hölderlin's late poems. Commentators almost always refer to the bright side of Apollo, who, while not himself Helios the sun, does represent brilliant daylight and all things visual and visionary. Fire from heaven, as we recall from the first letter to Böhlendorff, is what characterizes the ancient Greeks in general. One thinks of Empedocles on Etna, attempting to unite the lightning of the sky and the fiery magma of Etna's crater in his own body bound for incineration. For, as Hölderlin knew well, the sun can scorch, and daylight can dazzle. Moreover, Apollo is the god who strikes the Achaean Greek cities with

200 / Struck by Apollo

pestilence. He is the mouse and rat god Apollo Smintheos, and he is the lizard slayer Apollo Sauroctonus. One should above all recall that Apollo strikes Patroclus in the back during the latter's battle with Hector. Apollo strikes Patroclus with his fist precisely in that place where the armor—the armor of Achilles—is buckled; the armor falls from Patroclus, and Achilles' lover stands exposed to the spears of the enemy. "Struck," *geschlagen*, is a word that could mean being struck by an idea, an insight, or perhaps by a nightingale's song, which itself is *geschlagen*, or by the plucked and vibrating strings of a lyre; yet its first sense is that one is struck a blow, a blow that causes heroes to fall, since that is what heroes do.

> In the regions that border the Vendée, what interested me was the wild and the warlike, the sheer manliness whose lifelight shines directly in the eyes and limbs and that senses in the feeling of death something like a *virtù* that slakes its thirst to know [*das rein männliche, dem das Lebenslicht unmittelbar wird in den Augen und Gliedern und das im Todesgefühle sich wie in einer Virtuosität fühlt, und seinen Durst, zu wissen, erfüllt*].

Bertheau speculates that it was in the area bordering on the Vendée, in the Charente region, that Hölderlin was robbed, he and all the passengers of his *diligence*. What seems odd is Hölderlin's apparent admiration of the desperadoes—most likely deserters or the defeated rebels of the Vendée rebellion—whose savage aspect seems to him a *Virtuosität*, understanding this perhaps in terms of the Renaissance *virtù*, a kind of courageous and daring initiative to perform great deeds. What would make all this somewhat less strange are the reports, whether believable or not, that the brigands were interested only in seizing those moneys that were being transported by the civil authorities. According to such reports, the highwaymen, all Robin Hoods at heart, would leave the passengers and their valuables untouched. Yet if Hölderlin *was* robbed, so that he had to make the rest of his way home by foot as a vagabond, it would not have been Robin Hood who confronted him in the Charente. And yet if it had been the Merrymen, and if they had allowed Hölderlin to keep at least some of his earnings, it would mean that he continued to travel by post-coach, so that the twenty-eight-day timeline becomes more reasonable.

However that may be, Hölderlin here identifies "the thirst to know," which one may say characterizes his own life as a thinker and a poet, as also belonging to the men who risk death even as they threaten to deliver it. The letter's interweaving of *Lebenslicht*, "the light of life," and *Todesgefühl*, "the feeling of death," is striking. Freud uses the word *Lebenslicht* in a similar way in his *Interpretation of Dreams*, writing about a man who knows that he must soon die: "It is the lifelight [*das Lebenslicht*] that he can no longer augment" (SF 2/3:476). It is important to remember that in the Sophocles translations on which he was working in Bordeaux, Hölderlin comes to see that the Greek gods, who are the very essence of vitality, present themselves, at least in Sophoclean tragedy, *in der Gestalt des Todes*, precisely "in the figure of death." Hölderlin's letter continues, in passages we have seen earlier on:

> The athletic quality of southerly humanity, seen in the ruins of the spirit of antiquity, made me more familiar with the authentic essence of the Greeks; I came to know their nature and their wisdom, their bodies, the way they grew up in their climate and the rule by which they protected their exuberant genius [*den übermüthigen Genius*] from the overwhelming element.
>
> That is what constituted their sociability [*ihre Popularität*], the way they adapted themselves to foreign natures and communicated with them; that is why they have their peculiar individuality, which seems so full of life, inasmuch as supreme understanding in the Greek sense is a force of reflection, and this becomes comprehensible to us when we grasp the heroic body of the Greeks. It is tenderness, as in the quality of our own sociability.

To repeat, it is odd for us to think of Bordeaux as a city of "southern" people. We are more likely to see the ruins of antiquity in Arles or Nîmes or Nice, if not in the cities of Greece, coastal Turkey, and the Near East, cities that Hölderlin never saw. Yet by April, and certainly by May, Hölderlin would have experienced the warmth of the sun in the Gironde, a warmth that was new to him. He stresses that his was an embodied experience. Whereas the Germans of Swabia and Baden pride themselves on their inhabiting the sunniest part of Germany, with a warmth at least in the brief summer months that the north does not know, Hölderlin experiences here "the fire from heaven" that he has heretofore known only as an abstract principle, something learned from books. And it is true that his late poems are now full of references to a sun that scorches, a sun that produces arid wastelands. Some early editors and commentators speculated that Hölderlin himself suffered a sunstroke—indeed, sunstroke was one of the earliest explanations for his "madness," namely, that he was quite literally struck by the sun. Bertheau rejects the sunstroke theory, of course, as does everyone else nowadays, but

202 / Struck by Apollo

he speculates that Hölderlin ignored the warnings of his German hosts when he trudged across the Landes region west of Bordeaux to reach the sea. The Landes would have been a place to experience the "athletic quality" of the Greeks, whose wisdom is a wisdom of the body. Part of that wisdom is to recognize the need to protect oneself from the heat of the sun.

The Greeks' *Popularität* is not "popularity" in the modern sense but what characterizes the Greek people: their capacity not only to adapt themselves to the "overwhelming element" but to mix with the native populations on the Greek mainland and the islands, to say nothing about all the peoples of the ancient Near East, to communicate with them and accept them.[3] It is this "athletic" flexibility and agility of spirit and body that causes Hölderlin to marvel. The Greeks he has been reading and studying for many years now suddenly seem to him "so vital," so full of life, precisely because their intellect or *Verstand* is an organ not merely for mental calculation but for "supreme understanding," which "in the Greek sense is a force of reflection," *Reflexionskraft*. What sort of force is this? Whatever sort of "thought-fulness" characterizes it, it seems itself to be rooted in the Greek body. What historians have always called "the Greek miracle" becomes comprehensible to Hölderlin only when he grasps the heroic body of the Greeks. And what sort of athleticism is theirs? Hölderlin's answer continues to astonish us: "It is tenderness, as in the quality of our own sociability."

The heroic body as tender, *zärtlich*? I am still struck with amazement, and I cannot resist further comment on it. Hölderlin is surely thinking of Achilles, whom he characterizes not as the vengeful warrior who desecrates Hector's body but as the young man who runs to his mother and weeps. Achilles weeps because Agamemnon has claimed Briseïs as his prize, tearing her from Achilles' side. Six months after the dreadful scene in Frankfurt that results in Hölderlin's banishment from the Gontard household—and from his Diotima—he writes the following unfinished poem on Achilles and his mother Thetis:

---

3. Hölderlin's use of the word *Popularität* seems close to that of his young contemporary Novalis. In *Pollen*, no. 49, Novalis writes: "The nation is an idea. We should become a nation. An accomplished human being is a small nation. Genuine *Popularität* is the human being's supreme goal." Novalis and Hölderlin are thinking the Latin *popularitas* in its primary sense, as what comprises a "national character." Only when a populist demagogue flatters and deludes the people does the word take on its second meaning, today the common one. I have tried to capture Hölderlin's sense of the Greek (or southerly) character with the word *sociability*, even if that word too can be vulgarized. See Novalis (Friedrich von Hardenberg), *Werke, Tagebücher und Briefe*, 3 vols., ed. Hans-Joachim Mehl and Richard Samuel (Munich: Hanser Verlag, 1978), 2:247; cf. 2:252.

Splendid son of gods! when you lost the one you loved,
  You went to the ocean's rim, wept aloud into the flood,
Lamenting, your heart plunging into the depths of the holy abyss,
  Into the stillness. There, far from the embattled ships,
Far beneath the waves, in a peaceful grotto, azure Thetis
  Dwelled, she who protected you, goddess of the sea.
Mother she was to the young man, this powerful goddess;
  In earlier days on the rocky coast of the island she suckled
The boy lovingly, nourished him on the mighty song of the waves,
  Dipped him in the bath that lent him the strength of heroes.
And the mother heard the youth's lament, ascended mournfully
  From the seabed like a puff of cloud that climbs the sky;
With tender embrace she stilled the pains of her darling boy,
  And he heard the sweet nothings that meant she would
    help him.
Son of gods! would that I were like you, for then I could sing
  My secret suffering with confidence to one of the celestials.
I will not see that happen. I must bear humiliation, as though
    I belonged
  No more to her, though she's the one my tears remember,
You good gods! you who hear every human being who pleads
    with you.
  Ah! I have been loving you, holy light, intensely and so fervently,
Since the day I was born, and you, earth, with your fonts and
    forests;
  Father Aither, all too longingly and purely this heart of mine
Has felt you—oh, you who are beneficent, assuage my suffering,
  Lest the soul in me lose its tongue all too soon, [. . .]
                                        (CHV 1:200)

Frau Gock is evidently no Thetis. And, at least for Hölderlin, Achilles is
not the man of wrath. Rather, Hölderlin sings the tears of Achilles, the
hero who mourns Patroclus, killed by Hector, but also the hero who, after
he kills Hector in turn, restores the mutilated body to a tenderly grieving
father. He is above all the man who weeps over the loss of Briseïs. How
odd it is, Hölderlin must have thought, that the antiquities collection at the
Louvre contains no statues of Achilles. It is as though no sculptor dared to
portray the greatest and most tender of the heroes. No one could compel
Achilles to come out of his tent and serve as a model. Yet the sculptor of
Diomedes, the makers of all the Hermes statues, and above all the Praxiteles

204 / Struck by Apollo

who adores his Phryne down to the most luxuriant detail—all these artists seem to have learned the lesson of Homer's Achilles, the hero of tenderness.

One of the last poems Hölderlin tried to write, not long before he was taken to the Autenrieth Clinic, bears the title "Greece." He worked on it through three drafts but was unable to complete it. In it he searches for the "laws" that shape the development of the ancient culture that meant so much to him. He mentions several "laws" of development in the various drafts, "unity," "science," and "song," but there is one constant, namely, *Zärtlichkeit*, "tenderness."—It remains a central mystery for Hölderlin-studies and for much more than that.

Commentators often have great difficulty accepting the final clause of the paragraph's last sentence: *Zärtlichkeit* and the Greeks is one thing, but tenderness and the *Germans*? When we recall Hyperion's devastating portrait of the barbaric German, who is merely a shard of broken humanity, never complete enough for something like tenderness, it makes some of his editors want to add one word to Hölderlin's sentence, "and this is what our people *lack*." It may well be, however, that Hölderlin sees a possible connection between the "contraries" (as the stranger at Joué-les-Tours put it) of north and south, the German and the Greek, at least on better days. Perhaps Hölderlin thinks of it as a possibility for the future. It seems certainly true that if the name Hölderlin is a "test" that the German people have to confront, as Heidegger claims it is, no one would be more astonished than Heidegger to realize that the test is about how to embody tenderness. This would have been an incomprehensible addition to Heidegger's "Self-Assertion of the German University": the primary "service" of the German student body, as of the heroic body, would have to be the cultivation of tenderness.—But to return to the letter.

> When I saw the statues from antiquity, they made an impression that not only helped me to understand the Greeks more readily but also revealed to me the highest form of art, which, even though it is in extreme motion, phenomenalizing concepts and everything that we take seriously, nevertheless stands quite still and preserves everything for itself, such that certitude in this sense is the highest kind of sign.

These are the particular lines that encourage us to think that Hölderlin visited the antiquities section of the Louvre. As mentioned earlier, he also apparently saw there Michelangelo's *Slaves*, pieces that so impressed him that they gave him one of the pseudonyms that he used during the decades

Beyond Bordeaux and Back / 205

of his withdrawal and seclusion. His own isolation in the Tübingen Tower may have been "sculpted," as it were, in alternating forms of "rebellion" and "repose," both of them forms of a servitude, perhaps even of enslavement.—But, again, to return to Hölderlin's letter, for it suddenly strikes out a new direction. Hölderlin writes the following about his current situation:

> It was necessary for me, after several shattering experiences and matters that touched my soul, to get myself settled [*mich vestzusetzen*] for a time, and in the meantime, I am living in the town of my father [*in meiner Vaterstadt*].

These *Erschütterungen* surely include Susette's death, perhaps also his having been robbed during the journey home, and perhaps also his desperation about not being able to hold out in Bordeaux. Matters that touched his soul, or rather shattered it, probably include a scene that is said to have occurred upon his return to Nürtingen. I have referred to it briefly more than once in these pages. Before Hölderlin reached home, his luggage had arrived at Nürtingen, having been sent on ahead from Bordeaux and then from Strasbourg. His mother, going through it, found a small box hidden away beneath the false bottom of the chest. She opened it and found the letters to her son from Susette. She would have recognized the name as that of the wife of her son's former employer, Jacob Gontard, and the mother of Gontard's four children. She would also have recognized the feelings expressed in those letters and the details of their trysts. No doubt when Hölderlin crossed the threshold of the Nürtingen house, the mother lectured her son on the mortal sins of fornication and complicity in adultery. Tradition says that he flew into a rage and drove her and everyone else out of the house. From that point on he tried to avoid Nürtingen as much as he could, living for the most part in rooms his friend Sinclair arranged for him in Bad Homburg vor der Höhe. Yet it is clear that during the months Hölderlin spent in Sinclair's neighborhood, roughly from 1802 to 1804, both in Regensburg and then later in Bad Homburg, he was able to calm himself and pursue his work. This is the period during which, or rather at the beginning of which, the second letter to Böhlendorff is written—while he is still in Nürtingen. Yet the simple fact that Hölderlin's letter refers to his *Vaterstadt* may be telling.

Although it interrupts the narrative of the letter, I want to insert here some observations by Laplanche—derived from the theories of Jacques Lacan—concerning the roles of mother and father in Hölderlin's ostensible "schizophrenia." The title of Laplanche's work says it all, albeit by way of

206 / Struck by Apollo

indirection: *Hölderlin et la question du père*. Like Nietzsche and Jean-Paul Sartre after him, Hölderlin grew up without a father. Sartre, in *Les mots*, says that the absence of a father was the most beneficial and liberating factor of his life—no one was there to construct a punishing superego for him.[4] Why does this liberation not work for either Hölderlin or Nietzsche?

The prevailing Lacanian doctrine concerning the father is that the very *name* of the father is his "non!" to the son: the *nom-du-père* is the *non! du père*, especially where the child's desire for and dependence on the mother's affections are concerned. One might therefore suppose that the absence of a father can only mean a *yes* to life, a *yes* to the satisfaction of needs and the fulfillment of desires. Yet Laplanche's thesis is that the father's absence condemns Hölderlin to a certain helplessness in the face of womankind and love relationships in general. To use Lacan's language, which is based in part on the work of Melanie Klein, it is the absence of any integration of the phallus into Hölderlin's subjectivity, the absence of the *law* of the father, that disables him. According to Laplanche (JL 36, 43, 53–54, 89), Hölderlin's "forces" are "alienated in the mother" for his entire life. The mother "occupies" these forces or resources, one might say, somehow holding them in escrow; she absorbs them into her own schemes and plans for her boy. There is no law or "regulatory element" instituted by the father that would decree for the mother a more limited and more narrowly defined scope in the life of her son. Such a law, rather than being a mere negative for the son, rather than amounting to sheer prohibition, would have emancipated him from her tyranny.

We know that Nietzsche, toward the end of his active life, was able to rail against his mother and sister and to achieve at least a modicum of furious independence from their domination; in fact, after his breakdown, on two separate occasions, Nietzsche tried to strangle his mother. As far as we know, Hölderlin made no such attempt, even though his mother was far less generous than Nietzsche's had been. A handwritten note from Frau Gock lists all the monies she sent her son over the years to cover his expenses; these monies were in fact from Hölderlin's patrimony, an inheritance that his biological father had willed to him, not to her. The mother notes that these expenditures, which she regards as her son's debts to her, are to be "forgiven—as long as he remains obedient." During the first twenty years in which he was committed to the Tübingen Tower, years during which his mother was still alive, she never made the brief journey to visit her eldest son—reduced finally now to penury and strict obedience. He wrote her regularly, apparently on the insistence of

---

4. Jean-Paul Sartre, *Les mots* (Paris: Gallimard, 1964), 11.

his guardian Zimmer, signing himself as "your most obedient son." Yet he had frustrated her hopes, had sinned egregiously, and had disobeyed her, so that she never released to him his patrimony and never visited him. The last letter from her to him that survives is dated October 29, 1805, prior to his being seized and committed to the Autenrieth Clinic and his subsequent breakdown. Of all the "shattering" things that "touched" his soul, one may safely say, it was the lack of a loving mother and the absence of a protecting father that struck that soul with an unforgiving hand. It was a kind of blow, as though from Apollo, in the back, leaving him exposed to the lances and cudgels of the world.—But to return to the Böhlendorff letter, which now seems more paratactic than ever:

> Nature, here in my homeland, grips me ever more powerfully the more I study it. The storm, not merely in its extreme appearance, but already as a power and as a figure in the other forms of the sky, the light in its effects, shaping us as a nation, as a matter of principle, and as our very destiny [*nationell und als Prinzip und Schiksaalsweise bildend*], such that there is something holy for us, its compelling us in its coming and going, what is characteristic of our forests and the way in which in any given region all the various characteristics of nature come together, so that all the sacred places on Earth convene in one place, and the philosophical light that shines in my window is now my joy; so that I may preserve the way by which I have come to be here!

The struggle to think of his life as a way, a path, even if by virtue of what *Hyperion* calls "an eccentric orbit," is evident here, returning as he has from a different world back to the village of his childhood. The odd parataxis or sheer listing of natural events, especially the coming and going of storms, the experience of them as holy, and the sense of the forests and all of nature as coming together to meet in one place, the place in whose light he happens to be sitting and writing, is also something that appears from time to time in the final poems, the great hymns for which he is most remembered.

> Dear friend! I believe we will not want to be a footnote to the poets who have gone before; rather, I believe that our mode of song [*die Sangart*] will assume an altogether different character, and that we will not come into fashion because, since the Greeks, we are beginning once again to sing in a way that is appropriate to our fatherland, a natural way, an authentically original way.

208 / Struck by Apollo

Surely, Hölderlin is hoping for a *Sangart* that is appropriate to the land of his fathers—no matter how revelatory his voyage to France has been—and he is desiring to sing in an authentically original way. Yet his notion of "fatherland" is even more difficult to understand than his "father city"; commentators have been arguing the matter for generations now. One thing seems to be certain: he does not mean some sort of nationalism or German "exceptionalism," much less chauvinism. Nor does it seem to be the effort to found or ground a new history for the German people, as Heidegger, in his lecture course on Hölderlin's *Andenken*, takes it to be. Indeed, more French phrases appear now in Hölderlin's notes and sketches than ever before, so that it cannot be a matter of some sort of Nürtingen-Athens "axis." It is also true to say that Hölderlin's late hymns stretch the German language in a way that his more established colleagues found unheard of and even unhinged. His father tongue, as both Georg Trakl and Paul Celan would have agreed, and as Nietzsche certainly already knew, would never be the same after Hölderlin's productions—even if, during his years in the tower, it was only the younger people, most of them students in Tübingen, who recognized his greatness.—Now to cite the close of the letter.

> But write me soon. I need your clear-sounding tones. The psyche among friends, the genesis of thought in conversation and in letters, is necessary for artists. Otherwise we have no one for ourselves; rather, we belong to the holy image that we shape.
>
> Yours,
>
> H.

The "psyche among friends," an odd phrase, almost seems to refer to the French sense of *psyche*, namely, a full-length mirror: Hölderlin looks to whatever friends he can win to himself, especially older male friends, so that he can discern in them who he may be. If he seems to himself "odd," as Madame Salaberry thought, it is not merely because he is "a German." Though he may well be mirrored back to himself as a German, it is safe to say that whatever Hölderlin's "turn toward the fatherland" is, it has nothing to do with an underestimation of the foreign. His memories of the Gironde are too positive and too powerful for him to spurn France or the foreign in general. The issue is whether he can make his peace with his return, with his being back again at the point from which he started, not only on his voyage to Bordeaux but also on his life voyage. The light at his window is one thing; his memories of the foreign are another. Or perhaps those memories are that very light, a light shining out of the south to which the November sun has by that time flown.

Let me now turn to the question of Hölderlin's illness in greater detail. Laplanche reads Hölderlin's poems and prose texts with care and intelligence. This in itself is remarkable, inasmuch as most psychiatrists who pontificate on Hölderlin's illness, "analyzing" a patient they have never seen or interviewed, betray their complete innocence of any sense of what poetry is. An entire medical literature laments that Hölderlin's poems are disjointed, the syntax distended, and the word choice nothing short of bizarre, concluding that anyone who writes like this must be mad. I recall a story—I have no idea if it is true—that when T. S. Eliot sent an early draft of *The Wasteland* to Ezra Pound, that bolder poet struck out every other line of Eliot's draft; the result was not a series of coherent propositions but an epoch-making poem in which stark images loom one after the other with little or no readily discernible "logic." Indeed, the parataxis of the stark imagery constitutes the wasteland. Of Hölderlin, one may say that he had his Ezra at home. What makes the psychiatrists brood causes the lover of poetry to leap for joy. The fact that the very best parts of Laplanche's book are those in which he reads and comments on *Hyperion, The Death of Empedocles*, and the poems is therefore laudable. Less than laudable are the medical diagnoses and psychoanalytic speculations Laplanche engages in, which seem to me overhasty and sometimes downright sloppy.

Laplanche argues that Hölderlin's madness becomes evident already in June 1795 with his flight from Schiller's and Goethe's Jena. Laplanche follows the theme of that madness to the end of the first Homburg stay (September 1798 to June 1800). It is as though, not merely after 1806, but already by 1800, the case is closed. Yet there is an ambiguity, even an ambivalence, here. On the one hand, Laplanche does not hesitate to call Hölderlin's condition a form of "psychosis," and the diagnosis "schizophrenia" appears often in his text; on the other hand, he denies that what most psychiatrists designate under both terms applies without reservation to Hölderlin. Most importantly, he concedes that if psychosis is "the absence of the consciousness of one's morbid condition," an absence one may describe as "closure, the impenetrability of [the patient's] delirious certitude" (JL 3), then Hölderlin is never psychotic. Hölderlin hears no voices assuring him of his elevated mission. He does not see visions of either Dionysos or Diotima returning to him, except as figures of poetry. He does not possess what some would call the wretched euphoria of the mad. There is no illusory consolation in his life after 1806, but only the desperate need to hunker down, to conceal

210 / Struck by Apollo

and protect himself. However, Laplanche does not shy from saying that during the period of his greatest works, presumably from 1800 to 1806, "Hölderlin shows manifest signs of schizophrenic illness" (JL 13).

Early on in his study, Laplanche cites as corroboration of his diagnosis Schiller's nervousness about the state of mind of his young protégé (JL 17), along with Charlotte von Kalb's judgment that "a disorder of mind" is clearly evident by the end of the year 1794 (JL 28). Von Kalb's judgment is particularly important for Laplanche because it confirms his own sense of the underlying causes of Hölderlin's malady. Whereas the Waltershausen tutorship begins in January 1794 without incident, at some point during the year Hölderlin is given the assignment of night watches over his pupil Fritz, who is now in puberty and masturbating with great frequency and élan. Hölderlin, perhaps understandably, is unable to cope with the situation. Laplanche does not pause to wonder whether any mortal would flourish in the role of masturbation nightwatchman for a pupil. He takes Hölderlin's allergic reaction to young Fritz's jouissance to be extreme and as pointing to something he calls "the failed integration of a phallus into Hölderlin's subjectivity" (JL 29). The "unmastered phallus" looms in Hölderlin's own life at that very moment, according to Laplanche, with his brief but intense affair with Wilhelmine Kirms, the companion of Von Kalb. This affair ends in Kirms's pregnancy, which Hölderlin himself never seems to have learned of and certainly never acknowledged.

It would be sheer speculation to believe and to hope that the phallus makes a modest return—not to mastery but to tender intimacy—in the deeply loving relationship with Susette three years later. Whatever we may hope or believe, however, Laplanche stresses the repeated failure of Hölderlin's love relationships from boyhood on, and we do have to recall his willingness to "pass on" his early loves to a more capable lover. Following Lacan's theory, Laplanche understands this failure as marking the absence of a certain *loi*, which would be "the law of the father" (ibid.). As we remember, Hölderlin's father was absent twice over: his biological father died when Hölderlin was two, his stepfather at the end of the boy's eighth year. Virtually every biographer agrees that the search for a father figure dominates much of the poet's life. The prime instance of this search is Schiller, although one thinks too of Goethe, Herder, Immanuel Niethammer, Schubart, Heinse, and a large handful of other figures from whom Hölderlin seeks both protection and inspiration, always in vain. Laplanche's thesis, which we have already heard, and which has to be taken seriously, is that Hölderlin's "forces" are "alienated in the mother" throughout his life; there is no "law of the father,"

Beyond Bordeaux and Back / 211

no regulatory agency that would define and limit the role of the mother in his life (JL 33).

It is safe to say that this regulatory agency attributed by Laplanche and Lacan to "the law of the father" will not be clear to most readers. It is unclear—albeit intriguing—to me. To repeat, we are all familiar with the "name" and the "no!" of father, *le nom (non!) du père*, which interrupts and frustrates the child's need to possess the mother's affections entirely. Yet the "positive" side of the paternal no-saying is surely not so well understood. Lacan's thesis, based in part on Klein's notion of the devouring mother, is highly speculative but also highly suggestive. When the father is missing, writes Laplanche, as in the cases of Hölderlin, Gérard de Nerval, and Nietzsche, there is no possible "regulation" of the mother's role. If the usual Oedipus Complex has the father as an interloper, one the child wishes to make "the damaged third," that is, the one to be excluded from possession of the mother, the absence of the father inverts the entire situation: it is the mother who comes to possess her child exclusively. To put it in philosophical terms, terms Hölderlin would have heard at Jena, Laplanche speculates that the Fichtean *Nicht-Ich*, or "Not-I," which ought to define the ego as well as limit it, is in Hölderlin's case simply "nothing," *le rien*, so that something about the child's life will be permanently "foreclosed" or in default (JL 37). Even though Schiller is more than benign and helpful to him, Schiller being not only for Hölderlin but for an entire generation "the sovereign censor and arbiter of contemporary literature" (JL 38), Hölderlin feels under constant pressure from this "nothing" that defines him. This pressure will cause him to "flee" situations over and over again. His relation to the law of the father will always be that of the outlaw, that is, of one who is precisely outside the protection of the law, one in whom the lifelight is bright with death.

In a word, Hölderlin cannot possibly fulfill the demands of the mother, since those demands are not tempered by the law of the father. Hölderlin senses nothing more than his own abjection before the (missing) law. On the one hand, the young poet must flee to rescue his subjectivity, experienced as his "originality," from the overwhelming influence of the otherwise sought-after father figure; on the other hand, he has no faith in either the abiding love of that figure or his own talent, his own gifts. And his flight from the spectral father, felt always as the father's prior abandonment of the son's undeserving self, carries over into all his love relationships: for Hölderlin, "love implies this feeling of absolute indigence, this moment in which the subject finds himself literally annihilated, stripped of himself in

212 / Struck by Apollo

the presence of his object" (JL 40). As Schiller withdraws and becomes more reserved about his young protégé—and Goethe was always distant, even if Hölderlin describes him as a loving father—Hölderlin despairs of his worth as poet and man. The law of the father, which would have prevented the mother from wholly reabsorbing her "produced object," that is, her son, is somehow abrogated, his future foreclosed. The son succumbs to absolute possession by the mother (JL 42–43).

While these notions and analyses chafe, simply because of their absolutizing tendency and their claim of universal applicability, they do help us understand one of the most remarkable aspects of Hölderlin's relation to his mother. As I mentioned earlier, he never really seems to have understood—at least as far as the letters allow us to see—how tightfisted and tyrannical his mother has been with him during his entire life. Over and over again he writes about her generosity and her self-sacrifice on his behalf; he feels that he can never repay her. Meanwhile, it is clear that she has deprived him of his own patrimony, so that when he is finally incapacitated, incarcerated in the tower, as though he were a figure in a fairy tale, it is both a "moral" and a financial victory for her: she dies a devout and wealthy woman, having diverted her son's patrimony to her own securely invested accounts, transferring precious little of it to him to cover his meager expenses. During his active years she uses the patrimony to enforce her son's "obedience," and when, after his initial recalcitrance, he finally capitulates, collapsing into total submission, she applies to the local prince for a state pension for the patient, claiming falsely that she herself is insolvent. The state grants the pension, and the mother, investing that too, becomes even wealthier. By 1843, the year of Hölderlin's death, his paternal inheritance has tripled in value (JL 90). His widowed mother is thus the perfect integration of piety and capital, the happy marriage of Weber and Marx.

Laplanche's interpretation chafes most irritatingly, however, when the notions of *forclusion* and *manque*, "foreclosure and lack," are carried over into the region of *signification* (JL 43–44, 97). At times Laplanche seems to accept the traditional complaint that Hölderlin's verses lack a certain regulatory law and that this lack is a sign of his illness. What Knaupp recognizes as Hölderlin's skillful use of something like a middle voice, enabling our own astonishment at the mournful and splendid rising of the moon to be read as the moon's astonishment, as though the moon could see herself in a *psyche*, Laplanche interprets as unregulated mental confusion. Whereas Hölderlin marvels at the fact that "human beings dwell / In France," Laplanche can see only Hölderlin's abjection and disorientation. As I also mentioned earlier, Adorno's "Parataxis" is an effective antidote. As one works through the *Homburger Folioheft* and all its fragments and lists of isolated names and phrases, one has to remember that one is in the hands not of a madman but of a lover of language—one who perhaps paid heed to the names of every village he passed through on his way to and from Bordeaux, "meaningless" names, as it were, mere phonemes, mere chunks of language.

Yet certain of Laplanche's judgments make sense: it is true that the *Grundton* of Hölderlin's *Hyperion* is the rapid alternation of elation and dejection (JL 62), perhaps also true that the poet's desire in *The Death of Empedocles* is for an impossible "primordial Object" (JL 90). In the third and final version of the play, which depicts the conflict between Empedocles and Manes, the principal problem may be fruitfully described as an imaginary that suddenly becomes radically uncertain of itself (JL 119). Yet is the play for that reason a *pathographie*? Laplanche's genuine insight, it seems to me, is that the dissolution of the Empedocles project is instructive for our own situation as creative writers and poets. He notes Hölderlin's resistance to the identity philosophy of his former colleague and friend Hegel: instead of Hegel's "identity of identity and nonidentity," Hölderlin's is, in Laplanche's words, "the difference of difference and nondifference" (JL 116). However, Laplanche takes this to be a sign of schizophrenia, and not in the sense of Gilles Deleuze and Félix Guattari, who of course have not yet written their *Anti-Oedipus* at the time Laplanche is writing. Nor can Laplanche be aware of Derrida's "Différance," which will be delivered some six or seven years down the road. And yet at the very end of his reading of Hölderlin's *Empedocles* Laplanche writes something that seems to me to be undeniably true: "It is he [Hölderlin] who re-opens the question of schizophrenia as a universal problem," *la schizophrénie comme problème universel* (JL 133). Or, thinking of all philosophy since Aristotle, schizophrenia as the problem of universals, including the universals of psychoanalysis.

In short, Lacan's idea of *la loi du père*, when applied as a principle of the symbolic, of signification, or of literature, may well be a bizarre phantasm: the hypothesis that in addition to paternal prohibition there is a regulatory function that puts all the signifiers into place, so that delirium can be avoided, the imaginary yoked, and the symbolic achieved, sometimes seems to be as mad as its foreclosure putatively makes the schizophrenic. To squeeze the poet's universe into a ball and roll it toward some overwhelming question—this is what psychoanalysis always seems to risk. And yet mothers and fathers, whether present or absent, do have their way with the creators of literature along with the rest of us, do they not? Even and perhaps especially when they are absent. When the fathers go missing—even in a time that prides itself on the insignificance and irrelevance of paternity—who can

214 / Struck by Apollo

honestly say what the possible consequences are? Nietzsche, not long before he reflected on the "hard" yet "tender" wood from which a human being should be carved, called the conjunction of his dead father and his living mother the "riddle" or the "enigma" of his existence. He claimed that this mixed heritage was not only his "singularity" but also his "good fortune," his *Glück*: "As my father, I am already dead," he wrote; "as my mother I am still alive and am growing old."[5] Hölderlin brooded constantly over his own proclivity to mourn both of his defunct fathers, even as he begged his mother to stop her brooding. Perhaps, like both of his dead fathers, Hölderlin is doubly defunct, the victim of two absent fathers and one very present mother. This would be Laplanche's suspicion.

And yet. Reinhard Horowski, a retired neuropathologist and avid reader of Hölderlin, is impatient with all these psychoanalytic theories. And he is furious over all the psychiatric diagnoses of dead persons who were never patients of those very confident diagnositicians. The title of his book comes from some graffiti spray-painted on the Tübingen Tower—it was there on my first visit to Tübingen many years ago, but it has by now been removed, perhaps regrettably—announcing, in calligraphic dialect, *Der Hölderlin isch et verruckt gwä*, "Hölderlin was *not* crazy." Horowski's book is not a diatribe, however. He carefully reviews the library of books and articles that have speculated on the supposed causes of Hölderlin's illness and he roundly rejects all of them.

Important for his discussion of Hölderlin's illness is the autopsy report: Hölderlin's brain was in excellent condition for his seventy-three years of life, and there was no "liquefaction," as had been in the cases of Nietzsche and Nietzsche's father. (To be sure, however, nothing in an autopsy report would be likely to confirm or disconfirm a diagnosis of schizophrenia or psychosis.) What eventually killed Hölderlin—but also slowed him down considerably, to the point of apathy, during the final decades of his life— was, according to Horowski, a stenosis (or deterioration) of the aortic valve, the valve through which the heart pumps oxygen-enriched blood to brain and body. Horowski speculates that mercury poisoning (in the form of *Kalomel*, prescribed in massive doses as an emetic and purgative at the Autenrieth Clinic in 1805–1806) along with overdoses of belladonna and opium administered during those same months to quell the rages were the principal contributing factors to whatever confusion and apathy afflicted the poet during the final thirty-five years of his life (RH 113–15, 149).

---

5. Nietzsche, *Ecce homo*; KSW 6:264.

Horowski does not deny that Hölderlin's inherited disposition made him hypersensitive and that periods of depression regularly followed his manias and rages, nor does he deny that mental illness played a significant role in Hölderlin's ancestry, passed down not so much by the more mobile ministers and pastors in his family background as by the local sacristans and lay administrators of the churches who were bound to one locale and who hence contributed to a certain amount of inbreeding.

Yet what Horowski stresses has little to do with genetics—the current best hope of scientistic positivism, which seems to be conquering philosophers of every stripe nowadays—or even with neuropathology. He emphasizes the two major disappointments of Hölderlin's life: his failure, in his own eyes, to be welcomed among the greats of his time and to be acknowledged as a significant poet; and the death of Susette, a death he had both envisaged in his fiction—Susette had complained to Hölderlin about Diotima's death in *Hyperion*, but he replied that the plot of the novel required it—and predicted in his letters to her after their separation. These two losses or failures, these two abundant sources of grief, guilt, and feelings of inadequacy, against the backdrop of a mother he could never satisfy and the two fathers who vanished from his life over and over again, are, in Horowski's view, decisive for the rages and the eventual apathy.

There are flashes of insight and wit in the final verses Hölderlin wrote for his visitors, and there are many anecdotes that suggest the survival of irony and humor in the poet of the tower. Yet the powers that produced *Der Weingott, Andenken*, and *Patmos* are in abeyance after 1806. And not even the fondest memories of the gardens of Bordeaux or of the scent of lemon and olive oil up his nose when he was on the wharves of the Garonne, nor even memories of his incomparable Diotima, inexplicably transported in his imagination to the dunes of the Atlantic coast, could restore those powers.

If I truncate this discussion of Hölderlin's voyage "beyond" both Bordeaux and his homeland, "beyond" in the sense of the poet's ever-increasing remoteness and isolation after 1806, it is because such discussions do not seem to be fruitful for our appreciation of the poetry. Joe and I did not make our own trips to Bordeaux and back for the purpose of a diagnosis. In the end, it is not the long decline into twilight but the sunbursts of achievement that gripped us—the achievements of the poetry and the achievement of these adventurous voyages to and from the sea. As exhausting and as dangerous as these journeys were for him, they were also sometimes for him and almost always for us sources of immense joy. He himself tells us this. And so I want to append a joyous word to the conclusion of the project, if only in the form of an epilogue.

Photo 65. Terpsichore dances atop the National Theater of Bordeaux.

Epilogue

Viva la joia!

"Why does no one take joy in the sacred dance?" asks Hölderlin of his contemporaries—and of us. One sometimes wishes that Hölderlin had made his voyage to Bordeaux a generation earlier. He might then have crossed Tristram Shandy's path. Tristram, or his voluble "companion," Laurence Sterne, by that time had surrendered his post-chaise ticket for a mule. Plodding along somewhere in Gascogne, perhaps quite close to Bordeaux, Tristram comes across a group of country revelers. The revelers call out to him—they need him to complete their dance party. And so, the reluctant traveler who is fleeing Death, which is the ultimate foreclosure, is swept up into the celebration. Sterne depicts the scene at the end of the seventh volume of his shaggy novel:

> The youth struck the note upon the tabourin—his pipe followed, and off we bounded. . . .
>
> The sister of the youth, who had stolen her voice from heaven, sung alternately with her brother—'twas a Gascoigne roundelay.
>
>
>
> VIVA LA JOIA!
> FIDON LA TRISTESSA!
>
>
>
> The nymphs joined in unison, and their swains an octave below them—
>
> . . . *Viva la joia!* was in her lips—*Viva la joia!* was in her eyes. A transient spark of amity shot across the space betwixt us—She looked amiable!—Why could I not live, and end my days thus? Just disposer of our joys and sorrows, cried I, why could not a man sit down in the lap of contentment here—and dance, and sing, and say his prayers, and go to heaven with this nut-brown maid? (VII, 43; 512)

218 / Struck by Apollo

This is Sterne's *Andenken*, complete with *braunen Frauen*. Yet neither Sterne nor Hölderlin will end their lives dancing to a "Gascoigne roundelay." Hölderlin's powers, after 1806, are, to repeat, in abeyance. There is one poem, however, written apparently in 1808, or perhaps much later, possibly as late as the 1820s, that strikes us as reminiscent of the great elegies of Hölderlin's past. It is a long unfinished poem in which the narrative voice appears to belong to Hölderlin's Diotima, Susette herself. This remarkable poem surely has flashes of insight into love and catastrophe, and perhaps—Bertheau affirms this strongly—even a memory or two of gardens in either Frankfurt or Bordeaux, of the sea, and of the sand dunes near Arcachon, Lège, and Soulac, even if Hölderlin's Diotima was never there, at least not when he was. Hölderlin's Diotima approaches the poet from the realm of the dead and says, or sings (CHV 1:911–13):

> If, out of the remoteness, since we are parted,
> I am still known to you, if, out of the past,
> O you who shared my sorrows! I can
> Still paint for you a few good things,
>
> Then tell me, how does the woman who loves you
> Await you? In those gardens where, after a wretched
> And dark time, we found one another?
> Here by the streams of the holy, primeval world?
>
> This I must say, a few good things entered
> Into your ken, as off in the distance you
> Once happily gazed all around you, a
> Human being forever shuttered, with gloomy
>
> Aspect. How the hours flitted by, how
> Silent was my soul about the truth, that
> I had been so sundered.
> Yes! I confess it, I was yours.
>
> Truly! since everything that is known to you
> You want to write down and convey to my memory
> In letters, that is how it is with me as well,
> So that I, now gone, tell all touching the past.
>
> Was it spring? Was it summer? The nightingale,
> With its sweet song, lived among the birds
> That dwelled not far off in the bush, and
> Trees wafted their fragrances over us.

The unobstructed paths, the low-lying scrub and the sand
　　On which we trod, made me more joyful still,
　　　　And lovelier the hyacinths blossomed there,
　　　　　　Or the tulips, the violets, the carnations.

About the houses and up the walls sprouted ivy,
　　Green the blessed penumbra of long avenues. Often
　　　　In the evening, in the morning, we were there,
　　　　　　Said some things, happy to see one another.

In my arms the young man came alive, he who,
　　Abandoned, one day walked out of the landscape,
　　　　Which he showed me with a heavy heart,
　　　　　　Though the names of these rare places

And all their beauty he retained, whatever on those
　　Blessed shores meant so much to me as well,
　　　　All that burgeons in our homeland, or
　　　　　　Concealed even from a lofty prospect

From which one can usually espy the wide sea,
　　Yet no one wants to be that high. Be content,
　　　　And think of her who still takes pleasure in it,
　　　　　　Because the charming day shone down on us,

Commenced with a confession or a squeeze of the hand,
　　Which united us. Ah! woe is me!
　　　　They were beautiful days. But
　　　　　　Mournful twilight followed hard upon.

You are so alone in the lovely world,
　　That is what you always say, my beloved.
　　　　But here is something you do not know,
　　　　　　[. . .]

This is where the fragment ends. He knows that she who survives only in the land of the dead knows something that he does not know. And he knows that now that she is gone forever, he never will know it. And yet they did love. They did know. There *was* a heroism of tenderness. And he can remember that, along with the names of "these rare places / And all their beauty." The sea will return all these things to him, as divine beauty

220 / Struck by Apollo

spills sea spawn and sea wrack onto the shore. He recalls, however, that the sea both takes and gives memory. Perhaps that is why his poem seems to confuse the sands of Arcachon and Soulac with the gravel paths of the gardens at White Hart, the Gontard winter residence in Frankfurt where the lovers last met—at least if Hölderlin did not make his way to Frankfurt during the final days of her illness.

Confined now as he is to the tower on the banks of the Neckar, where he writes this last great elegy, he remembers what his own *Andenken* advises the rest of us, advises anyone who will listen, to do:

> But go now and greet
> The lovely Garonne
> And the gardens of Bordeaux. . . .

"I still think of that," he says of southern France during the thirty-five years of his deepening isolation, "laden with golden dreams," dreaming dreams of the heroic, tender body.

> But hand me
> One of those fragrant cups
> Full of darkling light,
> That I may rest; for slumber
> Would be sweet among the shadows.
> It is not good
> Soullessly to ponder
> Mortal thoughts. Good
> Is a conversation, saying
> Things the heart means, listening much
> About days of love
> And deeds that were done.

He does have the satisfaction of knowing that "what remains the poets institute." That was his life's work. But the need for repose, for slumber, the desire to be a shade among shadows becomes prominent once the stories of the "deeds that were done" have been told and the "days of love" (Viva la joia!) have flown. He ends "The Wine God," the poem that has accompanied us all the way to Bordeaux and back, and perhaps even beyond, by telling us that Dionysos lulls to sleep even the rancorous one, even Cerberus, the three-headed dog of *ressentiment* that guards the gates of hell. Sometimes that hellish underworld was called *Orkus* by the Greeks, which they opposed to *Elysium*. Yet Hölderlin's poem in the end dissolves the opposition of underworld and upperworld. Bitterness abates. All is now turned more decisively to the Earth and all the rare and beautiful places of Earth, such as the place, the old cemetery in Tübingen, where Hölderlin is buried. The final stanza of *Der Weingott* says of Dionysos:

> Yes! they rightly say he reconciles the day with the night,
>   Guides the stars of heaven eternally down, eternally up,
> Forever gay, like the needles on the evergreen pine,
>   Which he loves, and the wreath of ivy he chose to weave
> Because it endures and leaves a trace of the flown gods
>   Even for the godless ones who dwell in gloom.
> What the ancient song foretells of the life to come,
>   Behold! that is what we are, underworld is upperworld.
> Miraculously and precisely it is fulfilled, as with humankind;
>   Let him believe who examines! but so much happens and
> So little has any consequence, for we are shades deprived of heart
>   Till Father Aither knows each one and belongs to everyone.
> Meanwhile, as a herald of joy, the spirit of wine comes,
>   Sent by deity to us shades here below. The blessed wisemen
> Among us know that this is so: a smile illumines their
>   Incarcerated soul, the light warms their eyes to thaw.
> The Titan dreams and sleeps in the arms of the Earth; even the
>   Envious one, the three-headed dog, drinks and sleeps.
>   (CHV 1:319)

Illustrations

Maps

1	Post-Coach Map of Europe in 1812, reprinted with the kind permission of the Bibliothèque historique des postes et des télécommunications, Paris. All the remaining maps in the book are details, that is, enlarged portions, of this 1812 map.	34
2	Nürtingen-Strasbourg.	41
3	Strasbourg-Colmar.	41
4	Colmar-Besançon.	42
5	Besançon-Chalon.	43
6	Chalon-Lyon.	43
7	Lyon-Clermont.	44
8	Clermont-Limoges.	44
9	Limoges-Périgueux.	45
10	Périgueux-Bordeaux.	45
11	Bordeaux-Saintes.	146
12	Saintes-Niort.	149
13	Niort-Blois.	150
14	Blois-Paris.	162
15	Blois-Chartres-Paris.	163

224 / Illustrations

16 Paris-Châlons. 165

17 Châlons-Metz-Nancy. 166

18 Metz-Nancy-Strasbourg. 166

Photographs

1 January sunset at Soulac-sur-Mer, near Bordeaux. v

2 Tübingen cemetery. "Friedrich Hölderlin, born March 29,
1770; died June 7, 1843." xiv

3 Nürtingen on the Neckar River. 1

4 The Sankt-Remigius-Kapelle near Wurmlingen, not far from
Tübingen. 6

5 Main courtyard of the Tübinger Stift. 9

6 The Hôtel Meyer, Allées de Tourny, Bordeaux. 18

7 The swollen Saône River. 48

8 The garden across the Neckar where Hölderlin played as a
child. 50

9 Between Horb-on-Neckar and Freudenstadt in the Black
Forest. 54

10 Atop the Kniebis Mountain in the northern Black Forest. 56

11 The Maison des Tanneurs, Strasbourg. 61

12 Seventh-century crypt of St. Pierre-le-Jeune church, Strasbourg. 63

13 Notre-Dame-de-Strasbourg, at the main portal of the
Strasburger Münster. 64

14 The *Liebfrauenmünster*, the Strasbourg Cathedral. 67

15 A field near the Doubs River, between Belfort and Besançon. 74

16 The Pont de Navilly over the Doubs River. 77

17 The Saône River not far from Chalon. 79

18 The Lyon Cathedral, St. Jean-le-Baptiste. 84

19	A Tuscan-style courtyard off the rue St. Georges in Vieux Lyon.	86
20	The theater at Lugdunum, the Roman Lyon.	88
21	A funeral mask at Lugdunum.	90
22	Cybele, wearing the mural crown, at Lugdunum.	92
23	The Monts-Dore, dominated by the Sancy Massif, southwest Auvergne.	96
24	The Cathedral of Clermont, Notre-Dame-de-l'Assomption.	97
25	*The Virgin with Over-Size Hands*, Clermont Cathedral.	98
26	A *Black Virgin* in the crypt of Notre-Dame-du-Port, Clermont.	100
27	Pontarion, "Bridge over Le Thaurion."	101
28	An old mill at St.-Léonard-de-Noblat on the Vienne River.	103
29	Château des Bories, near Antonne, approaching Périgueux.	103
30	The cloister at the Cathedral of Périgueux.	105
31	At Sourzac-sur-l'Isle, the ruins of a church destroyed during the Hundred Years' War.	106
32	Abandoned farmhouse in Pomarède, not far from Mompon-Ménestérol.	107
33	Soulac-sur-Mer, near Bordeaux.	108
34	Château Fongravey, the spring and fall residence of Consul Meyer at Blanquefort.	116
35	At Soulac-sur-Mer, the moon rising "in mourning and in splendor."	118
36	Gull at Soulac-sur-Mer, early morning.	120
37	Early morning at Soulac, Joe walking south toward Bordeaux.	121
38	The strand at Soulac.	121
39	The Bay of Arcachon; in the distance, the Dune du Pilat.	122
40	Plaque on the side of the Hôtel Meyer, Bordeaux.	129
41	Hölderlin's apartment in Bordeaux at rue Saint-Rémi no. 2 (now no. 4).	129

226 / Illustrations

42	Place de la Bourse, Bordeaux.	131
43	The Atlantic coast near Lège, west of Bordeaux.	133
44	Scrivener on the north side of Chartres cathedral.	144
45	The cathedral at Saintes and the ruins of the Roman arena.	148
46	Parthenay-sur-le-Thouet, Nouvelle-Aquitaine.	151
47	St. Pierre-de-Vieux-Parthenay.	151
48	Pond at the now vanished Château Rabière in Joué-les-Tours.	159
49	Blois on the Loire River.	160
50	Cathedral of Orléans, interior.	161
51	*Bacchus*, the Wine God, second century CE.	170
52	*The Aphrodite of Arles*, presumably a copy of the *Thespian Aphrodite* by Praxiteles.	176
53	*The Hermes Richelieu*, copy of an original by Naucydes, ca. 370–360 BCE.	178
54	*Diomedes* capturing the Palladion from Troy.	179
55	The *Antinous of Écouen*, from the second century CE.	180
56	*Apollo the Lizard Slayer*, based on a statue by Praxiteles, ca. 350–340 BCE.	181
57	A *Maenad* or *Bacchante*, copy of a statue from the fourth century BCE.	183
58	*Bacchus*, a detail of photo 51.	187
59	*Silenos Carrying Dionysos (Bacchus), Son of Zeus*. A portrait of Michelangelo?	188
60	The *Jupiter of Smyrna*, casting a long shadow.	190
61	Detail from *The Three Graces*, second century BCE.	191
62	Michelangelo Buonarroti, *The Slaves*, here the "rebellious" slave.	192
63	Michelangelo Buonarroti, *The Slaves*, here the "expiring" slave.	193
64	The Tübingen Tower viewed from the banks of the Neckar.	196
65	Terpsichore atop the National Theater of Bordeaux.	216

Tables

1 Minimum distances between major stops from Nürtingen to
Bordeaux   47

2 Minimum distances between major stops from Bordeaux to
Strasbourg   168

Index

Achilles, 137, 200, 202–203
Adorno, Theodor W., 110, 115, 212
Aeschylus, 136, 189
Aglaia, 154–55, 157–58, 191
Aither, 125–26, 137, 140, 181, 189, 203, 221
Alsace, x, 58, 71, 74, 91
Antigone, 60, 133–34, 139–41
Aorgischere, das (the "more intense"), 21, 23
Apollo, 22, 135, 141, 173, 180–82, 194, 198–200, 207, 226
Arcachon, Bay of, 114, 119, 122, 132–33, 218, 220, 225
Ariadne, 89, 141, 184
Aristophanes, 10, 76
Artemis, 64
Athena, 64, 175, 177
Atlantic Ocean, v, x, xi, 17, 39, 70, 72, 94, 106, 111, 112, 114–15, 117, 119, 132–33, 137, 145, 215, 226; *see also* sea
Audeguy, Stéphane, 163–64
Autenrieth Clinic, 197–98, 204, 207, 214
Auvergne, iv, ix, xi, 29, 42, 47, 73, 94–96, 100–102, 125

Bacchae, Bacchus, 170, 182–84, 187–88, 192, 226

Beaujolais, 79, 80, 82, 92
Beck, Adolf, xii n. 1, 39–40, 47, 49, 60, 72 n. 5, 73, 158
Bertaux, Pierre, 59, 167, 198
Bertheau, Jochen, xii n. 1, 7–8, 32–33, 37, 47, 73, 83, 94–95, 109–12, 114–15, 119, 122–24, 127–28, 130, 132, 145–47, 152, 155, 158, 167, 169, 192, 199, 200–202, 218
Besançon, xi, 27, 35n. 1, 40–43, 46–47, 70–71, 73–74, 77, 223–24
Black Forest, ix, 54–56, 73, 101, 224
Böhlendorff, Casimir Ulrich, 21–23, 26–27, 91, 135, 172, 198–99, 205, 207
Bordeaux, ix–xiii, 1, 3, 7–9, 16–19, 24, 28–36, 38–39, 42, 45–47, 49, 52, 53, 57, 58, 60, 65, 68, 69, 71, 76, 78, 85, 87–88, 93, 94–95, 99, 101–102, 106, 109–43, 145–46, 149, 154, 156, 167–69, 171–72, 184, 186, 188, 191n. 10, 197–99, 201–202, 205, 208, 213, 215, 216–18, 220, 223, 224, 225, 226, 227
Buonarroti, Michelangelo, 50, 172, 174, 187–88, 192–93, 204–205, 226
Burgundy, x, 40–41, 79–80, 85, 92

Catholicism, 62, 64–66

230 / Index

Celtic, Celts, 62, 99
Charente, 145, 147, 200; *see also*
  Vendée
Christianity, 5, 23, 62, 66, 81, 89,
  99, 102, 141; *see also* Evangelical,
  Pietism
clarity of presentation (*Klarheit der
  Darstellung*), 21–22, 155
Clermont-Ferrand, xi, 36, 42–44,
  46–47, 49, 70, 94–100, 223, 225
compassion, 23, 153
crypts, 62–63, 77, 99–100, 224, 225
Cybele, 91–92, 125

Danaë, 64, 140, 189
Dastur, Françoise, xi, xiii, 13n. 3, 42n.
  4, 46n. 5, 95
death and dying, 2, 5, 10, 19, 23,
  25–26, 28–32, 69, 80–81, 89, 91,
  139, 140, 142, 162, 167, 185–86,
  194, 198–201, 205, 209, 211, 212,
  213, 215, 217
Deguy, Michel, 114–15
Demeter, 25, 64–65, 81, 94, 140, 147
Denkendorf, 2, 51–52, 62
departure (*Abschied*), 14, 18–19, 23,
  24, 28, 30, 31, 33, 35, 53, 60n. 2,
  109, 111, 128, 154, 197
Derrida, Jacques, 115, 162, 213
destiny, 21, 23–24, 31–32, 52, 65,
  76, 118–19, 125–26, 207; *see also*
  "school of destiny"
Diomedes, 177, 179, 182, 203, 194,
  226
Dionysos, 64, 80, 81–82, 89, 91, 94,
  138–39, 141, 147, 182, 184–88,
  192, 194, 209, 220–21, 226
Dordogne River, 39, 70, 104, 112–15,
  117, 131
Doubs River, 35n. 1, 39–41, 46, 59,
  68, 70, 71, 73–79, 102, 224

eccentric orbit, 7, 198, 207

Empedocles of Acragas, 21, 89, 139,
  156, 199–200, 209, 213
Enlightenment, the, 7, 11
eros, erotic, 2, 138–39, 175, 194
Euripides, 182–84
Evangelical, 3, 9, 24, 62, 89; *see also*
  Christianity, Pietism

fatherland, 9, 19–20, 26–27, 53
fathers, ix, 2–5, 16, 25, 65, 78, 80,
  125–26, 138, 140–42, 152–55, 157,
  159, 189, 198, 203, 205–15, 221
Fichte, Johann Gottlieb, xi, 11, 13,
  20, 211
fire from heaven (*Feuer vom Himmel*),
  21–24, 87, 123, 135, 169, 189,
  199, 201
food, 25, 91–93
foreign, the, x, 22–23, 28, 53, 59,
  91, 123n. 5, 124, 134–35, 201,
  208–209
French Revolution, the, xi, 7–9, 18,
  42n. 4, 59, 85, 104, 119, 126, 130,
  152, 163, 164, 170–72, 175, 177,
  199; *see also* Girondist, Jacobin,
  Terror
Freud, Sigmund, 174–75, 177, 181,
  182n. 4, 201
friendship, 24, 31, 46n. 5, 127
funeral masks, 89–90, 141, 225

Gallo-Roman, 62, 87; *see also*
  Lugdunum, Saintes
Garonne River, 39, 47, 65n. 3, 70,
  112–17, 119, 124, 127, 130–31,
  145, 193, 215, 220
Gascogne, x, 24, 71, 117, 122–23,
  137, 217
Gironde, Girondist, 7, 9–10, 39, 70,
  85, 112, 114–15, 117, 131–32,
  145–46, 201, 208
Gock, Carl, 3, 5, 10, 11, 15, 17,
  19–20, 27–29

Index / 231

Gock, Johanna Christiana, 4, 93, 203, 206; *see also* mothers
God, 2, 5, 7, 8, 9n. 2, 19, 25, 27, 29, 67, 91; *see also* Christianity, Evangelical, Pietism
gods, the, 25–26, 29, 53, 62, 76, 81, 91, 93, 125–26, 137–41, 154–56, 174, 177, 182, 185–86, 189, 194, 201, 203, 221
Goethe, Johann Wolfgang, xi, 8n. 1, 11–13, 15, 25n. 5, 66, 93–94, 109, 139, 209, 210, 212
Gontard, Henry, 16, 71, 205
Gontard, Jacob, 15–16, 33, 71, 102, 202, 205, 220
Gontard, Susette ("Diotima"), 15–16, 30–33, 59–60, 71, 81, 93, 109, 132, 138, 143, 156, 167, 168, 189, 198, 199, 205, 210, 215, 218–19
Gothic, 62, 66, 97, 164, 182
Graves, Robert, 25–26
Greece, x, 24, 53, 87, 118, 123n. 5, 125, 127–28, 234, 155–56, 174–75, 201, 204
Greek, the Greeks, xi–xii, 10, 17–18, 21–23, 26, 80, 81, 85, 87, 93, 109, 130, 133, 134–37, 141–42, 154–58, 169, 171–91, 194, 199–204, 207, 220–21
Guthrie, W. K. C., 185–86

Hartmann, Moritz, 152–55, 157–58
Hauptwil, Switzerland, 17–18, 30, 54, 69
"heavenly ones," the, 125–26, 137–38, 141, 159–60; *see also* gods, Greek
Hegel, Georg Wilhelm Friedrich, xi, 7, 8–10, 12, 21, 52, 59, 81, 132, 163, 213
Heinse, Johann Jakob Wilhelm, 60n. 2, 81, 138–39, 173, 210
Helvétius, Claude Adrien, 7–8
Hemsterhuis, Franz, 7n. 1

Hera, 22, 187; *see also* Juno
Herakles, 64, 185
Heraclitus of Ephesus, 89
Herder, Johann Gottfried, 12–13, 127n. 6, 210
Hermes, 177–78, 182, 203–204, 226
heroes, 7–8, 23, 59, 89, 128, 161, 171, 199–200, 203–204, 219
"heroic body," the, xii, 134–38, 171–95, 202, 204, 220; *see also* tenderness
Hoffmann, E. T. A., 152n. 1, 153, 157, 182
Hölderlin, Friedrich, works cited: "Bread and Wine" (*Brot und Wein*), xi, 60, 81, 93; *see also* vin rapé, wine; "Celebration of Peace" (*Friedensfeier*), 8, 60, 85, 167; "Columbus," 127–28, 132; *The Death of Empedocles*, 89, 139, 156, 209, 213; *see also* Empedocles of Acragas; "Half of Life" (*Hälfte des Lebens*), 50–51; *Homburger Folioheft*, 65, 110n. 1, 117, 118, 141, 149, 172n. 2, 186, 197, 213; *Hyperion*, 6, 8n. 1, 10, 123, 128, 141, 156, 189, 204, 207, 209, 213, 215; "Fragment of *Hyperion*," 11; "The Main," "The Neckar," 52–53; "The Next Best" (*Das Nächste Beste*), 110n. 1, 123, 141; "Notes on Antigone," 141; "Notes on Sophocles," 140n. 13, 140n. 13, 141, 201; "Remembrance" (*Andenken*), xi, 70, 99, 110, 111–12, 113–15, 123n. 5, 127, 129, 131–32, 191n. 10, 197, 208, 215, 218, 220; "To the Madonna," *An die Madonna*, 65–66, 95, 97–99, 119, 164, 172, 174; Translation of *Antigone*, 60, 133, 134, 139; *see also* Sophocles; Translation of *Oedipus the Tyrant*, 60, 133–34, 139–43; *see also*

232 / Index

Hölderlin, Friedrich *(continued)*
Sophocles; *Vom Abgrund nemlich,*
110–11, 122, 124; "The Wine
God" *(Der Weingott),* xi–xii, 60n.
2, 80–83, 89, 93, 117–18, 127,
137–39, 160, 170, 184–85, 189,
194, 220, 226; *Wenn aus der Ferne,*
111–12, 218–19
Hölderlin, Ulrike ("Rike"), 7–8, 13,
17, 28, 29, 36, 52
Homburg vor der Höhe, 31, 128, 197,
205, 209
Homer, 21–22, 53, 134, 136–37, 177,
181, 204
Horowski, Reinhard, 198, 214–15
hospitality, xiii, 26, 46n. 5, 127, 136

Iduna, 109, 134
illness, Hölderlin's, xi, 3, 13, 72, 91,
198, 209–15; Susette Gontard's,
30–33
immortality, 31, 156, 185

Jacobin, 7–8, 59, 85; *see also* French
Revolution, Terror
Jena, 10–15, 17, 18, 30, 36, 59, 109,
209, 211
Joan of Arc, 161–62
Jocasta, 142–43
Joué-les-Tours, 147, 152–60, 191, 204,
226
joy, xi, xiii, 5, 10, 12, 16, 21, 27, 29,
30, 36, 62, 82, 91, 93, 118, 123,
126–27, 137, 159, 184, 207, 209,
215, 217–21
Juno, "Junonian sobriety," 22, 175,
183; *see also* Hera

Kalb, Charlotte von, 11–13, 36, 210
Kant, Immanuel, xi, 7, 10–11, 13, 20
Keats, John, 175, 181, 182, 189, 194
"Killalusimeno," 71–72, 157, 193

Kirms, Wilhelmine Marianne, 13–14,
210
Knaupp, Michael, xii n.1, 51, 53, 60,
81, 110n. 1, 212
Kniebis, 40, 46, 47, 55–58, 72, 74,
101, 224
Knubben, Thomas, xii n. 1, 47, 73,
130n. 7

Lacan, Jacques, 205–206, 210–11, 213
Lacoue-Labarthe, Philippe, 139
Landauer, Georg Christian, 17–19, 24,
26, 51
Laplanche, Jean, 13, 111, 198,
205–206, 209–14
Laroche, Sophie, 124–25
Lebendige, das ("liveliness," "vitality"),
17, 134–36, 139, 141, 194
Lebenslicht ("the light of life"),
200–201
Lefebvre, Jean-Pierre, 65, 113–14, 128,
172n. 2
lightning, 25, 87, 123, 126, 199
Limoges, ix–xi, 36, 39, 42, 44–47, 49,
94, 96, 100–103, 223
Louvre, the, x, xi, xii, 33, 50, 87, 145,
163, 164, 169, 171–95, 203, 204
love, 10, 12, 51–52, 62, 66, 82, 93,
102, 115, 118, 124, 127, 205,
209, 210–11, 213; of family, 7, 20,
27–29, 194–95; of fatherland, 26; of
nature, 2, 65; romantic love, 2, 4,
14, 16–17, 31–33, 80, 82–83, 109,
111, 113, 115, 137, 138–39, 140,
153, 167, 175, 177, 186, 195, 203,
206, 210–11, 218–20; *see also* eros
Lugdunum, 37, 39, 85, 87–92, 94,
141, 147, 225
Lyon, ix, xi, 8, 24, 27–29, 35–39,
42–44, 46–47, 49, 58–59, 68,
70, 72–73, 79–80, 82–88, 91–92,
94–96, 102, 169, 199, 223–25

madness, 26, 93, 114, 198, 201, 209; *see also* illness, schizophrenia

madonnas, 65–66, 95, 97–99, 119, 164, 172, 174

Maenads, 82, 182–83, 186, 194, 226

Matthison, Friedrich, 51, 154

Maulbronn, 2–3, 52, 62

memory, x, 10, 51, 54, 76, 83–84, 104, 113–15, 132, 150, 158, 161, 177, 208–209, 215, 218–20

Mereau, Sophie, 14

Meyer, Daniel Christoph, x–xi, 18–19, 24, 33, 67–68, 88, 95, 116–17, 128–30, 133, 154, 199, 224, 225

Michelangelo, *see* Buonarroti

Midas, 141, 187–88

Montesquieu, Charles de Secondat, 7–8, 130

moon, the, 81–82, 117–19, 175, 212, 225

mothers, 14, 16, 65–67, 82, 91–92, 137, 141–43, 174, 184–85, 202–203, 206–207, 210–14; Hölderlin's mother, xiii, 2–7, 10–11, 13, 18–20, 27–29, 36, 49, 66, 68, 73, 89, 109, 143, 167, 197, 198, 205, 206, 210–14; *see also* Gock, Johanna Christiana

mourning, 4–5, 10, 82, 89, 117–18, 139, 159, 177, 194, 199, 203, 212, 214, 219, 225

Napoleon Bonaparte, xi, 7–8, 38, 59, 83, 85, 95, 167, 171–73

Nast, Louise, 3–4

Nationelle, das (the "native," "innate"), 21–23, 202

nature, 2, 7, 10, 17, 21, 42, 51, 62, 65, 72, 80, 96, 115, 135, 140, 161, 184, 199, 207; *see also* "school of nature"

Neckar River, 1–3, 5, 7, 27, 39, 47, 49–54, 72, 196, 220, 224, 226

Neuffer, Christian Ludwig, 5, 10, 12, 13, 14, 16, 91

Niethammer, Immanuel, 18, 210

Nietzsche, Friedrich, x, 15, 39, 84, 136, 143, 167, 183–84, 188–89, 206, 208, 211, 214

night, the, 29, 40, 54, 56, 74, 75, 76, 81–83, 93, 96, 112, 113, 126, 138–39, 142, 153, 157, 175, 197, 210, 221

Nürtingen, ix, xi, 1–2, 13, 17, 19, 27–28, 31, 33, 34, 35, 41, 46, 47, 49, 51, 109, 132, 133, 167, 197–98, 205, 208, 223, 224, 227

parataxis, 110, 149, 199, 207, 209, 212

Paris, ix–xi, xiii, 7, 8, 24, 28, 33, 34, 38, 42, 58–59, 77, 78, 85, 87, 95, 111, 130, 145, 152, 162–65, 168, 171–95, 223–24

passion, 21–22, 140, 189; *see also* eros, love

Patroclus, 200, 203

Perigord, Périgueux, ix–xi, 36, 39, 42, 45–47, 49, 70, 94, 101–105, 223, 225

Persephone, 25, 64–65

Pietism, 2, 8, 29, 66, 91, 93, 109, 141; *see also* Evangelical

pilgrimage, 95, 99, 150

Plato, 10, 186

polytheism, 62, 66, 81, 138

post-coaches, ix–xi, 27, 28, 34, 35, 37–40, 42, 46–47, 49, 62, 68–71, 73, 75–79, 94–95, 102, 145–46, 149, 151, 164, 200, 223

Praxiteles, 174–76, 180, 181, 203–204, 226

psyche, 208, 212

psychiatry, 13, 111, 197, 198n. 2, 209, 214

234 / Index

psychoanalysis, 117, 198n. 2, 209,
213–14
psychology, 5, 65, 123n. 5, 133

relais ("relay stations"), 42n. 4, 46, 68,
71, 76–78, 94, 95
Rhine River, 3, 39–40, 46, 49, 54,
57–59, 70–71, 73, 76, 167, 185–86
rivers, xi, 24, 28, 35, 37, 39, 53, 58,
68–70, 73, 75–77, 83, 115, 124
Roman, 37, 39, 58, 62, 66, 69, 80,
85, 87–89, 94, 99, 140, 147–48,
154, 155, 169, 171, 173–74, 177,
187, 189, 191, 194, 225, 226
Romanesque, 3, 62, 66, 95, 99, 104,
148, 150, 151, 164
Rousseau, Jean-Jacques, 7–8, 167

Sartre, Jean-Paul, 206
Sattler, D. E., xii n. 1, 49, 60, 68,
134, 167–68
Saône River, the, 35n. 1, 39, 46, 48,
59, 68, 70, 73, 76, 78–79, 83–85,
87, 102, 224
"Scardanelli," 49, 157, 167–68, 193,
198
Schelling, Friedrich Wilhelm Joseph,
xi, 7, 8, 9, 51, 52, 60, 62, 65, 81,
138, 174, 177, 181–82, 185, 186
Schiller, Friedrich, xi, 11–16, 18, 109,
126, 134, 209–12
schizophrenia, 13, 111, 205, 209–10,
213–14; *see also* illness, madness,
psychiatry
Schmidt, Jochen, xii n. 1, 60, 110n. 1
"school of destiny," the, 6, 52, 174; *see
also* destiny
"school of nature," the, 6–7, 174; *see
also* nature
Schubart, Christian Friedrich Daniel,
4, 210
sea, the, x, 4, 24, 54, 66, 76, 93,
94, 109, 113–19, 122, 123, 125,

127–28, 132–33, 136–37, 154n.
2, 156, 164, 172, 202, 203, 215,
218–20; *see also* Atlantic Ocean
Selene, 82, 175
Semele, 64, 82, 184–85
Silenos, 89, 141, 184, 187–89, 192,
226
Sinclair, Isaak von, 8, 31–32, 197,
198, 205
solitude, 2, 13n. 3, 15, 27, 53, 75,
102, 113
Sophocles, xi, 29, 60, 65, 88, 133–34,
139–43, 156, 174, 189, 201
Soulac-sur-Mer, v, 94, 108, 114,
117–21, 133, 145, 168, 218, 220,
224, 225
"southerly humanity," xii, 135–36,
194, 201, 202n. 3
spring, 4, 5, 29, 32, 36, 57, 60n. 2,
80, 94, 101, 116, 123, 126, 152,
165, 191n. 10, 218, 225
Stäudlin, Gotthold Friedrich, 11, 18,
19
Sterne, Laurence, 69, 83, 87, 217–18
Strasbourg, ix–xi, 17, 24, 27–28, 33,
35, 38–42, 46–47, 49, 55, 58–59,
61–64, 66–68, 70–72, 74–75, 85,
91, 109, 145, 164, 166, 167–68,
205, 223–24, 227
Swabia (*Schwaben*), 3, 50, 51, 54, 58,
109–10, 201

Tantalus, 25–27
tenderness (*Zärtlichkeit*), xii, 4, 16,
135–37, 171, 175–95, 201–204,
210, 214, 219–20
Terror, the, 7–8, 78, 102; *see also*
French Revolution, Jacobin
theater, 12, 87–89, 128, 130, 139,
225
thunder, 89, 119, 125, 126, 138, 159,
189–90
Tiresias, 141–42

translations, xi, xii n.1, 21, 29, 60, 66, 88, 112, 122, 124, 127, 133–34, 139–40, 143, 156, 174, 201

Tristram Shandy, see Sterne, Laurence

Tübingen, xi, 14, 3–4, 7, 17, 35, 40, 46, 47, 49, 51–52, 60, 71, 88, 157, 163, 196–97, 205–206, 208, 214, 221, 224, 226

Tübinger Stift, 7–10, 52, 62

Tuscan, 85–86, 225

tutorships, x, xi, 5, 10–11, 13, 15, 16–19, 24, 36, 71, 89, 102, 109–10, 128, 134, 188, 210

uncanny, the, 119, 142, 153, 177, 180, 181–82, 184, 187

"unity of life," 91, 186, 204

Vendée, the, 95, 145, 199–200; *see also* Charente

Verwandtschaft ("affinity," "kinship"), 15, 164

vin râpé, 124–25, 127; *see also* wine

wakefulness, 76, 81, 83

Weimar, 11–12, 36, 109, 139

Wieland, Christoph Martin, 2, 138

wine, xii, 3, 5, 18–19, 52, 79–81, 83, 89, 91–93, 115–18, 125, 127, 138–39, 155–56, 159, 170, 184–87, 189, 194, 221, 226; *see also* vin râpé, "Bread and Wine" and "The Wine God," *under* Hölderlin, works cited

winter, ix–xii, 1, 6, 15, 17, 29, 32, 35–37, 40, 51, 56–57, 60n. 2, 61, 73, 80, 82, 85, 101–102, 117, 123n. 5, 126, 133, 149, 182–83

Wurmlinger Kapelle, 6–7, 52, 224

Württemberg, 4, 7–9, 50, 59, 62, 85

Zeus-Pater (Jupiter), 25, 53, 64, 91, 140–41, 185, 187–89, 192, 226

Zimmer, Ernst, 52, 197–98, 207